Death Penalty in Decline?

EDITED BY AUSTIN SARAT

Death Penalty in Decline?

The Fight against Capital Punishment in the Decades since Furman v. Georgia

TEMPLE UNIVERSITY PRESS
Philadelphia • Rome • Tokyo

TEMPLE UNIVERSITY PRESS
Philadelphia, Pennsylvania 19122
tupress.temple.edu

Copyright © 2024 by Temple University—Of The Commonwealth System
of Higher Education
All rights reserved
Published 2024

Library of Congress Cataloging-in-Publication Data

Names: Sarat, Austin, editor.
Title: Death penalty in decline? : the fight against capital punishment in
the decades since Furman v. Georgia / edited by Austin Sarat.
Description: Philadelphia : Temple University Press, 2024. | Includes
index. | Summary: "This volume presents essays evaluating the
similarities and differences between the legal, political, ethical, and
practical landscapes confronted by the death penalty abolition movement
at the time of the Furman v. Georgia decision and subsequent reversal
and those confronted by the same movement today"— Provided by publisher.
Identifiers: LCCN 2023042556 (print) | LCCN 2023042557 (ebook) | ISBN
9781439924815 (cloth) | ISBN 9781439924822 (paperback) | ISBN
9781439924839 (pdf)
Subjects: LCSH: Capital punishment—United States. | Capital
punishment—United States—Cases. | BISAC: SOCIAL SCIENCE / Capital
Punishment | POLITICAL SCIENCE / American Government / General
Classification: LCC HV8699.U5 .D385 2024 (print) | LCC HV8699.U5 (ebook)
| DDC 364.660973—dc23/eng/20240213
LC record available at https://lccn.loc.gov/2023042556
LC ebook record available at https://lccn.loc.gov/2023042557

♾ The paper used in this publication meets the requirements of the
American National Standard for Information Sciences—Permanence
of Paper for Printed Library Materials, ANSI Z39.48-1992

Printed in the United States of America

9 8 7 6 5 4 3 2 1

To my son, Ben, who brings joy to my life as I study the grim reality of capital punishment.

Contents

Acknowledgments   ix

Introduction: The Death Penalty in Decline and Today's
Abolitionist Politics / AUSTIN SARAT   1

PART I LOOKING BACK AT *FURMAN V. GEORGIA*

1. What-Ifs and Missed Opportunities: The U.S. Supreme
   Court, Death Sentences and Executions, and the Fiftieth
   Anniversary of *Furman v. Georgia* / JOHN D. BESSLER   21
2. What Was "Unusual" in *Furman*? / LINDA ROSS MEYER   64
3. The Foreignness of *Furman* / CAROL S. STEIKER AND
   JORDAN M. STEIKER   92

PART II ON THE ROAD TO ABOLITION?

4. Catholicism and the Ongoing Struggle to End the Death Penalty,
   from *Furman v. Georgia* to the Present / SARA MAYEUX   135
5. Abolition Then and Now: The Role of *Furman*'s Failure in
   Today's Abolition Success / CORINNA BARRETT LAIN   167
6. When the Killing Law Stops Killing: Thoughts about *Furman* /
   JAMES R. MARTEL   196

Contributors   225

Index   227

Acknowledgments

For most of the fifty years that are the subject of this book, I have taught at Amherst College. It has been a wonderful intellectual home, filled with terrific colleagues and students. I am grateful to them and the college that brings us together.

This book emerged from an online conference in which each of the authors whose writings are collected here discussed each other's work. They each modeled a distinctive combination of rigor and generosity. I am lucky to have had the chance to collaborate with them.

Finally, I want to thank Hannah Dimas for her skilled research assistance.

Death Penalty in Decline?

Introduction

The Death Penalty in Decline and Today's Abolitionist Politics

AUSTIN SARAT

The year 2022 was an extraordinary one for America's death penalty. The use of the death penalty continued a decades-long decline, and the political climate favoring the restriction or abolition of capital punishment continued to improve.[1] Looking back, the last half century has witnessed extraordinary changes in how Americans think about the death penalty.

Fifty years ago, in 1972, the United States Supreme Court brought a temporary halt to capital punishment in *Furman v. Georgia*.[2] Four years later, however, the Court approved new procedures for deciding on death sentences and upheld the constitutionality of the death penalty.[3] And by the 1990s, fueled by a "tough on crime" political climate,[4] the number of death sentences and executions steadily climbed. Yet, over the last several decades, the tide has turned, and the death penalty is in decline.

Today, a conservative-dominated Supreme Court seems completely unsympathetic to the kind of constitutional challenges that the Court recognized in *Furman*.[5] In fact, it now seems eager to do whatever it can to ease the way when death penalty jurisdictions want to carry out executions.[6] Yet in this as in other areas, the Court seems to be out of step with the mood in the country.

The Death Penalty Information Center (DPIC), an organization that collects data about capital punishment, captured that mood in its 2022 year-end report,

In a year awash with incendiary political advertising that drove the public's perception of rising crime to record highs, public support for capital punishment and jury verdicts for death remained near fifty-year lows. Defying conventional political wisdom, nearly every measure of change—from new death sentences imposed and executions conducted to public opinion polls and election results—pointed to the continuing durability of the more than 20-year sustained decline of the death penalty in the United States.[7]

Even with the recent rise in violent crime, the death penalty is nowhere near the top of the list of America's current concerns.[8]

Looking first at the number of death sentences and executions reveals the magnitude of the death penalty's decline. Twenty-two people were sentenced to death in 2022, down from the peak of 315 who received death sentences in 1996, and the DPIC notes that "the five-year average of new death sentences, 27 per year, is the lowest in 50 years." Turning from death sentences to executions shows a similar pattern. Eighteen people were executed in 2022, down from the 98 who were executed in 1999 when executions reached their highest point in recent history. The number of executions in 2022 was the fewest in more than three decades. Moreover, thirty-seven states have either abolished the death penalty outright or not executed anyone in more than a decade.[9] In fact, more states have ended capital punishment in the last fifteen years than in any other comparable period in American history.

Further indications of the death penalty's decline occurred in July 2021 when Attorney General Merrick Garland announced a moratorium on federal executions[10] and in December 2022 when Oregon governor Kate Brown commuted the death sentences of the seventeen people on her state's death row and ordered correctional officials to dismantle its execution chamber.[11] In 2022, the number of people on death row across the nation "declined in size for the 21st consecutive year."[12] At the year's end, there were approximately 2,400 men and women awaiting execution in the United States. As the DPIC reports, "That number is down by nearly a quarter from a peak of nearly 3,600 at the turn of the 21st century."[13]

As registered in public opinion polls, support for the death penalty remained at or near a fifty-year low point.[14] Support for life without parole, as an alternative to the death penalty, has steadily increased—to the point where the country is now evenly split when people are asked whether they prefer the death penalty or life without parole as a punishment for murder.[15]

In spite of these clear trends, some jurisdictions seem to be doubling down on capital punishment. America's death penalty is now defined, as the DPIC noted in its 2021 year-end report, "by two competing forces: the continuing long-term erosion of capital punishment across most of the country, and extreme conduct by a dwindling number of outlier jurisdictions to continue to pursue death sentences and executions."[16]

That "extreme conduct" includes imposing death sentences arbitrarily and sometimes sentencing innocent people to death.[17] Moreover, it is seen when executions are carried out in a racially discriminatory way.[18] Looked at as a whole, capital punishment in the United States, as Amnesty International observes, is used "against the most vulnerable in society, including the poor, ethnic and religious minorities, and people with mental disabilities."[19]

This fact helps explain why many Americans now have serious doubts about the need for and wisdom of capital punishment, as well as about the way it is administered. Also fueling this changing sentiment is a growing awareness of the fallibility of the death penalty system. Today, exonerations from death row have become quite common. Since 1973, 190 people in twenty-five states have been released from death row with evidence of their innocence.[20]

These exonerations have had a great impact on the debate about the death penalty. Sixty-three percent of the American public now believe that an innocent person has been executed in the past five years, and confronting the sheer fact of miscarriages of justice has led many Americans to reconsider their views about the death penalty.[21] The fear of executing the innocent, the continuing specter of racial discrimination in the death penalty system, and the difficulties encountered with lethal injection executions have led to the perception that the death penalty system is broken from start to finish.

That perception has spurred the growth of a new abolitionist politics.[22] Opposition to the death penalty traditionally has been expressed in several guises. For instance, some abolitionists traditionally have opposed the death penalty in the name of the sanctity of life. Even the most heinous criminals, they urge, are entitled to be treated with dignity.[23] Other traditional abolitionists have emphasized the moral horror, the "evil," of the state's willfully taking the lives of any of its citizens. Still others believe that death as a punishment is always cruel.[24]

But over the last fifty years, abolitionists have come to focus less on moral than on legal values. They have used the familiar language of due process, equal treatment, fairness, and the simple but incontrovertible proposition that the innocent should not be executed. They try to speak in the language of the "American mainstream"—of scrupulous, fair-minded people committed to the view that even in death cases, and perhaps especially in death cases, justice must be done justly.[25]

Some scholars have tried to make sense of this development but generally have not looked at it through the lens of the last half century and the legacy of *Furman v. Georgia*.[26] Nonetheless, it is now conceivable to ask whether (and when) the death penalty might be ended in the United States. If it is, how will abolition occur, and what factors will bring it about? Fifty years after *Furman*, does that decision offer a model for people seeking to end capital punishment or a warning about the path forward?

This book offers some answers to those questions. It focuses more on providing an analysis of the enduring significance of *Furman* and the facts of the present moment than on trying to predict the future. This book comes at a time when the United States is in the midst of an unprecedented national reconsideration of the death penalty.[27] As this book shows, many of the terms on which Americans now talk about capital punishment can be traced back to *Furman*.

At the time when *Furman* was decided, death penalty statutes across the country gave great latitude to judges or juries in deciding who would be sentenced to death and who would be sentenced to life in prison. The lawyers who litigated the case saw that latitude as the avenue through which social prejudices, especially racial prejudice, were played out.[28] For them, capital punishment was a form of legal lynching, and ending the death penalty was a civil rights issue.

The *Furman* litigation was the culmination of a campaign conducted by a group of lawyers under the auspices of the NAACP Legal Defense Fund. They hoped the Supreme Court would strike down the death penalty once and for all because of its demonstrated racial discrimination and other inequities.[29] But the NAACP lawyers were unable to get a majority of the Court to agree on a set of reasons for their judgment.[30] The Court issued a cryptic and unusual per curiam decision—one that is given in the name of the Court rather than any specific judges. It read, "The Court holds that the imposition and carrying out of the death penalty in these cases constitute cruel and unusual punishment in violation of the Eighth and Fourteenth Amendments."[31]

The ruling was narrow in scope and was fragmented. It set out that if a death sentence was handed out in a capricious or discriminatory nature, then it would be unconstitutional. Five justices each wrote separate opinions concurring in the judgment of the Court. The four dissenters were similarly split in their views, though they generally agreed that the question of whether the death penalty should be ended was a legislative and not a judicial question.

Among those concurring with the judgment in *Furman*, Justice William Douglas, who did not think that the death penalty was always unconstitutional, used his opinion to condemn the arbitrary and discriminatory way in which death sentences were imposed under laws that gave complete discretion to the sentencing judge or jury.[32] Because judges or juries rarely handed down death sentences, Justice Potter Stewart wrote that any particular capital defendant would have to be very unlucky to get one. It was, Stewart said, like "being struck by lightning." Justice Byron White agreed and concluded that, because they were rarely imposed, they could serve no legitimate punitive purpose.

William Brennan and Thurgood Marshall were the only two justices who at the time *Furman* was decided believed that the death penalty itself was always unconstitutional.[33] As Justice Marshall wrote,

> To arrive at the conclusion that the death penalty violates the Eighth Amendment, we have had to engage in a long and tedious journey. The amount of information that we have assembled and sorted is enormous. . . . In striking down capital punishment, this Court does not malign our system of government. On the contrary, it pays homage to it. Only in a free society could right triumph in difficult times, and could civilization record its magnificent advancement. In recognizing the humanity of our fellow beings, we pay ourselves the highest tribute. We achieve "a major milestone in the long road up from barbarism" and join the approximately 70 other jurisdictions in the world which celebrate their regard for civilization and humanity by shunning capital punishment.[34]

Similarly, Justice Brennan argued,

> Death is truly an awesome punishment. The calculated killing of a human being by the State involves, by its very nature, a denial of the executed person's humanity. The contrast with the plight of a person punished by imprisonment is evident. An individual in prison does not lose "the right to have rights." . . . A prisoner remains a member of the human family. . . . His punishment is not irrevocable. Apart from the common charge, grounded upon the recognition of human fallibility, that the punishment of death must inevitably be inflicted upon innocent men. . . . The punishment itself may have been unconstitutionally inflicted, yet the finality of death precludes relief. An executed person has indeed "lost the right to have rights."[35]

Brennan concluded,

> In sum, the punishment of death . . . is an unusually severe and degrading punishment; there is a strong probability that it is inflicted arbitrarily; its rejection by contemporary society is virtually total; and there is no reason to believe that it serves any penal purpose

more effectively than the less severe punishment of imprisonment. The function of these principles is to enable a court to determine whether a punishment comports with human dignity. Death, quite simply, does not.[36]

The *Furman* decision was both a remarkable achievement for the NAACP lawyers and a disappointment for those seeking to abolish capital punishment in this country. It was remarkable because, for the first time in American history, the Court insisted that if the United States were going to use death as a punishment, the government had to take extraordinary steps to ensure that it was administered fairly. It was a disappointment because the Court did not follow Marshall and Brennan and say, once and for all, that capital punishment could not be squared with the Constitution.[37]

Reaction to the *Furman* decision was swift.[38] Death penalty states worked hard to discern its meaning and to ascertain what they could do to restore capital punishment. Some states, such as Louisiana and North Carolina, enacted mandatory death penalty statutes, eliminating discretion entirely from the death penalty system. Others—Georgia, Florida, and Texas—chose a different path, retaining the punishment but guiding discretion by narrowing and specifying the class of death-eligible crimes.

Four years after *Furman*, the death penalty was back before the Supreme Court. The question then was whether either of those approaches adequately addressed the concerns expressed by the justices who concurred with the *Furman* decision. This time the Court's verdict was less equivocal, though no less divided. In a 5–4 decision, it struck down mandatory death sentencing statutes.[39] In addition, a seven-justice majority found guided-discretion statutes to be constitutional.[40]

Despite compelling evidence that narrowing and specifying the class of death-eligible defendants did not cure the problems of unfairness identified in *Furman*, the Supreme Court again upheld the death penalty in 1987. In *McCleskey v. Kemp*, it ruled that statistical evidence could not be used to prove that racial discrimination persisted even after the implementation of the *Furman*-inspired reforms.[41]

In the fifty years since *Furman*, doubts about the appropriateness of capital punishment have from time to time been expressed by justices who had earlier supported it. Thus, just before his retirement from the Supreme Court, Justice Harry Blackmun, in the 1994 decision *Callins v. Collins*,[42] determined that, despite the Court's effort to insure the fairness and reliability of the death penalty, it remained deeply and irretrievably flawed. Justice Blackmun used his dissent in *Callins* to make clear that his views on capital punishment had evolved:

From this day forward, I no longer shall tinker with the machinery of death. For more than 20 years I have endeavored—indeed, I have struggled—along with a majority of this Court, to develop procedural and substantive rules that would lend more than the mere appearance of fairness to the death penalty endeavor. Rather than continue to coddle the Court's delusion that the desired level of fairness has been achieved and the need for regulation eviscerated, I feel morally and intellectually obligated simply to concede that the death penalty experiment has failed. It is virtually self-evident to me now that no combination of procedural rules or substantive regulations ever can save the death penalty from its inherent constitutional deficiencies. The basic question—does the system accurately and consistently determine which defendants "deserve" to die?—cannot be answered in the affirmative. It is not simply that this Court has allowed vague aggravating circumstances to be employed. The problem is that the inevitability of factual, legal, and moral error gives us a system that we know must wrongly kill some defendants, a system that fails to deliver the fair, consistent, and reliable sentences of death required by the Constitution.[43]

Blackmun's opinion, focusing as it did on problems in the administration of capital punishment, was a milestone in the history of capital punishment over the last half century.[44] He was, however, not the only justice to express misgivings about state-sponsored execution during that time. In public comments, other justices, echoing *Furman*, voiced their doubts about fairness in the way capital punishment is administered in this country.

For example, in a 2001 speech at the University of the District of Columbia David A. Clarke School of Law, Justice Ruth Bader Ginsburg said, "In the United States, the most daunting of those criminal matters currently are cases in which death may be the punishment. I have yet to see a death case, among the dozens coming to the Supreme Court on eve of execution petitions, in which the defendant was well represented at trial."[45]

That same year, Justice Sandra Day O'Connor expressed concerns about the application of the death penalty in a speech to Minnesota Woman Lawyers. She cited the fact that, as of that time, ninety people had been exonerated from death row. She noted, "Serious questions are being raised about whether the death penalty is being fairly administered in this country. . . . Perhaps it's time to look at minimum standards for appointed counsel in death cases and adequate compensation for appointed counsel when they are used."[46]

Doubts about the death penalty also have surfaced from time to time in the opinions of the Court. In the 2002 case *Atkins v. Virginia*,[47] the Supreme

Court ruled that "mentally retarded" defendants could not be put to death. In his majority opinion, Justice John Paul Stevens wrote,

> Our independent evaluation of the issue . . . concluded that death is not a suitable punishment for a mentally retarded criminal. We are not persuaded that the execution of mentally retarded criminals will measurably advance the deterrent or the retributive purpose of the death penalty. Construing and applying the Eighth Amendment in the light of our "evolving standards of decency," we therefore conclude that such punishment is excessive and that the Constitution "places a substantive restriction on the State's power to take the life" of a mentally retarded offender.[48]

In *Roper v. Simmons*,[49] decided in 2005, the Court used similar logic to conclude that executing juvenile offenders is unconstitutional. Justice Anthony Kennedy said,

> The differences between juvenile and adult offenders are too marked and well understood to risk allowing a youthful person to receive the death penalty despite insufficient culpability. An unacceptable likelihood exists that the brutality or cold-blooded nature of any particular crime would overpower mitigating arguments based on youth as a matter of course, even where the juvenile offender's objective immaturity, vulnerability, and lack of true depravity should require a sentence less severe than death. In some cases, a defendant's youth may even be counted against him.

Justice Kennedy also wrote the opinion in *Kennedy v. Louisiana*,[50] in which the Court ruled that the possibility of death as a punishment had to be limited to the crime of murder. When striking down a Louisiana law that said that a defendant could be sentenced to death for the rape of a juvenile, Kennedy wrote,

> Confirmed by repeated, consistent rulings of this Court, the ["evolving standards of decency"] principle requires that use of the death penalty be restrained. The rule of evolving standards of decency with specific marks on the way to full progress and mature judgment means that resort to the penalty must be reserved for the worst of crimes and limited in its instances of application. In most cases justice is not better served by terminating the life of the perpetrator rather than confining him and preserving the possibility that he and the system will find ways to allow him to understand the enormity

of his offense. Difficulties in administering the penalty to ensure against its arbitrary and capricious application require adherence to a rule reserving its use, at this stage of evolving standards and in cases of crimes against individuals, for crimes that take the life of the victim.[51]

Justice David Souter's dissent in the 2005 case *Kansas v. Marsh*,[52] in which the Court upheld the constitutionality of Kansas's death penalty law, reveals his own disillusionment with the justice system's ability to fairly apply capital punishment. He wrote,

In the face of evidence of the hazards of capital prosecution, maintaining a sentencing system mandating death when the sentencer finds the evidence pro and con to be in equipoise is obtuse by any moral or social measure. And unless application of the Eighth Amendment no longer calls for reasoned moral judgment in substance as well as form, the Kansas law is unconstitutional.[53]

Justice Stevens used his concurrence in *Baze v. Rees*, a 2008 case about the constitutionality of lethal injection, to again register his doubt about the death penalty. As he put it,

The thoughtful opinions written by The Chief Justice and by Justice Ginsburg have persuaded me that current decisions by state legislatures, by the Congress of the United States, and by this Court to retain the death penalty as a part of our law are the product of habit and inattention rather than an acceptable deliberative process that weighs the costs and risks of administering that penalty against its identifiable benefits, and rest in part on a faulty assumption about the retributive force of the death penalty. . . . Full recognition of the diminishing force of the principal rationales for retaining the death penalty should lead this Court and legislatures to reexamine the question recently posed by Professor Salinas, a former Texas prosecutor and judge: "Is it time to Kill the Death Penalty?" . . . The time for a dispassionate, impartial comparison of the enormous costs that death penalty litigation imposes on society with the benefits that it produces has surely arrived.[54]

And in 2015, Justice Stephen Breyer's dissenting opinion in the lethal-injection case *Glossip v. Gross* offered a Blackmun-like indictment of capital punishment.[55] Breyer focused on what he called "three fundamental constitutional defects" that he said plagued the death penalty. Those defects, he said, were its "serious unreliability," including "convincing evidence... that innocent people have been executed"; its arbitrary and discriminatory application; and "unconscionably long delays that undermine the death penalty's penological purpose." Those constitutional defects, Breyer concluded, "lead me to believe that the death penalty, in and of itself, now likely constitutes a legally prohibited 'cruel and unusual punishmen[t].'"

Beyond the views of Supreme Court justices, other milestones in the death penalty's decline over the last half century include the founding of the Innocence Project in 1992 and its remarkable work in highlighting the problem of false convictions in capital cases,[56] the mass clemency granted in 2001 by then Illinois governor George Ryan that emptied his state's death row,[57] the well-publicized horror of Clayton Lockett's botched execution in 2014,[58] and the election in 2020 of President Joe Biden, which made him the first American president to run and win as a death penalty abolitionist.[59]

Today, more than fifty years after *Furman*, arbitrariness and discrimination remain persistent features of America's death penalty system. Americans are still arguing about fairness in that system. And some believe that the case against the death penalty continues to be made on the terms that *Furman*'s concurring opinions articulated.

But the legacy of *Furman* is contested by scholars who now find it to be dated and out of step with the current realities of capital punishment in the United States. Others think that it initiated a process that lent a veneer of legal respectability to the death penalty system.[60] As they see it, *Furman* has allowed death penalty states to keep the machinery of death running by making procedural changes rather than addressing the injustices that continue to plague capital punishment in the United States. As sociologist and law professor David Garland puts it, *Furman* and the court decisions that took up its mantle have served "to enhance the perceived lawfulness and legitimacy of capital punishment" and acted "as a force for its conservation."[61]

Death Penalty in Decline? The Fight against Capital Punishment in the Decades since Furman v. Georgia revisits *Furman v. Georgia* to assess its meaning and contribution to the current situation of capital punishment in the United States. Focusing on the legacy of Furman and its implications for the abolitionist politics today, the book highlights some of the factors that are propelling the decline of the death penalty and others that stand in the way of abolition. Among other things, it highlights the tactics and politics of abolitionism today, the current state of the concerns *Furman* raised about arbitrariness and discrimination in the death penalty's application, differences in the culture of life and death that have emerged in the fifty years since *Furman* was decided, and new perspectives on the prospects for abolition of the death penalty.

The three chapters in Part I look back at *Furman* and provide three different frames for understanding how it has shaped the contemporary death penalty landscape. They emphasize how the human-rights-and-dignity framing introduced by Justice Brennan in *Furman* has evolved in both death penalty jurisprudence and politics. Together, they help readers understand the elements of continuity and change that mark the last half century of capital punishment.

The first chapter, by John Bessler, examines what he calls the "missed opportunities" that have marked the fifty years of death penalty history since *Furman*. Bessler argues that *Furman* offered a framework that could have ushered in what he calls "a whole new era of criminal justice reform—one focused on respect for human dignity, freedom from discrimination, and the protection of universal human rights."

But the Court did not follow that path. Instead, Bessler claims, the Supreme Court's 1976 decision in *Gregg v. Georgia* and two companion cases—judicial decisions allowing the resumption of American executions—undercut the foundation set in *Furman* and set the stage for the *McCleskey v. Kemp* decision that upheld the constitutionality of Georgia's discriminatorily administered death penalty.

Bessler focuses on the post-*Furman* cruelty of capital punishment, including "death row syndrome," botched execution, and wrongful conviction. Moreover, in his view, each of those factors means that the death penalty is a form of torture. In addition, death sentences and executions are torture because the condemned are subjected to a continuous death threat. These sentences are like mock executions (where someone is led to believe that an execution is about to occur), which have already been banned by international law. Modern death sentences constitute a form of psychological torture.

Bessler concludes that in the fifty years since *Furman*, the jurisprudence of capital punishment and the abolitionist movement have failed by not making explicit the connection of the death penalty with torture or cruel, inhuman, or degrading treatment, which are prohibited under international human rights law. He ends by citing Justice Blackmun's ideas: "Just as nonstate actors are prohibited by law from killing and making death threats, so too must state actors be prohibited from gratuitously killing prisoners and making death threats of the kind now routinely made in the context of the death penalty's administration."

Chapter 2, by Linda Meyer, offers a different take on *Furman*. Instead of focusing on the issue of torture or cruelty, she suggests that the most useful way to understand the decision and its legacy is to focus on what is unusual about America's death penalty. "How did the Supreme Court hear 'unusual'

12 / Austin Sarat

in *Furman*," Meyer asks, "when it decided to prohibit a death penalty that was not, at the time, unusual at all?"

Meyer argues that the justices understood the word *unusual* in several different ways: "infrequent now, infrequent at the founding, unlawful, unruly, and 'simply not done.'" She traces these different understandings in the *Furman* opinions and the jurisprudence of the death penalty. She says that, unlike the other justices who concurred in *Furman*, Justice Brennan treated *unusual* as a normative term, not a descriptive one. As she suggests, Brennan understood that judges have a front-row seat to the application of law, and that as applied, the death penalty cannot be administered in any usual human way but always asks the impossible and unusual of judges and juries.

In her view, Brennan was right to see that what was unusual about the death penalty, and always will be, is that the death penalty does not treat "'human beings as human beings.' 'Unusual' is a violation of the imperative to treat humans 'alike' as part of the human community"—respecting the humanity in others. No set of procedural adjustments of the kind initiated in response to *Furman* can ever address that primal fact about capital punishment. For Meyer, the real lesson of *Furman* (a lesson that, fifty years later, this country has not yet learned) is that it is "normatively 'unusual' to treat humans as things; it is simply not done."

The next chapter, by Carol Steiker and Jordan Steiker, states flatly that "reading *Furman v. Georgia* today can be a jarring experience." It offers an extended analysis of why that is the case. They acknowledge continuities between *Furman* and today, including "the dramatic decline in the use of capital punishment in the years immediately preceding *Furman* and in the present day, as well as the shadow of race discrimination that influenced the Court then and influences it now."

But the Steikers argue that the situation of capital punishment in the United States today is radically different than it was in 1972 when *Furman* was decided. In their words, "Both the jurisprudential landscape and the shape of capital practices have changed dramatically over the past fifty years, to the point that much of *Furman*'s framing, analysis, and politics fails to track contemporary circumstances or understandings." They argue that "*Furman*'s account of what was wrong with the death penalty in 1972 is not congruent with the chief concerns that courts and others are most likely to raise about the practice of capital punishment today. This central discontinuity," they suggest, "is in large part the product of *Furman* itself. The decision and its progeny changed capital practices and influenced the shape of constitutional and wider discourse about the death penalty."

This chapter highlights, among other things, what the Steikers call the Supreme Court's "changing constitutional methodology." This includes "differences in the Court's reliance on international comparisons, its use of empirical evidence, and its reliance on social-scientific experts in its Eighth Amendment jurisprudence." They also note that the political context of today is also very different from what it was fifty years ago. Here they highlight what they call "the increasingly dynamic environment of capital punishment practices in the states, the influence of late-stage litigation on the Court's current approach to capital issues, and the changed nature of what constitutes a 'liberal' versus a 'conservative' justice on the Supreme Court."

The Steikers conclude that a modern-day *Furman*-like decision, were it ever to come to pass, "would look much different from its predecessor." And, given that the death penalty is falling out of favor in many parts of the country, they suggest that when nationwide abolition occurs, "there is little likelihood that . . . [it] will evoke the kind of outraged backlash that greeted *Furman* in 1972. It has been, and remains, a long and winding road, but the journey toward enduring constitutional abolition begun a half century ago will eventually arrive at the charted destination, albeit by means not fully imagined then."

The three chapters in the next part of the book, "On the Road to Abolition?" look at the shape of the death penalty debate today and ask how it differs from what it was at the time *Furman* was decided. They introduce us to the ways social movements and individual actors have brought their perspectives to bear in the death penalty debate and ask readers to consider whether abolition of capital punishment will significantly reshape relations between citizens and their government.

The first, Sara Mayeux's "Catholicism and the Ongoing Struggle to End the Death Penalty, from *Furman v. Georgia* to the Present," examines the relationship between anti-death-penalty activism and Catholicism. It assesses the contribution of Catholic doctrine to the past fifty years of abolitionist activity and compares it to the issue of abortion.

Mayeux notes that, like abortion, the death penalty is offensive to Catholic doctrine and has been roundly condemned by recent popes. But the Church had not yet issued a categorical condemnation of the death penalty at the time of *Furman*. In fact, throughout history, it had acknowledged the right of civil authorities to execute criminal offenders. In addition, Mayeux highlights survey evidence and suggests that Catholics were significantly more supportive of the death penalty than non-Catholics in 1974. Mayeux's chapter pays particular attention to Justice Brennan, who was the only Catholic on the Supreme Court at the time of the *Furman* decision. She contends that his religion did not influence his *Furman* opinion. Mayeux says that Brennan kept his religious views separate from his work, emphasizing his fidelity to his oath to the Constitution. And, shortly after *Furman*, he joined the majority opinion in *Roe v. Wade*, which announced a constitutional right to abortion in defiance of Church teaching.

Mayeux notes that there was a shift in the position of the Catholic Church on the death penalty dating to 1980. That year, American bishops called on "Christians and all Americans to support the abolition of capital punishment." They explained that abolition would manifest "our belief in the unique worth and dignity of each person from the moment of conception, a creature made in the image and likeness of God."

Since then, the Church has embraced and supported a "culture of life." Mayeux says that today, in the Church's eyes, the dignity of the person is not lost even after the commission of very serious crimes. For the Church, "the death penalty is inadmissible because it is an attack on the inviolability and dignity of the person."

But Church doctrine has not been fully reflected in popular mobilization against capital punishment. While there are certainly many Catholic activists and organizations working against the American death penalty, the issue, Mayeux argues, has not animated a mass popular campaign of religious activists seeking to remake constitutional law on par with the pro-life movement. In fact, she claims, the Church's desire to maintain an alliance against abortion with Evangelical Protestant groups (which mostly support capital punishment) explains why Catholic theological objections to the death penalty have not been translated into the same kind of mass mobilization as they have in the pro-life movement.

The next chapter, by Corinna Barrett Lain, takes issue with the Steikers' argument in Chapter 3. Lain argues that there are striking similarities between the social and political contexts of 1972 and today. At the time *Furman* was decided, the United States had a de facto moratorium on executions. In fact, no one was put to death from 1967 to 1977. Today, Lain contends, the death penalty is dying. "History," she says, "it would seem, is repeating itself."

But unlike fifty years ago, today's abolition strategy does not focus on the Supreme Court. Now, death penalty opponents are pursuing an incremental, state-by-state strategy. They have succeeded, as noted earlier, in dramatically reducing the number of death sentences and executions and achieving de jure abolition in many states. *Furman*, Lain argues, helped bring about this change in strategy.

As noted earlier, it produced a political and legal backlash that undid the substantial progress abolitionists had made before *Furman*. For decades after the decision, that backlash shored up capital punishment. But death penalty opponents learned a hard lesson from those developments. As a result, as Lain puts it, "instead of aiming high, abolitionists are aiming low."

That lesson has framed the work of the present moment. In addition, *Furman* and *Gregg* launched a "regulatory project" that "created a mass of complicated doctrine, and that gave rise to a cadre of specialized capital defenders to navigate it," which in turn had "cascading effects of its own."

Today, Lain contends, "abolition is once again on the horizon, and this time it is coming from the states themselves." She thinks that this offers a better approach for those seeking the death penalty's end. In many parts of the country, abolition now has taken hold at the grass roots. This means that it will be less easily derailed than it was in the aftermath of *Furman*. Maybe, Lain concludes, once the death penalty has died its own slow, torturous death, this time it will be "dead for good."

The last chapter in this book, by James Martel, departs from and disagrees with Lain's assessment of the prospects for abolition as well as her discussion of *Furman*'s legacy. Rather than celebrating that possibility and that legacy, Martel wants us to look beyond them to examine the broader issue of state-sanctioned violence. To do so, he brings the writing of the philosopher Walter Benjamin to bear on understanding the last half century of abolitionist efforts.

For Benjamin, the law, in its formulation as mythic violence, *must* kill in order to demonstrate that it has authority. This is as true of law in liberal democracies as it is in authoritarian regimes. Yet Martel acknowledges that there are vast areas of the law that have nothing to do with killing and large areas of law that address the remediation or prevention of violence. While he recognizes that the death penalty has been eliminated in a huge number of countries all over the world, he argues that the state's need to kill is ever present.

Benjamin's understanding of the law, in its mythic instantiation, is akin to what Martel calls "archism," the belief that life without a domineering state and social hierarchy is impossible. The state's assertion of a right to kill is a key aspect of life in an archic condition. As a result, Martel argues that this is not a right that the law will give up readily (except in the partial and limited ways that occurred in *Furman*).

Martel warns his readers to be wary of treating *Furman* as an example of progress. Instead, it should be understood as a deflection from the essential logic of state killing. And, even as the last fifty years have seen some progress in the effort to end the death penalty, at the same time the violence of the archist state has been relocated in police killings and mass killings by private individuals. Both, Martel argues, reinforce the same regime as does the death penalty.

Martel concludes that as long as a commitment to the maintenance of social and political hierarchies exists, the decline of the death penalty will not mean the end of the killing state. In those conditions, killing in some form, he concludes, will remain at the heart of the law.

Taken together, the work collected in *Death Penalty in Decline? The Fight against Capital Punishment in the Decades since* Furman v. Georgia does not offer a singular or simple assessment of *Furman* or of the situation of the death penalty today. If *Furman*'s legacy is still relevant today, it is not because

16 / Austin Sarat

in the ensuing fifty years, the death penalty has not taken some unexpected twists and turns. In the end, while the direction of change seems clear to all of the authors whose work is collected here, it is not yet certain whether and when this period of decline might bring an end to America's death penalty.

NOTES

1. Frank Baumgartner, Suzanna L. DeBoef, and Amber Boydstun, *The Decline of the Death Penalty and the Discovery of Innocence* (New York: Cambridge University Press, 2008).

2. Furman v. Georgia, 408 U.S. 238 (1972).

3. Gregg v. Georgia, 428 U.S. 153 (1976).

4. Jonathan Simon, *Governing through Crime: How the War on Crime Transformed American Democracy and Created a Culture of Fear* (New York: Oxford University Press, 2009).

5. Adam Liptak, "The Supreme Court's Growing Hostility to Arguments of Death Row Inmates," *New York Times*, November 15, 2021, https://www.nytimes.com/2021/11/15/us /politics/supreme-court-death-penalty.html.

6. *Id.*

7. Death Penalty Information Center, *The Death Penalty in 2022: Year End Report*, December 16, 2022, https://deathpenaltyinfo.org/facts-and-research/dpic-reports/dpic -year-end-reports/the-death-penalty-in-2022-year-end-report.

8. Julie Bosman et al., "Fear of Crime Looms Large for Voters, to Republicans' Advantage," *New York Times*, November 3, 2022.

9. Death Penalty Information Center, *Death Penalty in 2022*.

10. U.S. Department of Justice, "Attorney General Merrick B. Garland Imposes a Moratorium on Federal Executions," July 1, 2021, https://www.justice.gov/opa/pr/attorney -general-merrick-b-garland-imposes-moratorium-federal-executions-orders-review.

11. Ed Pilkington, "Oregon Governor Commutes Sentences of Everyone on Death Row in State," *Guardian*, December 14, 2022.

12. Death Penalty Information Center, *Death Penalty in 2022*.

13. *Id.*

14. Jeffrey Jones, "Death Penalty Support Holding at Five Decade Low," Gallup, November 18, 2021, https://news.gallup.com/poll/357440/death-penalty-support-holding-five -decade-low.aspx.

15. *Id.*

16. Death Penalty Information Center, *The Death Penalty in 2021: Year End Report*, December 16, 2021, https://deathpenaltyinfo.org/facts-and-research/dpic-reports/dpic -year-end-reports/the-death-penalty-in-2021-year-end-report.

17. Phillip Morris, "Sentenced to Death but Innocent: These Are the Stories of Justice Gone Wrong," *National Geographic*, February 18, 2021.

18. Scott Phillips and Justin Marceau, "Whom the State Kills," *Harvard Civil Rights— Civil Liberties Law Review* 55 (2020): 2–69, https://journals.law.harvard.edu/crcl/wp-con tent/uploads/sites/80/2020/08/08.10.2020-Phillips-Marceau-For-Website.pdf.

19. Amnesty International, "The Death Penalty—Your Questions Answered," accessed October 11, 2023, https://www.amnesty.org/en/what-we-do/death-penalty/the -death-penalty-your-questions-answered/.

20. As of December 2022. See Death Penalty Information Center, "Innocence," accessed October 11, 2023, https://deathpenaltyinfo.org/policy-issues/innocence.

21. Pew Research Center, *Most Americans Favor the Death Penalty Despite Concerns about Its Administration*, June 2, 2021, https://www.pewresearch.org/politics/2021/06/02/most-americans-favor-the-death-penalty-despite-concerns-about-its-administration/.

22. Austin Sarat et al., "The Rhetoric of Abolition: Continuity and Change in the Struggle against America's Death Penalty, 1900–2010," *Journal of Criminal Law and Criminology* 107, no. 4 (2007): 757–80, https://scholarlycommons.law.northwestern.edu/cgi/viewcontent.cgi?article=7616&context=jclc.

23. *Id.*

24. *Id.*

25. *Id.*

26. Baumgartner et al., *Decline of the Death Penalty.*

27. "Use of the Death Penalty in the U.S. May Be Ending," *Economist*, January 21, 2021, https://www.economist.com/united-states/2021/01/21/use-of-the-death-penalty-in-america-may-be-ending.

28. Evan Mandery, *A Wild Justice: The Death and Resurrection of Capital Punishment in America* (New York: W. W. Norton, 2014).

29. Michael Meltsner, *Cruel and Unusual—the Supreme Court and Capital Punishment* (New York: Random House, 1973).

30. Mandery, *Wild Justice.*

31. *Furman*, 408 U.S. 238.

32. Steven Smith, "Justice Douglas and the Death Penalty: A Demanding View of Due Process," *American Journal of Criminal Law* 20, no. 1 (1992): 135–61.

33. Some of what follows borrows from Charles Ogletree and Austin Sarat, "Introduction: Toward and beyond the Abolition of Capital Punishment," in *The Road to Abolition? The Future of Capital Punishment in the United States*, ed. Charles Ogletree and Austin Sarat (New York: NYU Press), 1–16.

34. *Furman*, 408 U.S. at 371 (Marshall, J., concurring).

35. *Id.* at 290 (Brennan, J., concurring).

36. *Id.* at 305.

37. Mark Hurwitz, "Give Him a Fair Trial, Then Hang Him: The Supreme Court's Modern Death Penalty Jurisprudence," *Justice System Journal* 29, no. 3 (2013): 243–56.

38. David Oshinsky, "Stay of Execution," *New York Times*, August 30, 2013, https://www.nytimes.com/2013/09/01/books/review/a-wild-justice-by-evan-j-mandery.html.

39. Woodson v. North Carolina, 428 U.S. 280 (1976).

40. *Gregg*, 428 U.S. 153.

41. McCleskey v. Kemp, 481 U.S. 279 (1987).

42. Callins v. Collins, 510 U.S. 1141 (1994).

43. *Id.* (Blackmun, J., dissenting).

44. Austin Sarat, "Recapturing the Spirit of Furman: The American Bar Association and the New Abolitionist Politics," *Law and Contemporary Problems* 61, no. 4 (1998): 5–28.

45. Ruth Bader Ginsburg (speech, University of the District of Columbia David A. Clarke School of Law, Washington, DC, April 9, 2001).

46. Sandra Day O'Connor (speech to Minnesota Woman Lawyers, Minneapolis, MN, July 3, 2001).

47. Atkins v. Virginia, 536 U.S. 304 (2002).

48. *Id*. at 16–17 (Stevens, J.).

49. Roper v. Simmons, 543 U.S. 551 (2005) (Kennedy, J.).

50. Kennedy v. Louisiana, 554 U.S. 207 (2008).

51. *Id*.

52. Kansas v. Marsh, 548 U.S. 163 (2006).

53. *Id*. at 9 (Souter, J., dissenting).

54. Baze v. Rees, 553 U.S. 35 (2008) (Stevens, J., concurring).

55. Glossip v. Gross, 576 U.S. 863 (2015) (Breyer, J., dissenting).

56. See https://innocenceproject.org/.

57. Austin Sarat, *Mercy on Trial: What It Means to Stop an Execution* (Princeton, NJ: Princeton University Press, 2007).

58. Jeffrey Stern, "The Cruel and Unusual Execution of Clayton Lockett," *Atlantic*, June 2015.

59. Austin Sarat, "Joe Biden Is the First President to Openly Oppose the Death Penalty," *Slate*, January 21, 2021.

60. Hurwitz, "Give Him a Fair Trial."

61. David Garland, *Peculiar Institution: America's Death Penalty in an Age of Abolition* (Cambridge, MA: Harvard University Press, 2012).

I

Looking Back at
Furman v. Georgia

1

Looking Back at
Furman v. Georgia

1

What-Ifs and Missed Opportunities

The U.S. Supreme Court, Death Sentences and Executions, and the Fiftieth Anniversary of Furman v. Georgia

JOHN D. BESSLER

Introduction

On June 29, 1972, the U.S. Supreme Court issued its landmark decision in *Furman v. Georgia*. In a terse per curiam opinion, the Supreme Court held that the "carrying out of the death penalty" in three cases—of William Furman, a Black man convicted of killing a white homeowner during a burglary, and of two other Black men, Lucious Jackson and Elmer Branch, convicted of raping white women—"constitutes cruel and unusual punishment in violation of the Eighth and Fourteenth Amendments."[1] Although the Supreme Court's six-sentence per curiam opinion made no reference to race, the long history of America's death penalty is completely intertwined—indeed, bound up—with both overt racial prejudice and more subtle forms of racial bias.[2] The U.S. Constitution's Eighth Amendment—adopted in an era of slavery and modeled on similarly worded provisions of the English Bill of Rights (1689) and revolutionary-era state constitutions[3]—provides, "Excessive bail shall not be required, nor excessive fines imposed, nor cruel and unusual punishments inflicted."[4] It was the Fourteenth Amendment, ratified in 1868 in the Civil War's aftermath, that ultimately guaranteed equality of treatment under the law and, in time, made various provisions of the U.S. Bill of Rights, including the Eighth Amendment, applicable against the states.[5] The Fourteenth Amendment reads in part, "No State shall make or enforce any law which shall abridge the privileges or immunities of citizens of the United States; nor shall any State deprive any person of life, liberty, or property, without due process of law; nor deny to any person within its jurisdiction the equal protection of the laws."[6]

Furman's concurring and dissenting opinions both refer to the concept of torture,[7] the aggravated form of cruelty.[8] But neither set of opinions treated death sentences and executions *as* torture in spite of the inherently torturous characteristics of capital punishment, which uses state-sanctioned death threats against those accused of committing crimes. Instead, the battle in *Furman* was fought largely over the arbitrariness of capital sentences and the role of judges versus legislators in America's criminal justice system. In *Furman*, Justice Potter Stewart famously wrote that the death penalty's administration was "cruel and unusual in the same way that being struck by lightning is cruel and unusual," while Justice Lewis Powell—joined by Chief Justice Warren Burger and Justices Harry Blackmun and William Rehnquist—wrote in dissent that the justices' "personal views" should not usurp the role of legislatures and juries in authorizing and imposing capital sentences. Justice Blackmun expressed his personal repugnance of the death penalty but chose not to vote to declare that punishment unconstitutional in *Furman*. Wanting his personal beliefs to be known publicly, Blackmun took this swipe at capital punishment in his 1972 dissent: "Cases such as these provide for me an excruciating agony of the spirit. I yield to no one in the depth of my distaste, antipathy, and, indeed, abhorrence, for the death penalty, with all its aspects of physical distress and fear and of moral judgment exercised by finite minds."[9]

The Supreme Court's *Furman* decision, which drew headlines across the country, did not materialize out of nowhere. In fact, the seed for it was planted centuries earlier, during the Enlightenment, when the Western world's anti-death-penalty movement began. That movement started with Quaker opposition to executions in England and William Penn's "Great Law" of 1682 in the province of Pennsylvania.[10] It then accelerated with the publication of Italian philosopher Cesare Beccaria's *Dei delitti e delle pene* (1764), translated into French as *Traité des délits et des peines* (1765) and into English as *An Essay on Crimes and Punishments* (1767). As Enlightenment ideas proliferated, two European locales—Tuscany in 1786 and Austria in 1787—abolished the death penalty close to the Constitutional Convention in Philadelphia (May–September 1787) that produced the U.S. Constitution. As avid readers of Beccaria and other penal reformers, many of America's own founders openly sought to dramatically curtail the use of executions or—in a few cases—opposed them altogether, including for the crime of murder.[11]

Furman v. Georgia was a successful byproduct of human rights campaigns and a growing judicial awareness and recognition of human rights violations in the post–World War II period. Before *Furman*, the Third Geneva Convention (1949) prohibited acts of both physical and mental torture against prisoners of war under international humanitarian law.[12] In 1958, the U.S. Supreme Court had ruled in *Trop v. Dulles* that stripping a deserter of American citizenship was "a form of punishment more primitive than torture, for it destroys for the individual the political existence that was centuries in the development."[13] Then, in 1961, Amnesty International—the London-based human rights organization—was founded. Its leaders and members exposed acts of cruelty and torture worldwide and launched an international campaign against the death penalty in the 1970s.[14] In the United States, the NAACP's Legal Defense Fund also began a "moratorium strategy" in the 1960s to contest every death warrant throughout the country.[15] Indeed, by the mid-twentieth century, the law's prohibition of mental or psychological torture was crystallizing, gaining traction among American jurists alongside the traditional prohibition against physical torture.[16] Just the year before Justice Felix Frankfurter dissented in *Solesbee v. Balkcom* (1950), where he observed that "the onset of insanity while awaiting execution of a death sentence is not a rare phenomenon,"[17] he wrote about mental torture in *Watts v. State of Indiana* (1949). In *Watts*, the Supreme Court held that a coerced confession to murder, obtained by depriving the detainee of sleep and adequate food, violated applicable law. As Frankfurter wrote, "There is torture of mind as well as body; the will is as much affected by fear as by force. And there comes a point where this Court should not be ignorant as judges of what we know as men."[18] The Court decided *Watts* the same year that article 17 of the Third Geneva Convention—the Geneva Convention Relative to the Treatment of Prisoners of War (1949), to use its full title—broadly barred acts of "physical or mental torture."[19]

The incongruity of American law outlawing coerced interrogations as well as nonlethal corporal punishments while permitting the use of death sentences, which constitute credible death threats and lead to more severe punishments than nonlethal acts, has not been lost on jurists and legal commentators. "Surely the fear and distress of a man who knows he is about to be killed is at least as great as that of an expatriate," Justice Arthur Goldberg and his former law clerk, Alan Dershowitz, wrote in their influential 1970 *Harvard Law Review* article, "Declaring the Death Penalty Unconstitutional." That article recalled the facts of *Trop* and quoted what Justice Frankfurter had previously written in dissent: "Is constitutional dialectic so empty of reason that it can be seriously urged that loss of citizenship is a fate worse than death?"[20] In the plurality opinion in *Trop*, the Supreme Court itself recognized the anomaly of striking down a nonlethal punishment while continuing to allow the use of a lethal one. As the *Trop* plurality observed, "At the outset, let us put to one side the death penalty as an index of the constitutional limit on punishment. Whatever the arguments may be against capital punishment, both on moral grounds and in terms of accomplishing the purposes of punishment—and they are forceful—the death penalty has been employed throughout our history, and, *in a day when it is still widely accepted*, it cannot be said to violate the constitutional concept of cruelty." "But it is equally plain," the *Trop* judgment emphasized, "that the existence of the death penalty is not a license to the Government to devise any punishment short of death within the limit of its imagination."[21]

In reflecting on the legacy of *Furman v. Georgia*, the landmark judicial decision that later inspired the postapartheid Constitutional Court of South Africa to declare unconstitutional that country's death penalty in 1995,[22] *Furman* should be celebrated even though tremendous disappointment followed in its wake. The death penalty has been used for centuries, with American executions dating back to colonial times and continuing, if only sporadically, to this day.[23] But *Furman*, at least temporarily, broke the death penalty's age-old spell on American law, holding out the prospect and promise of a far more fair and just American criminal justice system—one based on respect for human dignity and that does not tolerate arbitrariness or discrimination in criminal cases. Before *Furman*, capital punishment had traditionally been treated as a lawful sanction and as a "crime-control" tool,[24] just as the nonlethal corporal punishments of a bygone era (e.g., the pillory, the stocks, and whipping) had once been authorized by law to punish offenders, with the lash, for example, frequently employed against offenders and on southern plantations against the enslaved.[25] Indeed, throughout the history of its use, the death penalty had customarily been treated *as something other than torture* in spite of its main immutable characteristic: the state's intentional use of credible death threats in criminal matters, whether to extract confessions or guilty pleas or—when carried out—to deliberately take lives.[26]

While *torture* was once understood to refer principally to the continental European civil-law juridical practice of inflicting excruciating physical pain to extract confessions to secure convictions,[27] in the post–World War II period that legal concept took on a much broader meaning—one understood to encompass the infliction of either physical *or* mental severe pain or suffering for a broad variety of purposes. To this day, both international law and international humanitarian law continue to explicitly prohibit both physical and mental torture,[28] with the UN Convention against Torture and Other Cruel, Inhuman and Degrading Treatment or Punishment (1984)—in addition to barring cruel, inhuman, or degrading treatment or punishment—prohibiting *both* varieties of torture for purposes of punishment, extracting information or confessions, or discrimination.[29] Although the often-heated public debate in the United States and before the U.S. Supreme Court over capital punishment has long focused on whether death sentences are a *cruel and unusual* punishment, it has been suggested more recently that the death penalty, in all of its forms and regardless of the method of execution, should be seen as a *torturous* practice.[30] With at least 28,282 people under sentence of death worldwide at the end of 2022, including more than 2,330 death row inmates in the United States, the life-or-death implications of the capital punishment debate are clear.[31]

The law is constantly evolving, as it is wont to do, with both lawmakers and judges laying down applicable rules of law. Not only has torture been barred by international law for decades, but it is expressly prohibited by existing provisions of the U.S. Code,[32] the Supreme Court's long-standing Eighth Amendment jurisprudence,[33] and various state statutes and accompanying case law.[34] The U.S. Code, for example, already criminalizes torture "outside the United States."[35] While the definition of torture in the Convention against Torture varies from the language in the U.S. Code (and federal regulations) intended to implement that international convention,[36] federal law itself explicitly defines *torture* as "an act committed by a person acting under the color of law specifically intended to inflict severe physical or mental pain or suffering (other than pain or suffering incidental to lawful sanctions) upon another person within his custody or physical control."[37] The Torture Victim Protection Act[38] passed by Congress likewise provides victims of torture with a private right of action against perpetrators of torture,[39] with federal law prohibiting the entry into the United States of anyone involved in "any act of torture";[40] authorizing the president of the United States "to provide assistance for the rehabilitation of victims of torture" in "the form of grants to treatment centers and programs that are carrying out projects or activities specifically designed to treat victims of torture for the physical and psychological effects of the torture";[41] and containing a "torture" exception to the Foreign Sovereign Immunities Act, thus allowing victims of torture, including of mock executions, to obtain damages against state sponsors of terrorism.[42] The Eighth Amendment itself has long been interpreted to prohibit torture,[43] with American states classifying *torture-murder* as an aggravated form of murder. What is crystal clear: for decades, both physical and psychological forms of torture have been outlawed by international and domestic law. In 1971, the year before *Furman*, the venerable *Oxford English Dictionary* specifically defined torture as "severe or excruciating pain or suffering (of body or mind)."[44] Today, the question that must be confronted head-on: Does the death penalty, because of its inherent or immutable characteristics, including its systematic use of credible death threats, inflict severe pain or suffering amounting to torture?

The *Furman* Decision and the Culmination of the NAACP's Litigation Strategy

Furman v. Georgia, which temporarily halted America's death penalty, rendered a final judgment in the consolidated appeals of three criminal cases. The Supreme Court had granted certiorari in all three cases, but for each one, the central question was the same: "Does the imposition and carrying out of the death penalty . . . constitute cruel and unusual punishment in violation of the Eighth and Fourteenth Amendments?" Although the 5–4 *Furman* decision came in the form of a one-paragraph per curiam order, the case generated nine separate opinions—a rarity—and became, at the time, with all of its concurring and dissenting opinions, the longest Supreme Court decision ever issued. Justices William Douglas, William Brennan, Potter Stewart, Byron White, and Thurgood Marshall each wrote separate concurrences to articulate their individual views. Those opinions stressed the death penalty's arbitrary and discriminatory administration, the highly discretionary nature of capital sentencing, the infrequency and irrevocability of executions, the availability of imprisonment as a less severe alternative, the lack of justification or necessity for death sentences, and capital punishment's cruelty, severity, and violation of human dignity and contemporary standards of decency.[45]

Actually, *Aikens v. California* was initially "the lead case in the *Furman* litigation until it was mooted out when the California Supreme Court declared the state's death penalty unconstitutional under the state constitution" in *People v. Anderson* (1972).[46] Anthony Amsterdam, who argued both the *Aikens* and *Furman* cases before the U.S. Supreme Court as part of the Legal Defense Fund's team of litigators, was the principal author of the briefs in those two cases.[47] The U.S. Supreme Court's one-paragraph per curiam ruling in *Aikens v. California* (1972), finding that convicted rapist and murderer Earnest Aikens no longer faced "a realistic threat of execution" and that his appeal had become "moot," is just over 150 words in length. It was the California Supreme Court's *People v. Anderson* decision that thus—by fate—made the U.S. Supreme Court's *Furman* decision so well known, with the *Aikens* decision gradually drifting into obscurity.[48] Justice William Brennan later spoke about the NAACP's pivotal role in bringing about the *Furman* decision. As he emphasized in a 1986 lecture at Harvard, "In the mid-1960s, lawyers for the NACCP Legal Defense and Education Fund, Inc., began to mount a sustained challenge to the constitutionality of the death penalty in America." "Prior to 1972," he pointed out, "no American court, federal or state, had rendered a decision striking down the death penalty."[49]

The rationales offered in the *Furman* concurrences for the death penalty's unconstitutionality varied widely. Five justices concluded that the three death sentences under review violated the Eighth and Fourteenth Amendments, but they could not agree on a joint opinion as to the justification for that result. Instead of reaching a consensus, the five concurring justices focused principally on the history of the Eighth Amendment's cruel and unusual punishments clause, the rationales for punishment (e.g., deterrence and retribution), and equal protection and the role of racial discrimination in the death penalty's administration. The justices in the narrow *Furman* majority also examined whether executions violated human dignity and contravened the Eighth Amendment's "cruel and unusual punishments" prohibition.[50] That legal proscription, found in the U.S. Bill of Rights (1791), was first applied against American states in *Robinson v. California* (1962) by virtue of the Fourteenth Amendment—the Reconstruction-era amendment ratified in 1868. America's founders, embracing the "cruel and unusual punishments" prohibition found in the English Bill of Rights (1689), had incorporated that prohibition into early American state constitutions and, after the First Congress, into the U.S. Bill of Rights.

While eighteenth-century American lawmakers renounced arbitrariness, cruelty, and torture, they did not, in that era, fully reject capital punishment. However, Dr. Benjamin Rush—a signer of the Declaration of Independence—called the death penalty an improper punishment for any crime at Benjamin Franklin's house shortly before the 1787 Constitutional Convention. Treason and murder remained universally punishable by death in America even as legislators—inspired by Enlightenment thinkers such as Cesare Beccaria—curtailed the use of death sentences and executions. Early American lawmakers mainly thought of torture as it had been used by civil-law jurists in continental Europe and, for a time, by England's tyrannical monarchs—rulers who sought to exercise absolute power, including through notorious, by-then-defunct prerogative courts. Civil-law systems authorized judicial torture to extract confessions, and Tudor and Stuart monarchs—asserting the "divine right of kings" and exercising royal power through the Privy Council, the Court of Star Chamber, and its ecclesiastical counterpart, the Court of High Commission—resorted to barbarous corporal punishments (e.g., branding and nailing ears to the pillory before cutting them off) and torture, even though England's common law disavowed torture. American founders such as George Washington, Patrick Henry, and Thomas Jefferson specifically renounced torture, though like others in that bygone era, they did not conceive of capital punishment as torture, even as some founders forthrightly described executions as "cruel" and the product of "sanguinary" laws. In opposing England's draconian "Bloody Code," which made scores of crimes punishable by death, America's founders actively sought to restrict and limit capital punishment's use on American soil.[51] This antigallows activity led Alexis de Tocqueville to conclude in *De-*

mocracy in America (1840) that "the Americans have almost expunged capital punishment from their codes."[52]

In his concurrence in *Furman*, Justice Brennan observed that "we have very little evidence of the Framers' intent in including the Cruel and Unusual Punishments Clause among those restraints upon the new Government enumerated in the Bill of Rights." The absence of such a restraint in the Constitution as originally drafted, Brennan pointed out, "was alluded to, so far as we now know, in the debates of only two of the state ratifying conventions." Members of Congress, anti-Federalist Abraham Holmes protested at the Massachusetts convention in 1788, were "nowhere" restrained "from inventing the most cruel and unheard-of punishments" to "be inflicted on persons convicted of crimes." "There is no constitutional check on them, but that racks and gibbets may be amongst the most mild instruments of their discipline," he said.[53] "Holmes' fear that Congress would have unlimited power to prescribe punishments for crimes was echoed by Patrick Henry at the Virginia convention," Brennan added, providing the historical context. "Congress," Henry declared at Virginia's ratifying convention in 1788, "may define crimes and prescribe punishments." "But when we come to punishments," he warned, "no latitude ought to be left, nor dependence put on the virtue of representatives." As Henry stressed: "What says our (Virginia) bill of rights?—'that excessive bail ought not to be required, nor excessive fines imposed, nor cruel and unusual punishments inflicted.'" Fearing the lack of a constitutional constraint on Congress in authorizing punishments in the absence of a provision like the one in Virginia's bill of rights, Patrick Henry asked this question: "What has distinguished our ancestors?" His answer: "That they would not admit of tortures, or cruel and barbarous punishment."

In *Furman*, Justice Brennan—after reviewing the Eighth Amendment's history—emphasized, "We know that the Framers' concern was directed specifically at the exercise of legislative power. They included in the Bill of Rights a prohibition upon 'cruel and unusual punishments' precisely because the legislature would otherwise have had the unfettered power to prescribe punishments for crimes." "Yet we cannot now know exactly what the Framers thought 'cruel and unusual punishments' were," Justice Brennan observed more than two hundred years after the fact, offering this assessment in alluding to a speech made at the First Congress by Representative Samuel Livermore of New Hampshire: "Certainly they intended to ban torturous punishments, but the available evidence does not support the further conclusion that only torturous punishments were to be outlawed. As Livermore's comments demonstrate, the Framers were well aware that the reach of the Clause was not limited to the proscription of unspeakable atrocities." Livermore raised the possibility that the "cruel and unusual" language might later be used to bar then-authorized punishments for crime. "Nor did they intend simply to forbid punishments considered 'cruel and unusual' at the time," Brennan wrote in his *Furman* concurrence, citing the U.S. Supreme Court's decision in *Weems v. United States* (1910), which struck down *cadena temporal*, a Filipino corporal punishment, as a cruel and unusual punishment.[54] That punishment involved ordering a prisoner to perform "hard" and "painful" labor for twelve to twenty-one years "for the benefit of the state" while always—"night and day"—carrying "a chain at the ankle, hanging from the wrists."

The Eighth Amendment's cruel and unusual punishments clause, the Court in *Weems* noted of the sparse legislative history, "received very little debate in Congress," with Representative William Loughton Smith of South Carolina objecting to the words as "being too indefinite" and Representative Samuel Livermore of New Hampshire resisting the clause's inclusion in the U.S. Bill of Rights. "The clause," Livermore said, "seems to express a great deal of humanity, on which account I have no objection to it; but, as it seems to have no meaning in it, I do not think it necessary."[55] Both *Weems* and the *Furman* concurrences of Justices Douglas and Brennan took note of Smith and Livermore's remarks at the First Congress—speeches followed by that legislative body agreeing "by a considerable majority"[56] to what ultimately became the Eighth Amendment.[57] In the congressional debate, Livermore raised these questions and offered this perspective: "What is meant by the terms 'excessive bail?' Who are to be the judges? What is understood by 'excessive fines?' It lays with the court to determine." Articulating his concerns and his own view of the law, Livermore added, "No cruel and unusual punishment is to be inflicted; it is sometimes necessary to hang a man, villains often deserve whipping, and perhaps having their ears cut off; but are we, in future, to be prevented from inflicting these punishments because they are cruel?" "If a more lenient mode of correcting vice and deterring others from the commission of it could be invented," he observed, "it would be very prudent in the legislature to adopt it; but until we have some security that this will be done, we ought not to be restrained from making necessary laws by any declaration of this kind."

In interpreting the Constitution, the *Weems* Court pragmatically looked beyond eighteenth-century history, calling the Eighth Amendment prohibition "progressive" and "not fastened to the obsolete," even though *Wilkerson v. Utah* (1879) and *In re Kemmler* (1890) had upheld the death penalty's constitutionality. The cruel and unusual punishments clause, the *Weems* Court concluded after citing various cases and legal commentators, "may acquire meaning as public opinion becomes enlightened by a humane justice." As the Court in *Weems* observed, "Time works changes, brings into existence new conditions and purposes. Therefore a principle, to be vital, must be capable of wider application than the mischief which gave it birth.

This is particularly true of constitutions."[58] The founding era had itself witnessed much advocacy against both capital and corporal punishments—now seen as barbaric vestiges of the past in most societies. Under the influence of Enlightenment writers such as Voltaire, Cesare Beccaria, William Blackstone, and John Howard, the founding era was, in fact, in great flux in terms of what societal or punishment practices were seen as acceptable. Inspired by Beccaria and other penal reform advocates, America's founders authorized the construction of penitentiaries and made substantial efforts to curtail executions and nonlethal corporal punishments. States restricted the number of capital crimes, and in 1793—just two years after the Eighth Amendment's ratification—John Hancock, the governor of Massachusetts, called on legislators to abolish branding, ear cropping, and "the Public Whipping Post," what he called an "indignity to human nature." Hancock—now most famous for his flamboyant signature on the Declaration of Independence—believed that "a sentence to hard labor will perhaps have a more salutary effect than mutilating or lacerating the human body."[59]

Although *Wilkerson* and *In re Kemmler* upheld as constitutional the methods of execution of shooting to death and electrocution, both of those judicial decisions simultaneously renounced torture as an Eighth Amendment violation. In *Wilkerson*, the Court found it "safe to affirm that punishments of torture . . . and all others in the same line of unnecessary cruelty, are forbidden," citing legal treatises and mentioning various modes of execution used for high treason (i.e., beheading, disemboweling while alive, and drawing and quartering) and "treason committed by a female" (i.e., "burning alive").[60] In *In re Kemmler*, the Court cited the language in *Wilkerson* about the prohibition of torturous punishments and similarly declared of the Eighth Amendment prohibition—albeit in dicta—that "if the punishment prescribed for an offense against the laws of the state were manifestly cruel and unusual as burning at the stake, crucifixion, breaking on the wheel, or the like, it would be the duty of the courts to adjudge such penalties to be within the constitutional prohibition." In the late nineteenth century, the Supreme Court—in hindsight—simply failed to conceive of death sentences and executions as cruel or torturous acts. "Punishments are cruel when they involve torture or a lingering death; but the punishment of death is not cruel within the meaning of that word as used in the constitution," the Court wrote in *In re Kemmler*, contending that the word *cruel* implies "something more than the mere extinguishment of life."[61]

Almost needless to say, torture and cruelty come in many forms, with the justices in the *Furman* majority classifying the death penalty, as applied, as cruel and unusual. In his *Furman* concurrence, Justice Brennan—looking back at the history of American law—pointed out that "the physical and mental suffering inherent in the punishment of *cadena temporal* was an obvious basis for the Court's decision in *Weems v. United States* that the punishment was 'cruel and unusual.'"[62] "No other existing punishment is comparable to death in terms of physical and mental suffering," Justice Brennan emphasized, noting that, closer to home, flogging—a punishment with a long and sordid history closely associated with slavery and military discipline[63]—had been discontinued as a punishment. The Eighth Circuit's decision in *Jackson v. Bishop* (1968), written by then-circuit-judge Harry Blackmun, had specifically used the Eighth Amendment to outlaw the lashing of prisoners in Arkansas. "We know," Brennan wrote, "that mental pain is an inseparable part of our practice of punishing criminals by death, for the prospect of pending execution exacts a frightful toll during the inevitable long wait between the imposition of sentence and the actual infliction of death." Brennan's *Furman* concurrence, in fact, discussed both acute physical pain and the infliction of "severe mental pain." "The barbaric punishments condemned by history, 'punishments which inflict torture, such as the rack, the thumb-screw, the iron boot, the stretching of limbs, and the like,' are, of course, 'attended with acute pain and suffering,'" Justice Brennan underscored of physically excruciating punishments.[64]

Undergirding Justice Brennan's *Furman* concurrence was the concept of human dignity—what the Supreme Court's plurality opinion in *Trop v. Dulles* (1958) had referred to as "the dignity of man" in finding that the Eighth Amendment "stands to assure" that the power to punish "be exercised within the limits of civilized standards." In *Trop*, decided nearly fifteen years before *Furman*, the Court had declared it unconstitutional to strip a wartime deserter of citizenship following a dishonorable discharge. In that case, the Supreme Court, by way of Chief Justice Earl Warren's plurality opinion, found that the Eighth Amendment's prohibition on "cruel and unusual punishments" should be gauged by the "evolving standards of decency that mark the progress of a maturing society."[65] "The Cruel and Unusual Punishments Clause prohibits the infliction of uncivilized and inhuman punishments," Brennan wrote in *Furman*, adding this observation: "The State, even as it punishes, must treat its members with respect for their intrinsic worth as human beings. A punishment is 'cruel and unusual,' therefore, if it does not comport with human dignity." Brennan stressed that the infliction of physical pain "may be a factor in the judgment" that a particular punishment is cruel and unusual, but he added, "More than the presence of pain, however, is comprehended in the judgment that the extreme severity of a punishment makes it degrading to the dignity of human beings." In speaking of long-antiquated barbarous punishments, Brennan wrote, "When we consider why they have been condemned, however, we realize that the pain involved is not the only reason. The true significance of these punishments is that they treat members of the human race as nonhumans, as objects to be toyed with and discarded." Barbaric punishments, he concluded, are "inconsistent with the fundamental premise" of the cruel and unusual punishments clause "that even the vilest criminal remains a human being possessed of common human dignity." "A punishment may be degrading to human dignity solely because it is a punishment" or "simply by reason of its enormity," Brennan wrote, citing *Trop* for the proposition that "expatriation" is a "punishment more primitive than torture."[66]

In contrast to Justice Brennan's concurrence, Chief Justice Warren Burger and Justices Harry Blackmun, Lewis Powell, and William Rehnquist each wrote separate dissents in *Furman*. Those dissents emphasized, among other things, that the "cruel and unusual punishments" prohibition cannot be construed to bar the death penalty's imposition, that Americans used executions throughout the country's history, that death sentences had not previously been viewed as an Eighth or Fourteenth Amendment violation, and that a court's role differs from that of legislatures. The statutes of lawmakers, the dissenters stressed, were entitled to deference, with the *Furman* dissenters contending that lawmakers were free to eliminate or curtail capital punishment if desired, that the concepts of retribution and deterrence justified capital punishment, and that the Court's per curiam ruling did not declare capital punishment to be a per se Eighth Amendment violation.[67] The dissenters thus saw capital punishment as a legislative prerogative. "I still believe the death penalty is a cruel and unusual punishment," a seventy-three-year-old William Furman—the subject of the *Furman* case—said in 2006 in Macon, Georgia, after being released from state prison after spending a quarter-century behind bars for his crimes. "Why did I pull that trigger?" Furman was still asking himself, recalling how—as a younger man—he'd broken into a Savannah, Georgia, home and fired a pistol through a closed door, tragically killing twenty-nine-year-old William Joseph Micke Jr.[68]

Justice Blackmun's dissent in *Furman* noted that the U.S. Supreme Court's ruling had been "somewhat propelled toward its result" by the California Supreme Court's decision in *People v. Anderson*,[69] with that state supreme court ruling on February 18, 1972, "We have concluded that capital punishment is both cruel and unusual as those terms are defined under article I, section 6, of the California Constitution, and that therefore death may not be exacted as punishment for crime in this state." "The cruelty of capital punishment," California's high court had ruled, "lies not only in the execution itself and the pain incident thereto, but also in the dehumanizing effects of the lengthy imprisonment prior to execution during which the judicial and administrative procedures essential to due process of law are carried out." "Penologists and medical experts agree," the state supreme court wrote, "that the process of carrying out a verdict of death is often so degrading and brutalizing to the human spirit as to constitute psychological torture."

"The brutalizing psychological effects of impending execution," it declared, "are a relevant consideration in our assessment of the cruelty of capital punishment." At the end of its opinion, the California Supreme Court summed up its ruling: "We have concluded that capital punishment is impermissibly cruel. It degrades and dehumanizes all who participate in its processes. It is unnecessary to any legitimate goal of the state and is incompatible with the dignity of man and the judicial process."[70]

After multiple generations of Americans had advocated against capital punishment,[71] culminating in the *Furman* decision, it seemed at least plausible in 1972 that America had witnessed its last execution.[72] Indeed, on July 2, 1968, four years before *Furman*, U.S. attorney general Ramsey Clark—with executions in the United States having ground to a halt, in large part because of the NAACP's litigation strategy—had forcefully testified against the death penalty before a U.S. Senate Judiciary Committee's subcommittee. "Surely the abolition of the death penalty," Clark told Congress, "is a major milestone in the long road up from barbarism." "Today," he testified, "more than 70 nations and 13 of our States have generally abolished the death penalty." Clark recounted just how inactive or dormant state-sanctioned killing had become in the United States: "While most States and the Federal system reserved the ultimate sanction, it has been rarely used in recent years. There were 199 executions in the United States in 1935. There was only one in 1966; two in 1967." Clark continued, "Only one person has been executed under any of the 29 Federal statutes authorizing death in the past 10 years. He can be the last." "The death penalty should be abolished," Clark optimistically concluded.[73]

However, those seeking the death penalty's permanent abolition in the United States were soon disappointed after *Furman*. Death penalty proponents mobilized, and the *Furman* decision prompted a legislative backlash, with thirty-five American states reenacting death penalty laws to try to comply with the dictates of *Furman*, however muddled its holding because of the fractured nature of the five concurrences in that case. "*Furman*," the Supreme Court later wrote in *Maynard v. Cartwright* (1988), "held that Georgia's then-standardless capital punishment statute was being applied in an arbitrary and capricious manner; there was no principled means provided to distinguish those that received the penalty from those that did not."[74] Reacting to the backlash, just four years after *Furman*, the Supreme Court again took up the issue of the death penalty's constitutionality in the year of America's bicentennial. In *Gregg v. Georgia* (1976) and two companion cases, *Jurek v. Texas* and *Proffitt v. Florida*,[75] the Supreme Court—charting a very different course—then upheld death penalty laws purporting to guide juror discretion. Those cases thereby resurrected the American death penalty, although the Court struck down Louisiana and North Carolina statutes that made the death penalty mandatory for certain crimes.[76] At oral argument before the Supreme Court in 1976, then-solicitor-general Robert Bork defended the death penalty, arguing that it could not be considered unconstitutional because "the men who framed the Eighth Amendment" had "framed the procedures which must be followed in inflicting it." Justice Potter Stewart—wrestling once more with the cruel and unusual punishments concept—asked the solicitor general, "What if a state said for the most heinous kind of first-degree murders we are going to inflict breaking a man on the wheel and then disemboweling him while he is still alive and then burning him up. What would you say to that?" Bork responded, "I would say that that practice is so out of step with modern morality and modern jurisprudence that the state cannot return to it. That kind of torture was precisely what the framers thought they were outlawing when they wrote the cruel and unusual punishment clause."[77]

After 1976, the U.S. Supreme Court and lower courts frequently considered new Eighth Amendment challenges, including in capital cases, often using the "evolving standards of decency" test in their judgments.[78] In the post-*Gregg* period, the Supreme Court emphasized that the Eighth Amendment bars prison officials from using excessive force, engaging in physically abusive conduct, and subjecting inmates to inhuman conditions of confinement.[79] For example, the Supreme Court recognized the government's duty to protect prisoners from harm and to provide them with their basic needs: food, shelter, medical care, safety, and the like.[80] "When prison officials maliciously and sadistically use force to cause harm," the Court ruled in *Hudson v. McMillian* (1992), "contemporary standards of decency always are violated."[81] "That the Eighth Amendment protects against future harm to inmates is not a novel proposition," the Supreme Court ruled in *Helling v. McKinney* (1993), finding a viable Eighth Amendment claim where an inmate had been exposed to environmental tobacco smoke, with the Court adding that inmates have a constitutional right to "reasonable safety."[82] "It is well settled that the Eighth Amendment protects the mental health of prisoners no less than their physical health," one federal district court wrote in 2016, citing yet another case about the problematic nature of governmental conduct that crosses "into the realm of psychological torture."[83]

In capital cases, the Supreme Court has used the Eighth Amendment and the "evolving standards of decency" test to forbid the execution of non-homicidal rapists,[84] those suffering from insanity[85] and intellectual disabilities,[86] juvenile offenders,[87] and those who neither kill nor intend to kill.[88] "Since *Furman*," the Supreme Court observed in *Maynard v. Cartwright*, "our cases have insisted that the channeling and limiting of the sentencer's discretion in imposing the death penalty is a fundamental constitutional requirement for sufficiently minimizing the risk of wholly arbitrary and capricious action."[89] In the post-*Gregg* milieu, however, the Supreme Court has consistently reiterated the right of the federal government and states to impose death sentences.[90] The Court has upheld the constitutionality of lethal injection protocols in Kentucky, Oklahoma, and Missouri[91] and now forces any death row inmate attempting to challenge a state's planned method of execution (1) to show that the method presents a "substantial risk of serious harm" amounting to "severe pain over and above death itself" and (2) to identify "an alternative" method that is "feasible" and "readily implemented" and that would significantly reduce the risk of harm.[92] The latter requirement, turning the adversarial system on its head, forces a death row inmate and the inmate's counsel to choose—in effect, stipulate to—a method by which the inmate could be executed. While the Eighth Amendment is generally interpreted to safeguard prisoners from physical harm and mental distress,[93] the Supreme Court's unwillingness to stick with its ruling in *Furman* and forbid executions altogether has led to an Eighth Amendment jurisprudence that has a decidedly Dr. Jekyll and Mr. Hyde character to it. In short, while the Eighth Amendment ordinarily protects prisoners from harm, it also simultaneously permits some offenders to be subjected to state-sanctioned death threats and, ultimately, execution. As presently interpreted by the Supreme Court, the Eighth Amendment thus has a "split personality"—on the one hand, protective, and on the other, destructive.

The "evolving standards of decency" test—derided by self-described "originalists" on the U.S. Supreme Court[94] even though the U.S. Constitution itself gives no guidance on how to read the Eighth Amendment—was regularly cited by American courts after that test's creation in 1958.[95] Not only did Justices Douglas, Brennan, and Marshall invoke that language from *Trop* in their *Furman* concurrences,[96] but the "evolving standards" concept was later used to declare unconstitutional the mandatory death penalty in 1976.[97] Likewise, in *Graham v. Florida*, the Supreme Court wrote, "To determine whether a punishment is cruel and unusual, courts must look beyond historical conceptions to the evolving standards of decency that mark the progress of a maturing society."[98] But in a sign of the Supreme Court's ideological shift in recent years (driven in large part by Donald Trump's appointment of new justices), in *Bucklew v. Precythe* (2019) the Court—without citing the "evolving standards of decency" test—held that the Eighth Amendment's "cruel and unusual punishments" prohibition should be interpreted "as a reader at the time of the Eighth Amendment's adoption would have understood those words."[99] Citing that language from *Bucklew*, the Sixth Circuit went so far as to conclude in 2022 that the "evolving standards of decency" test was thereby "largely repudiated" as "a constitutional barometer" of the Eighth Amendment's contours.[100] With the "evolving standards" test last invoked by the U.S. Supreme Court in a dissent written by Justice Sonia Sotomayor in

2021 and joined by Justices Stephen Breyer and Elena Kagan,[101] the Sixth Circuit so concluded even though Justice Samuel Alito's majority opinion in *United States v. Briggs* (2020) had taken note of the Supreme Court's "evolving standards of decency" line of cases.[102] Of course, America's twenty-first-century society differs substantially from eighteenth-century life when lawmakers commuted to work on horseback and in horse-drawn carriages. Also, the judicial philosophy of "originalism" runs completely contrary to what Thomas Jefferson, the principal author of the Declaration of Independence, once said: "The earth belongs to the living, and not to the dead."[103]

The Death Penalty's Arbitrary and Discriminatory Application: The Rarity of Executions and the Supreme Court's Atrocious *McCleskey v. Kemp* Decision

Although the U.S. Supreme Court rejected a due process challenge to capital punishment in *McGautha v. California* (1971),[104] the death penalty's arbitrary and discriminatory administration is a recurring theme of the *Furman* concurrences. This leads one to ask "what if" questions about how American law and society might have developed if only the Supreme Court had, post-*Furman*, insisted on nonarbitrary, nondiscriminatory applications of the law instead of allowing arbitrariness and systemic racism to persist, including in life-and-death matters.[105] In his *Furman* concurrence, Justice Stewart, in comparing the imposition of death sentences to "being struck by lightning," referred to the three petitioners in the case as "among a capriciously selected random handful" sentenced to death.[106] "My concurring Brothers," he wrote at a time before the first woman, Sandra Day O'Connor, had been appointed to the nation's highest court, "have demonstrated that, if any basis can be discerned for the selection of these few to be sentenced to die, it is the constitutionally impermissible basis of race."[107] Justice Thurgood Marshall—also examining English and American history—himself concluded that America's founders "intended to outlaw torture and other cruel punishments." "Regarding discrimination," Justice Marshall wrote, "it has been said that '(i)t is usually the poor, the illiterate, the underprivileged, the member of the minority group—the man who, because he is without means, and is defended by a court-appointed attorney—who becomes society's sacrificial lamb.'"[108] Marshall had represented men accused of capital crimes and fought tirelessly for civil rights, including in the Deep South, so he had seen racial discrimination up close.[109] "[A] look at the bare statistics regarding executions is enough to betray much of the discrimination," Marshall pointed out, citing data on those executed since 1930, evidence of racial and gender discrimination, and how the death penalty falls on the most vulnerable.[110]

The death penalty's abolition, Professor Brandon Garrett writes in *End of Its Rope: How Killing the Death Penalty Can Revive Criminal Justice* (2017), "will be a catalyst for reforming our criminal justice system." Noting that miscarriages of justice and the exposure of flaws in capital cases "are making headlines and shocking the public," he aptly points out that such tragedies not only "sow doubts about the death penalty" but "can also drive reforms for all types of criminal cases." Writing before the 2020 murder of George Floyd in Minneapolis, Minnesota, Garrett observed what abolition might portend for more systemic criminal justice reform: "The decline and fall of the death penalty will save lives, but more important it provides an opportunity to revive the broken American justice system." As Garrett puts it, "The death penalty's demise will allow us to focus on remedying inept lawyering, overzealous prosecution, inadequate mental health treatment, race discrimination, wrongful convictions, and excessive punishments."[111] It is impossible to rewind the clock back to the 1970s, but had the Supreme Court in *Furman* simply declared the death penalty to be a per se violation of the U.S. Constitution, the country would have forever jettisoned and moved beyond a plainly torturous, arbitrary, and discriminatory punishment. How the law might have developed in a death-penalty-free America is rank speculation, but it certainly would have been a more just country had it been devoid of arbitrary and racially discriminatory state-sanctioned killing.

For decades now, the death penalty—with all its arbitrariness, racial discrimination, and geographic disparities, with present-day death sentences coming from only a handful of American counties—has corrupted the way American lawmakers and jurists think about human rights and the criminal justice system. Ironically, while the words *torture, tortures,* or *torturous* are used more than fifty times in *Furman* in various contexts, the death penalty, in 1972, remained an unacknowledged torturous practice hiding in plain sight, with the judicial debate in *Furman* focused on whether death sentences and executions constituted cruel and unusual punishments, not torture. Both concurring and dissenting justices in *Furman* recognized that the Eighth Amendment prohibited torture and that America's founders had rejected torture,[112] yet the death penalty itself was not classified in 1972 under the legal rubric of torture. That's because, even then, U.S. Supreme Court justices were using an outdated conception of torture that failed to consider the psychologically torturous nature of state-sanctioned death threats in and of themselves. In wrestling with the meaning of the Eighth Amendment's prohibition of cruel and unusual punishments, the Supreme Court sadly missed the opportunity to accurately classify the death penalty for what it truly is: an act of torture.

In spite of all the arbitrariness and discrimination associated with capital punishment, the Supreme Court upheld its constitutionality in 1976 in a series of cases after thirty-five states had reenacted laws authorizing death sentences.[113] And in spite of a massive statistical study known as the "Baldus study," definitely showing the death penalty's discriminatory administration, including on the basis of the race of the victim,[114] the U.S. Supreme Court in *McCleskey v. Kemp* (1987)[115] turned a blind eye to what Justice Thurgood Marshall so cogently called capital punishment's "gross injustices."[116] In a five-to-four vote, the *McCleskey* Court held that Georgia's capital punishment law did not violate the U.S. Constitution's equal protection clause or the Eighth Amendment's cruel and unusual punishments clause. The Baldus study, taking into account 230 variables, concluded that defendants charged with killing white victims were 4.3 times as likely to receive a death sentence, that Black defendants were 1.1 times as likely to receive death sentences as other defendants, and that Black defendants who killed white victims had the greatest likelihood of being sentenced to death.[117] The *McCleskey* decision, which has been compared to other horrific Supreme Court decisions such as *Dred Scott v. Sandford* (1857) and *Plessy v. Ferguson* (1896), was yet another missed opportunity to advance the cause of justice.[118]

The *McCleskey* opinion came about only because the U.S. Supreme Court had upheld the death penalty's constitutionality in *Gregg v. Georgia* and then allowed executions to resume after 1976. By failing to outlaw capital punishment, the Supreme Court thereby allowed the carrying out of many hundreds of executions in the post-*Furman* period. "*Furman* and pre-*Furman* anti-death penalty litigation," Jack Greenberg (the then-director-counsel of the NAACP Legal Defense and Educational Fund) wrote in the *Yale Law Journal* in 1982, "resulted in vacated death sentences for about 860 defendants, including all 629 persons on death row at the time of *Furman*."[119] As one source explains of American history, "The Court's judgment in *Furman* not only invalidated the death sentences of the actual litigants in the case, but also the death sentences of all offenders awaiting execution throughout the country."[120] But the mass commutation of death sentences in *Furman*'s wake abruptly ended with *Gregg*, and American executions resumed on January 17, 1977, when the State of Utah executed Gary Gilmore by firing squad.[121] The Washington, DC–based Death Penalty Information Center (DPIC) reports that, since *Furman*, more than 9,700 death sentences have been imposed in the United States.[122] Since 1976, there have been more than 1,570 executions in the United States. In addition, DPIC has documented 195 exonerations from American death rows.[123] The National Registry of Exonerations, founded in 2012 and run by American universities, has itself documented more than twenty DNA exonerations of people who served time on death row, the first of whom was Kirk Bloodsworth, a former U.S. marine wrongfully convicted of the murder of nine-year-old Dawn Hamilton in Maryland.[124] Both the guilty and the innocent can be tortured, but just imagine the distinctive terror of being put on death row knowing full well that one committed no crime.

The composition of America's death row changes with every execution, exoneration, or natural death—and there are many of the latter these days, as inmates often spend decades on death row awaiting execution. Justice Brennan's concurrence in *Furman* also noted that death row populations change with conviction reversals, grants of new trials, orders for resentencing, and deaths by suicide or natural causes,[125] and those realities continue,[126] with lots of serious mental health issues—even self-mutilation—among inmates.[127] California death row inmates are more likely to die by natural causes and suicide than by execution;[128] a comprehensive study of U.S. capital cases from 1973 to 1995 led by Professor James Liebman at Columbia Law School found an overall error rate of 68 percent;[129] and another study, led by David Dow and Eric Freedman after Congress's passage of the Anti-Terrorism and Effective Death Penalty Act of 1996, found that, nationwide, death row inmates had a 12 percent success rate in capital litigation for the period between January 2000 and January 2007, with the success rate—in yet another demonstration of arbitrariness—ranging from below 5 percent in the Fourth, Fifth, and Eleventh Circuits to approximately 35 percent in the Ninth Circuit.[130] The American death penalty remains as arbitrary as ever, even as more and more countries around the world abandon the death penalty's use and vote for a moratorium on executions. Ninety countries have ratified or acceded to the Second Optional Protocol to the International Covenant on Civil and Political Rights aiming at the abolition of the death penalty.[131] And in December 2022, in a UN General Assembly vote, a record number of countries—125—voted for a global moratorium on executions, while the United States voted no.[132]

Since *Furman* failed to put the nail in the death penalty's proverbial coffin and executions resumed after *Gregg*, every death sentence sought or imposed in the United States reflects a situation in which an individual was subjected to a credible death threat (and for anyone presently on death row, still is). Capital prosecutions expose people to official, state-sponsored threat of deaths, and those convicted of capital crimes and sentenced to death are subjected to living under continuous threats of death while they await execution, exoneration, or a new trial or a natural death in prison. Indeed, because of the way the American death penalty is administered through execution warrants,[133] condemned inmates often face multiple, highly credible threats of execution over the years—even decades—they spend on death row.[134] The amount of time inmates spend on death row in the United States has increased exponentially over time,[135] with those confined on death row often spending two decades,[136] or even more, before execution (or exoneration).[137] By contrast, a large number of national constitutions and judicial systems, including Ger-

40 / John D. Bessler

many's Basic Law and Hungary's and South Africa's constitutional courts,[138] have declared the death penalty incompatible with fundamental human rights and found the death penalty to be unconstitutional.[139]

In fact, an immutable characteristic of any capital punishment regime is that it makes use of official death threats—the kinds of threats that in other contexts (e.g., custodial interrogations and mock executions) are already classified as Eighth and Fourteenth Amendment violations[140] or plainly torturous acts.[141] For example, in *Burton v. Livingston* (1986), the Eighth Circuit considered a prisoner's complaint alleging that a sergeant had "pointed a lethal weapon at the prisoner, cocked it, and threatened him with instant death." This death threat, alleged to have been "accompanied by racial epithets," came after the prisoner had given testimony against another guard in a section 1983 action, with the complaint describing "a wanton act of cruelty which, if it occurred, was brutal despite the fact that it resulted in no measurable physical injury to the prisoner." As the Eighth Circuit ruled in that case, "The day has passed when an inmate must show a court the scars of torture in order to make out a complaint under § 1983. We hold that a prisoner retains at least the right to be free from the terror of instant and unexpected death at the whim of his allegedly bigoted custodians."[142] Likewise, in *Northington v. Jackson* (1992), the Tenth Circuit found a viable section 1983 claim where a state actor had "put a revolver" to an inmate's head and "threatened to kill him." "The ensuing psychological injury," the Tenth Circuit emphasized in that case, "may constitute pain under the Eighth Amendment excessive force standard."[143] Mock amputations and mock executions are, themselves, already classified as torturous acts, and other cruel, inhuman, and degrading acts form the basis for many other legal violations.[144] In *Taylor v. Riojas* (2020), the U.S. Supreme Court held that an inmate stated a viable Eighth Amendment claim where the inmate was confined "in a pair of shockingly unsanitary cells," with the first cell "covered, nearly floor to ceiling," in "massive amounts" of feces, compelling the inmate to not eat or drink for nearly four days for fear that the food and water would be contaminated.[145]

Death penalty regimes use death threats in multiple contexts. In custodial interrogations in death penalty jurisdictions, law enforcement authorities—whether in attempts to extract confessions, information, or guilty pleas—sometimes make veiled or not-so-veiled threats about the prospect of a death sentence or, say, the electric chair.[146] Such threats can plainly result in false confessions (one of the leading causes of wrongful convictions), as multiple studies have shown.[147] Jurists now freely concede—and recent reports prove beyond a shadow of a doubt—this can and does occur (and with considerably frequency, it turns out). "Threatening a suspect that if she maintains her innocence she will die in the electric chair," a federal district court acknowledged in 2002, "could easily" produce a "false confession."[148]

For years, DPIC—in its regular posts—has been reporting on the clear connection between threats of the death penalty and false confessions.[149] Not only does *any* capital charge amount to a serious death threat, but those sentenced to death face unremitting threats of death throughout their confinement. These threats of death—as exonerations prove—are made not only against those accused of crimes who have engaged in criminal acts but also against those who know they are innocent of criminal wrongdoing because they are, in fact, totally innocent of the capital charges.

Prolonged stays on death row—the terms *death row phenomenon* and *death row syndrome* were coined to describe their adverse effects[150]—exacerbate the torturous cruelty of being subjected to a credible death threat.[151] But it is crystal clear that simply being exposed to a death threat *on a single occasion* can and does amount to psychological torture, as laws and judicial decisions in the criminal law context amply illustrate.[152] In the non-state-actor context, death penalty states already define *psychological torture* as an awareness of one's impending death and a helplessness to prevent that death.[153] Of course, death row inmates are made aware in advance of their impending deaths and are helpless to prevent their deaths. Some get reprieves or commutations or new trials, but their fate is ultimately out of their hands and up to others to decide. Before retiring, Justice Thurgood Marshall himself dissented from the denial of certiorari in a capital case, noting that the Missouri Supreme Court had a "narrowing construction" of the so-called "depravity of mind" aggravating circumstance under which the following factor was considered: "infliction of physical or psychological torture on the victim as when the victim has a substantial period of time before death to anticipate and reflect upon it."[154] Those subjected to capital sentences always have a substantial period of time to contemplate their impending deaths at the hands of the state.

The meaning of psychological torture should be judged objectively. And in assessing whether a state actor is engaged in a torturous act, the focus must be on the state actor making the threat of death, not on what someone did (or is alleged to have done) in the past. A credible death threat is a credible death threat, whether made by a perpetrator of a crime in the context of a heinous criminal act or by a state official using a piece of paper (e.g., a death warrant or a "Notice of Intent to Seek the Death Penalty"). Anytime someone held in confinement, whether due to being kidnapped or being arrested and put behind bars, is threatened with death, that threat is bound to inflict severe pain and suffering not only on the target of it but on others close to that individual who are aware of the threat. When death row inmates are asked about burial arrangements in advance of a state-sanctioned killing as part of an execution protocol, or when their family members are contacted about such matters (or have to deal with a medical examiner's request for an autopsy after the fact) or must wrestle with the anxiety and torment of an impending execution, the severity of the psychological pain or suffering is exacerbated, if not off the charts.[155] The bottom line: each and every threat of death against a detained person inevitably inflicts severe pain and suffering amounting to torture, not only on the offender but also on the offender's close family members. Like the specific target of a death threat, the family members of death row inmates are helpless to stop an execution from moving forward; only a state official can grant relief or a commutation or reprieve.

In essence, American courts, while recognizing the torts of intentional and negligent infliction of emotional distress and the tortious nature of death threats,[156] have failed to take psychological torture seriously in the death penalty context.[157] For example, in *Faulder v. Johnson* (1999), the Fifth Circuit rejected a death row inmate's claim that he was subjected to psychological torture because of the nine separate execution dates and repeated stays of his execution over twenty-two years. However, while conceding that the inmate had endured "a gruesome and disturbing ordeal," that court found no cognizable torture or cruel and unusual punishment claim because "the stays were the result" of the inmate's multiple appeals, failing to address the fact that every scheduled execution date, in and of itself, constitutes a torturous death threat.[158] The failure of the Supreme Court in *Furman* and other cases to address head-on the psychological torture inherent in every capital charge and death sentence constitutes a missed opportunity to label state-sanctioned death threats as cruel and torturous acts. The United States regularly excoriates totalitarian or authoritarian regimes, such as China and Iran, for imposing death sentences or carrying out executions that it sees as violations of human rights,[159] but the United States should be doing so from a position of strength and a well-settled understanding that *all* death sentences and executions inherently run afoul of universal human rights and human dignity. All executions, whenever and wherever carried out, inflict severe pain and suffering, and the United States should be a leader in the field of human rights, not a violator of them. If the United States were to abolish capital punishment, U.S. officials could speak with more moral clarity when they criticize the use of executions in China, Iran, Saudi Arabia, North Korea, or elsewhere.

Because the U.S. Supreme Court has, since *Furman*, declined to outlaw the death penalty, literally thousands of people in the United States have been subjected to state-sanctioned death threats.[160] Likewise, in nearly two hundred capital cases, there have been wrongful convictions leading to exonerations, and those are just the ones we know about already.[161] As of October 2023, death row inmate Richard Glossip has had two trials, ordered three last meals, and yet was still alive after nine separate execution dates because of late-minute stays, driven, in part, by serious doubts about his guilt after extensive after-the-fact investigations of his conviction and death sentence.[162] Family members—mothers and fathers, brothers and sisters, and sons and daughters—are routinely subjected to the torment of living through capital trials, appeals, and the lengthy postconviction process (as are judges, jurors, and the lawyers representing capital defendants and death row inmates). For some, there have been terror-inducing executions, with mothers wailing in execution chambers as their adult children get put to death even though maximum-security prisons exist to house violent offenders.[163] While the Supreme Court has, for many decades, held that the U.S. Constitution's Eighth Amendment prohibits torture,[164] by continuing to allow death sentences (which, at a minimum, inflict psychological torture), it has permitted torturous acts even though international law and existing provisions of domestic law purport to absolutely bar physical and mental torture.[165] "In light of the universal condemnation of torture in numerous international agreements, and the renunciation of torture as an instrument of official policy by virtually all of the nations of the world (in principle if not in practice)," the Second Circuit pointed out more than four decades ago in *Filártiga v. Peña-Irala* (1980), "we find that an act of torture committed by a state official against one held in detention violated established norms of the international law of human rights, and hence the law of nations."[166]

The U.S. Supreme Court has, quite literally, consciously ignored or failed to consider the modern, post–World War II definition of torture. Not only does the Third Geneva Convention bar acts of physical and mental torture, but in 1975, the UN General Assembly adopted the Declaration on the Protection of All Persons from Being Subjected to Torture and Other Cruel, Inhuman or Degrading Treatment or Punishment. That international declaration specifically defines *torture* to mean "any act by which severe pain or suffering, whether physical or mental, is intentionally inflicted" by a state actor for a prohibited purpose (e.g., obtaining information or a confession, punishment, or intimidation).[167] The subsequently adopted UN Convention against Torture—a binding treaty with the force of law—similarly defines *torture* as "any act by which severe pain or suffering, whether physical or mental, is intentionally inflicted" by "a public official or other person acting in an official capacity" for a prohibited purpose (i.e., obtaining "information or a confession," punishment, intimidation or coercion, "or for any reason based on discrimination of any kind").[168] For Supreme Court justices to ignore the modern-day understanding of torture, they must put their heads in the sand—clearly not what modern jurists should do when interpreting laws absolutely prohibiting torture. Common sense dictates that when mock executions are already considered torturous acts, actual state-sanctioned killings must be barred, too, as torturous acts.

The U.S. Supreme Court's Eighth Amendment jurisprudence must recognize the death penalty's torturous nature if the law is ever to be interpreted in a consistent and principled manner. Long before *Furman*, article 17 of the Geneva Convention Relative to the Treatment of Prisoners of War (1949) barred "physical or mental torture,"[169] with the U.S. Army Field Manual (1992) later stating that military interrogations must occur within the "constraints" of the Uniform Code of Military Justice and the Geneva Conventions. That field manual specifically prohibits "physical or mental torture and coercion," defining *torture* as "the infliction of intense pain to body or mind to extract a confession or information, or for sadistic pleasure." Examples of "physical torture" listed in the manual include "electric shock," "infliction of pain through chemicals or bondage," and "forcing an individual or stand, sit, or kneel in abnormal positions for prolonged periods of time." Likewise, prohibited "mental torture" includes "mock executions."[170] Credible death threats have been found to constitute "persecution" or torture in the context of immigration cases;[171] federal and state laws criminalize acts of torture and make death threats criminal acts;[172] courts routinely uphold criminal threat convictions, including even where a defendant lacks the immediate ability to act on the threat;[173] and U.S. law already defines torture to include "prolonged mental harm caused by or resulting from . . . the intentional infliction or threatened infliction of severe physical pain or suffering; . . . the threat of imminent death; or . . . the threat that another person will immediately be subject to death."[174] It is, of course, an absolute certainty that a threat of death in the death penalty context will cause prolonged mental harm and become a threat of imminent death as an execution date approaches.

While offenders commit crimes, it is state actors who bring capital charges, conduct capital trials, schedule executions, issue death warrants, and set up execution protocols—acts and protocols that inevitably inflict severe pain or suffering, whether physical, mental, or both (and almost certainly both, as psychological terror, whether prolonged or not, is bound to affect one's physical health). Studies have shown that state-sanctioned executions are regularly botched, thus resulting in the infliction of excruciating physical pain when planned executions are carried out by state officials. Austin Sarat—an internationally recognized expert—estimates that approximately 3 percent of executions carried out from 1890 to 2010 were botched in some way or another.[175] While "execution teams" may spend time planning for executions to reduce the risk of botched executions, the risk of physically torturous punishments is ever-present. And death row inmates preparing to die have no doubt heard the stories about botched executions, further aggravating the psychological torment they face as they await their own executions.

At Clayton Lockett's April 29, 2014, execution—to use but one example—Oklahoma officials used a three-drug protocol: midazolam (intended to render him unconscious), vecuronium bromide (to paralyze him), and potassium chloride (to stop his heart). The EMT selected a vein in his groin area as the injection site, but after the executioners administered the first drug at 6:23 P.M. and he was declared unconscious at 6:33 P.M., he unexpectedly began "twitching and convulsing" on the table at 6:36 P.M. He raised his head and said, "Oh, man," "I'm not . . .," and "Something's wrong." Lockett was not pronounced dead until 7:06 P.M., later prompting a lawsuit by Lockett's estate alleging torture and an Eighth Amendment violation—a lawsuit ultimately dismissed due to the "qualified immunity" of government officials even though the Tenth Circuit candidly wrote that "the Supreme Court's death-penalty opinions recognize that executions can go awry" and that "everyone acknowledges that Lockett suffered during his execution." "While Lockett's Estate takes issue with the three-drug protocol and the midazolam amount used in Lockett's execution," the Tenth Circuit stressed, "everyone agrees that Lockett's suffering arose from IV infiltration: the drugs leaked into the surrounding tissue rather than into his bloodstream, keeping Lockett from receiving full doses of the drugs." Although the Tenth Circuit accepted that Lockett's execution was "unnecessarily prolonged and horribly painful," it blithely characterized it as an "isolated mishap."[176] Not so, as Sarat and others have determined. "Several botched executions, including Clayton Lockett's killing," another respected academic, William Berry, writes, "have added more evidence that the effect of midazolam may be to torture the inmate to death."[177]

In her book *The Death of Innocents: An Eyewitness Account of Wrongful Executions* (2005), Sister Helen Prejean—the Roman Catholic nun and death row spiritual advisor known around the globe for her abolitionist stance—wrote of the adverse psychological effects of facing a sentence of death: "Mental torture is harder to see than physical torture but is nonetheless real. Half a century of research has taught us that mental torture may cause more suffering than physical pain." In *Dead Man Walking: An Eyewitness Account of the Death Penalty in the United States* (1993), she further highlighted the critical importance of what has been called the *rule of law*, the idea that legal rules must apply equally to those in positions of power: "If we are to have a society which protects its citizens from torture and murder, then torture and murder must be off-limits to *everyone*. No one, for any reason, may be permitted to torture and kill—and that includes government." "Torture is intrinsic to the death penalty," Sister Prejean emphasized, pointing out that death row inmates die "a thousand times mentally" before they physically die because they "anticipate" their deaths, imagine their deaths, and "vicariously experience" their deaths "many, many times."[178] In short, mental torture is inherent to any capital punishment regime anywhere in the world; it is simply part and parcel of the death penalty's administration.[179]

The continued failure of the United States and its highest court to outlaw capital punishment is unacceptable. While the concept of torture was once associated primarily with civil law systems and the infliction of excruciating physical pain or suffering, the UN Convention against Torture (to which the United States is a party)[180] and provisions of American law now make clear that both physical and mental forms of torture are forbidden.[181] The U.S. Code, in fact, specifically defines *torture* to mean "an act committed by a person acting under the color of law specifically intended to inflict severe physical or mental pain or suffering (other than pain or suffering incidental to lawful sanctions) upon another person within his custody or physical control."[182] Prior to the Enlightenment, death sentences and executions were universally accepted worldwide as a lawful means of punishing offenders. But capital punishment is no longer lawful in many countries and American states,[183] and many categories of offenders (e.g., juveniles, those suffering from insanity or intellectual disabilities, and those who neither kill or planned to kill) are no longer subjected to execution in the United States.[184] Ultimately, it is clear that the death penalty—when objectively considered—must be considered torturous in nature because it systematically (and unalterably) makes use of death threats. Mock executions (where someone is led to believe an execution is about occur) are already banned by the U.S. Code and the U.S. Army Field Manual, and they are regularly described by jurists as acts of psychological torture.[185] "Sham executions," one book on trauma emphasizes, are "a widely practiced form of torture."[186]

By refusing to declare the death penalty unconstitutional and off limits, the U.S. Supreme Court has thus allowed the ongoing use of a plainly torturous punishment.[187] In contravention of long-standing legal principles, the nation's highest court has also continued to allow the arbitrary and discriminatory infliction of that punishment—what has long been known as the state's "ultimate sanction."[188] Arbitrariness and discrimination are anathema to the U.S. Constitution's due process and equal protection clauses, and by permitting the death penalty to be administered in an arbitrary and discriminatory way, the Supreme Court has undermined the nation's expressed commitment to "EQUAL JUSTICE UNDER LAW"—the promise made on the façade of the Supreme Court's building in Washington, DC.[189] Death sentences and executions are frequently the product of racial prejudice and bias, as well as geographic and other disparities, and in reality America's death penalty has never been administered in a nonarbitrary or equal manner throughout the nation's history. In colonial and antebellum America, for instance, the death penalty was ruthlessly used to quash slave rebellions (e.g., Gabriel's Rebellion [1800] and Nat Turner's Rebellion [1831] in Virginia) and to terrify the enslaved.[190] Indeed, death sentences have never been imposed in a manner consistent with the Civil Rights Act of 1866, which requires "like punishment" for persons convicted of crimes regardless of the color of their skin.[191] Studies have shown that capital punishment is, in fact, actively used by just a small fraction of the nation's counties,[192] with just 2 percent of the nation's counties accounting for the majority of the country's executions.[193]

Conclusion

The Universal Declaration of Human Rights and the International Covenant on Civil and Political Rights prohibit torture and other acts of cruelty. Article 5 of the Universal Declaration and article 7 of the International Covenant both provide, "No one shall be subjected to torture or to cruel, inhuman or degrading treatment or punishment."[194] General prohibitions of torture were made more specific (i.e., to explicitly cover both physical and mental varieties) by the Third Geneva Convention, the UN Convention against Torture, and various provisions of domestic law. It is simply no longer the case that torture is narrowly defined as civil-law-style judicial torture or exclusively physical torment. Instead, torture now plainly includes a wide variety of acts, whether inflicting physical or mental torture. In the twenty-first century, physical and mental varieties of torture are prohibited by law, so it should be self-evident that credible threats of death by state officials should therefore be strictly prohibited in the criminal justice system.

When the California Supreme Court in *People v. Anderson* (1972) and the U.S. Supreme Court in *Furman v. Georgia* (1972) declared death penalty laws unconstitutional, some thought—or at least hoped—that America might have witnessed its last execution.[195] That sentiment, however, proved to be wishful thinking and premature, with Proposition 17 restoring California's death penalty in November 1972,[196] thirty-five states enacting new death penalty statutes in *Furman*'s wake,[197] and the U.S. Supreme Court, in *Gregg* and two companion cases, upholding the death penalty's constitutionality in spite of *Furman*.[198] As a result, American legal systems have carried out more than 1,570 executions—the vast majority of those in the South, where lynchings were once so prevalent[199]—since 1976.[200] Each of those executions—and every case of every death row exoneree, and they all have first and last names and family members—necessarily involved the use of state-sanctioned threats of death. Such threats of death inevitably produce severe torment and fear and, like the lynch mobs of yesteryear, predictably produce psychological terror as the prospect of an unnatural death approaches.[201] After decades of failed legislative efforts, acts of lynching finally became a federal crime in 2022 when the Emmett Till Antilynching Act was signed into law.[202] It is high time—indeed, well past time—for capital punishment to be outlawed and stigmatized, too.

The right to be free from torture and other forms of cruelty is a nonderogable right,[203] and that right is reflected in international law,[204] American case law,[205] and the U.S. Supreme Court's Eighth Amendment jurisprudence.[206] That both physical and mental forms of torture are forbidden by international law and international humanitarian law now dates back many decades.[207] Indeed, the prohibition of torture has already achieved jus cogens status alongside the strict international law prohibitions of maritime piracy, slavery, racial discrimination, and genocide.[208] Legal commentators and jurists, citing the UN Convention against Torture, have repeatedly emphasized that the prohibition against physical and mental torture is absolute—that it admits of no exceptions whatsoever. No public emergency, and not even war or imminent threat of war, is considered a justification for torture.[209] By failing to classify the death penalty as torture and by failing to declare the death penalty to be a per se violation of the Eighth and Fourteenth Amendments, the U.S. Supreme Court missed an important opportunity in *Furman* and later cases to put an end to the death penalty once and for all. Justices William Brennan and Thurgood Marshall—both of whom sought to classify the death penalty as a per se Eighth Amendment violation—regularly dissented after *Gregg* reauthorized the death penalty's use.[210] But a majority of Supreme Court justices, deliberately looking away from the reality of what the death penalty truly is, have consistently failed to recognize what Justices Brennan and Marshall saw so clearly: that the death penalty is inherently cruel, no matter the circumstances of its use.[211] If a simulated execution is a torturous act (and it is), it is clear that a real execution should be treated as a torturous act, too. Whether an act amounts to torture must be gauged by what the state actor is doing in real time, not by what an offender did in the past, no matter how heinous the offender's crime.

The UN Convention against Torture was not drafted and ratified by the United States until after *Furman* was decided.[212] But even before *Furman*, American jurist Harry Blackmun—then an Eighth Circuit judge—persuasively wrote in *Jackson v. Bishop* (1968) that the nonlethal corporal punishment of whipping violating the Eighth Amendment's cruel and unusual punishments clause. As Blackmun, declaring unconstitutional the lashing of Arkansas prisoners, wrote for the Eighth Circuit in that case, "We have no difficulty in reaching the conclusion that the use of the strap in the penitentiaries of Arkansas is punishment which, in this last third of the 20th century, runs afoul of the Eighth Amendment." As he stressed in his opinion, "Corporal punishment generates hate toward the keepers who punish and toward the system which permits it. It is degrading to the punisher and to the punished alike."[213] If the rights to be free from torture and cruelty are universal rights (and they are), and if credible death threats are already treated as unlawfully coercive or torturous acts in other contexts (and they are), then *no one*—whether guilty or innocent—should be subjected to such treatment or such torture or cruelty. In short, the death penalty must be reclassified as a torturous practice and its use strictly proscribed by international and domestic law. The rule of law, requiring equality of treatment and that those in power be subjected to the same laws and rules as those in society at large, demands no less. Just as nonstate actors are prohibited by law from killing and making death threats, so too must state actors be prohibited from gratuitously killing prisoners and making death threats of the kind now routinely made in the context of the death penalty's administration.[214]

In the twenty-first century, the U.S. Supreme Court—tasked with interpreting the U.S. Constitution—need not label the death penalty as a torturous act in order to declare it unconstitutional (although torture aptly describes capital punishment when objectively considered). Just as the Supreme Court in *Furman* found that the death penalty, as then applied, constituted a violation of the Eighth Amendment's cruel and unusual punishments clause, today's Supreme Court justices—if they so choose—could simply proclaim that capital punishment amounts to a "cruel and unusual punishment." The death penalty is certainly cruel, and it has certainly become very rare—or unusual—as the number of American death sentences and executions has dwindled, making the punishment, when inflicted, more freakish and arbitrary than ever.[215] Already, many nonlethal corporal punishments have been invalidated on Eighth Amendment grounds, with many of those cases involving far less severe punishments than the death penalty. For example, in *Hope v. Pelzer* (2002), the Supreme Court described an inmate's mistreatment as an "obvious" Eighth Amendment violation, where the Alabama inmate had been shackled to a hitching post for several hours in the hot sun without water, becoming dehydrated and sunburned.[216] What's really obvious in light of such past rulings? That the death penalty must be outlawed as a violation of the Eighth and Fourteenth Amendments.

One provision of the existing U.S. Code—10 U.S.C. § 855, titled "Cruel and Unusual Punishments Prohibited"—already associates the concept of cruel or unusual punishments with nonlethal corporal punishments. A provision of federal law, article 55 of the Uniform Code of Military Justice (one rooted in protecting military service members from antiquated punishments),[217] reads, "Punishment by flogging, or by branding, marking, or tattooing on the body, or any other cruel or unusual punishment, may not be adjudged by any court-martial or inflicted upon any person subject to this chapter. The use of irons, single or double, except for the purpose of safe custody, is prohibited."[218] Of course, international treaties to which the United States is already a state party prohibit both cruel, inhuman, and degrading treatment (CIDT) and torture, so whether acts are classified as CIDT or torture (cruelty's aggravated form), they are repugnant and unlawful.[219] Whether the death penalty is classified as a cruel and unusual punishment or under the more stigmatizing rubric of torture, the result—a declaration of the death penalty's unconstitutionality, one that would take off the table the state's right to kill—would be exactly the same.

Still, it is logical to classify and forever stigmatize the death penalty for what it is: an act of torture. Article 1 of the UN Convention against Torture defines *torture* as "any act by which severe pain or suffering, whether physical or mental, is intentionally inflicted upon a person for such purposes as obtaining from him or a third person information or a confession, punishing him for an act he or a third person has committed or is suspected of having committed, or intimidating or coercing him or a third person, or for any reason based on discrimination of any kind."[220] That description fits the death penalty to a tee because the punishment intentionally inflicts severe pain and suffering; the threat of its use has, over the years, been proved to extract false confessions because of the terror associated with threats of death; and it continues to be administered in an arbitrary, highly discriminatory fashion. "Some wrongs are more blameworthy than others," the U.S. Supreme Court wrote in 1996, pointing out the distinction between "nonviolent crimes" and those "marked by violence or the threat of violence."[221] Whereas a crime, whether heinous or petty, is always about what an offender has done, a punishment is always about how a society and the state choose to behave in response. With any capital punishment regime, it is state actors (lawmakers and prosecutors) who authorize and bring capital charges, it is members of society and state actors (jurors and judges) who impose death sentences, and it is state actors (governors, wardens, and executioners) who sign death warrants, plan executions, and carry out the state-sanctioned threats of death made by the state officials.

Torture is the aggravated form of cruelty, and the death penalty—as the state's ultimate sanction—should be classified not as state officials euphemistically choose to *characterize* it (i.e., as a "lawful sanction") but according to its inherent and immutable *characteristics*. There is, in fact, no way for the death penalty to be administered without resorting to the use of credible death threats—the kind of threats that, in other contexts, are already treated as inflicting severe pain or suffering that amounts to unlawful psychological torture. In the non-state-actor context, an offender's torturous conduct plainly aggravates the nature of the crime. Ironically, by using capital punishment, the state resorts to the very same technique—threats of death— that governments, in their laws, properly classify as tortious, torturous, and criminal conduct. As the Alabama Supreme Court, overseeing a locale that unfortunately still makes use of capital punishment, has held, "One factor this Court has considered particularly indicative that a murder is 'especially heinous, atrocious or cruel' is the infliction of psychological torture.

Psychological torture can be inflicted where the victim is in intense fear and is aware of, but helpless to prevent, impending death."[222] Just as it constitutes psychological torture for the perpetrator of a heinous crime to make someone aware of his or her impending death where that victim is then helpless to prevent that death, it is psychological torture to subject a person who is already in custody to a state-sanctioned death threat because the person subjected to that threat is also helpless to prevent that death.

In a world that adheres to a robust understanding of the rule of law, it is totally hypocritical for state officials, on the one hand, to condemn and criminalize death threats (as they rightfully do to deter nonstate actors from making them) and, on the other, to then turn around and use state-sanctioned death threats in their judicial systems. The all-powerful state does not order the rape of rapists or the maiming of those who maim, and neither should the state resort to killing those who kill or using death threats to intentionally inflict severe pain or suffering on those suspected or convicted of crimes or their families.[223] "Many laws consider a premeditated crime more serious than a crime of pure violence," the Nobel Prize–winning writer Albert Camus once observed, adding this coda in the form of a question: "But what then is capital punishment but the most premeditated of murders, to which no criminal's deed, however calculated it may be, can be compared?" A state that kills in the name of society, in fact, simultaneously mars both the state and its citizenry. In his influential essay "Reflections on the Guillotine," one presciently cited by Justice Brennan in *Furman*, Camus specifically warned against the evil of state-sanctioned killing and the death penalty's disproportionate and grotesque nature even in relation to heinous acts of violence in the non-state-actor context: "For there to be equivalence, the death penalty would have to punish a criminal who had warned his victim of the date at which he would inflict a horrible death on him and who, from that moment onward, had confined him at his mercy for months. Such a monster is not encountered in private life."[224]

NOTES

1. Furman v. Georgia, 408 U.S. 238, 239–40 (1972).

2. John D. Bessler, *Cruel and Unusual: The American Death Penalty and the Founders' Eighth Amendment* (Boston: Northeastern University Press, 2012); Carol S. Steiker and Jordan M. Steiker, *Courting Death: The Supreme Court and Capital Punishment* (Cambridge, MA: Belknap Press of Harvard University Press, 2016).

3. John D. Bessler, "From the Founding to the Present: An Overview of Legal Thought and the Eighth Amendment's Evolution," in *The Eighth Amendment and Its Future in a New Age of Punishment*, ed. Meghan J. Ryan and William W. Berry III (Cambridge: Cambridge University Press, 2000), 11.

4. U.S. Const. amend. VIII.

5. Timbs v. Indiana, 139 S. Ct. 682, 687 (2019).

6. U.S. Const. amend. XIV, § 1.

7. *Furman*, 408 U.S. at 260, 263–65, 271–73, 279, 281, 288 (Brennan, J., concurring); *id*. at 316, 318–23, 345 (Marshall, J., concurring); *id*. at 377–78, 380, 391–92 (Burger, C.J., dissenting); *id*. at 422 (Powell, J., dissenting).

8. Declaration on the Protection of All Persons from Being Subjected to Torture and Other Cruel, Inhuman or Degrading Treatment or Punishment, G.A. Resolution 3452 (XXX), Dec. 9, 1975, art. 1(2).

9. *Furman*, 408 U.S. at 309 (Stewart, J., concurring); *id*. at 418, 458 (Powell, J. dissenting); *id*. at 405 (Blackmun, J., dissenting).

10. John Bessler, *The Death Penalty's Denial of Fundamental Human Rights: International Law, State Practice, and the Emerging Abolitionist Norm* (Cambridge: Cambridge University Press, 2023), 34, 45–46.

11. John D. Bessler, *The Birth of American Law: An Italian Philosopher and the American Revolution* (Durham, NC: Carolina Academic, 2014); John D. Bessler, "The Marquis Beccaria: An Italian Penal Reformer's Meteoric Rise in the British Isles in the Transatlantic Republic of Letters," *Diciottesimo Secolo* 4 (2019): 107.

12. Geneva Convention Relative to the Treatment of Prisoners of War (hereinafter "GC III"), Aug. 12, 1949, 6 U.S.T. 3316, 75 U.N.T.S. 135.

13. Trop v. Dulles, 356 U.S. 86, 101 (1958).

14. Jutta Brunnée and Stephen J. Toope, *Legitimacy and Legality in International Law: An Interactional Account* (Cambridge: Cambridge University Press, 2010), 226.

15. E.g., Michael Meltsner, "Litigating Against the Death Penalty: The Strategy Behind *Furman*," *Yale Law Journal* 82, no. 6 (1973): 1111.

16. E.g., Lisenba v. People of State of California, 314 U.S. 219, 237 (1941).

17. Solesbee v. Balkcom, 339 U.S. 9, 14 (1950) (Frankfurter, J., dissenting).

18. Watts v. State of Indiana, 338 U.S. 49, 51–54 (1949); *id*. at 60 (Jackson, J., concurring in part and dissenting in part); Colombe v. Connecticut, 367 U.S. 568, 620 (1961) (Frankfurter, J.).

19. GC III, art. 17; David Weissbrodt and Cheryl Heilman, "Defining Torture and Cruel, Inhuman, and Degrading Treatment," *Law and Inequality* 29, no. 2 (2011): 343, 349.

20. Arthur J. Goldberg and Alan M. Dershowitz, "Declaring the Death Penalty Unconstitutional," *Harvard Law Review* 83 (1970): 1773, 1786–87.

21. *Trop*, 356 U.S. at 99 (emphasis added).

22. State v. Makwanyane 1995 (3) SA391 (CC) (S. Afr.).

23. John D. Bessler, "Foreword: The Death Penalty in Decline: From Colonial America to the Present," *Criminal Law Bulletin* 50, no. 3 (2014): 245.

24. John D. Bessler, "Taking Psychological Torture Seriously: The Torturous Nature of Credible Death Threats and the Collateral Consequences for Capital Punishment," *Northeastern University Law Review* 11, no. 1 (2019): 89.

25. John D. Bessler, "The Anomaly of Executions: The Cruel and Unusual Punishments Clause in the 21st Century," *British Journal of American Legal Studies* 2 (2013): 297.

26. John D. Bessler, "The Abolitionist Movement Comes of Age: From Capital Punishment as a Lawful Sanction to a Peremptory, International Law Norm Barring Executions," *Montana Law Review* 79 (2018): 37.

27. Andrew Kent, "Piracy and Due Process," *Michigan Journal of International Law* 39 (2018): 400.

28. Jesselyn Radack, "Tortured Legal Ethics: The Role of the Government Advisor in the War on Terrorism," *University of Colorado Law Review* 77 (2006): 22–23.

29. Convention against Torture and Other Cruel, Inhuman or Degrading Treatment or Punishment, Dec. 10, 1984, 1465 U.N.T.S. 85, 113 (hereinafter "CAT"), arts. 1 and 16.

30. Juan E. Méndez, "The Death Penalty as the Absolute Prohibition of Torture and Cruel, Inhuman, and Degrading Treatment or Punishment," *Human Rights Brief* 20, no. 1 (2012): 1; John D. Bessler, *The Death Penalty as Torture: From the Dark Ages to Abolition* (Durham, NC: Carolina Academic, 2017).

31. Amnesty International, *Death Sentences and Executions 2022* (May 2023), https://www.amnesty.org/en/documents/act50/6548/2023/en/, p. 12; DPIC, "Facts about the Death Penalty," accessed October 16, 2023, https://dpic-cdn.org/production/documents/pdf/FactSheet.pdf.

32. E.g., Sotloff v. Syrian Arab Republic, 525 F. Supp. 3d 121, 126, 137 (D. D.C. 2021).

33. William W. Berry III and Meghan J. Ryan, "Cruel Techniques, Unusual Secrets," *Ohio State Law Journal* 78 (2017): 413.

34. Tania Tetlow, "Criminalizing 'Private' Torture," *William and Mary Law Review* 58 (2016): 229–33.

35. 18 U.S.C. § 2340A(a), (c).

36. David Luban and Henry Shue, "Mental Torture: A Critique of Erasures in U.S. Law," *Georgetown Law Journal* 100 (2012): 823.

37. 18 U.S.C. § 2340(1)–(2); 18 U.S.C. § 1111(c)(6).

38. Pub. L. No. 102–256, 106 Stat. 73 (1992) (codified at 28 U.S.C. § 1350 note); *accord* 28 U.S.C. § 1605A(h)(7).

39. Xuncax v. Gramajo, 886 F. Supp. 162, 175–76 (D. Mass. 1995).

40. 8 U.S.C. § 1182(a)(3)(E)(iii).

41. 22 U.S.C. § 2152(a)-(b).

42. 28 U.S.C. § 1605A(a)(1); Bessler, *Death Penalty's Denial*, 14, 161, 171–72, 174, 177, 271–72.

43. Meghan J. Ryan, "Does the Eighth Amendment Punishments Clause Prohibit Only Punishments That Are Both Cruel and Unusual?," *Washington University Law Review* 87 (2010): 574, 582–83, 615.

44. Bessler, "Taking Psychological Torture Seriously," 3n1.

45. *Furman*, 408 U.S. at 240–57 (Douglas, J., concurring); *id.* at 257–306 (Brennan, J., concurring); *id.* at 306–10 (Stewart, J., concurring); *id.* at 310–14 (White, J., concurring); *id.* at 314–74 (Marshall, J., concurring).

46. Steiker and Steiker, this volume.

47. Linda H. Edwards, *Readings in Persuasion: Briefs That Changed the World* (Burlington, MA: Aspen, 2014), pt. 2, chap. 11; Scott W. Howe, "The Futile Quest for Racial Neutrality in Capital Selection and the Eighth Amendment Argument for Abolition Based on Unconscious Racial Discrimination," *William and Mary Law Review* 45 (2004): 2154–55.

48. Aikens v. California, 406 U.S. 813 (1972).

49. William J. Brennan Jr., "Constitutional Adjudication and the Death Penalty: A View from the Court," *Harvard Law Review* 100 (1986): 313–14.

50. *Furman*, 408 U.S. at 240–44, 253–57 (Douglas, J., concurring); *id.* at 257–63, 274, 300–305 (Brennan, J., concurring); *id.* at 306–8 (Stewart, J., concurring); *id.* at 310–12 (White, J., concurring); *id.* at 316–22, 330–33, 342–65 (Marshall, J., concurring).

51. See generally Bessler, *Cruel and Unusual*; Bessler, *Birth of American Law*.

52. David Garland, *Peculiar Institution: America's Death Penalty in an Age of Abolition* (Oxford: Oxford University Press, 2010), 114.

53. *Furman*, 408 U.S. at 258–59 (Brennan, J., concurring); Bessler, *Cruel and Unusual*, 186; Benjamin White, "Pain Speaks for Itself: Divorcing the Eighth Amendment from the Spirit of the Moment," *San Diego Law Review* 58 (2021): 460–61.

54. *Furman*, 408 U.S. at 259–60, 263, 377, 283 (Brennan, J., concurring).

55. Weems v. United States, 217 U.S. 349, 363–64, 366–69 (1910); Bessler, *Cruel and Unusual*, 186.

56. 1 Annals of Cong. 754 (1789).

57. *Weems*, 217 U.S. at 368–69; *Furman*, 408 U.S. at 244 (Douglas, J., concurring); *id.* at 266 (Brennan, J., concurring).

58. *Weems*, 217 U.S. at 369–71, 373, 378.

59. Bessler, *Cruel and Unusual*, 54; see also Bessler, *Birth of American Law.*

60. Wilkerson v. Utah, 99 U.S. 130, 135–36 (1879).

61. In re Kemmler, 136 U.S. 436, 446–47 (1890).

62. *Furman*, 408 U.S. at 271–72 (Brennan, J., concurring).

63. See, e.g., Frederick Bernays Wiener, "Courts-Martial and the Bill of Rights: The Original Practice II," *Harvard Law Review* 72 (1958): 291.

64. *Furman*, 408 U.S. at 271–72, 287–88 (Brennan, J., concurring).

65. *Trop*, 356 U.S. at 100–101.

66. *Furman*, 408 U.S. at 270–73 (Brennan, J., concurring).

67. *Id.* at 375–405 (Burger, C.J., dissenting); *id.* at 405–14 (Blackmun, J., dissenting); *id.* at 414–65 (Powell, J., dissenting); *id.* at 465–70 (Rehnquist, J., dissenting).

68. David Beasley, "Georgia Inmate in Historic Death Penalty Case Gains Perspective," Reuters, April 27, 2016, https://www.reuters.com/article/us-usa-georgia-furman/georgia-inmate-in-historic-death-penalty-case-gains-perspective-idUSKCN0XO2FM#.

69. *Furman*, 408 U.S. at 411 (Blackmun, J., dissenting).

70. People v. Anderson, 493 P.2d 880, 882, 894–95, 899 (Cal. 1972).

71. E.g., John D. Bessler, "The Long March toward Abolition: From the Enlightenment to the United Nations and the Death Penalty's Slow Demise," *University of Florida Journal of Law and Public Policy* 29, no. 1 (2018): 1.

72. Before *Furman*, executions had fallen into disuse, with a de facto moratorium in place. Carol S. Steiker and Jordan M. Steiker, "Cost and Capital Punishment: A New Consideration Transforms an Old Debate," *University of Chicago Legal Forum*, no. 1 (2010): 132–33.

73. Statement of Attorney General Ramsey Clark, U.S. Senate, Subcommittee on Criminal Laws and Procedures of the Committee on the Judiciary, Washington, DC, July 2, 1968.

74. Maynard v. Cartwright, 486 U.S. 356, 362 (1988).

75. Gregg v. Georgia, 428 U.S. 153 (1976); Jurek v. Texas, 428 U.S. 262 (1976); Proffitt v. Florida, 428 U.S. 242 (1976).

76. Roberts v. Louisiana, 428 U.S. 325 (1976); Woodson v. North Carolina, 428 U.S. 280 (1976).

77. Martin Clancy and Tim O'Brien, *Murder at the Supreme Court: Lethal Crimes and Landmark Cases* (Amherst, NY: Prometheus Books, 2013), 47–48.

78. E.g., Tessa M. Gorman, comment, "Back on the Chain Gang: Why the Eighth Amendment and the History of Slavery Proscribe the Resurgence of Chain Gangs," *California Law Review* 85, no. 2 (1997): 469n243. ("Federal courts have cited the 'evolving standards of decency' language used in *Trop* over 500 times.")

What-Ifs and Missed Opportunities / 55

79. Wilkins v. Gaddy, 559 U.S. 34, 36–40 (2010); Hudson v. McMillian, 503 U.S. 1, 5–10 (1992); Whitley v. Albers, 474 U.S. 312, 318–26 (1986); Graham v. Connor, 490 U.S. 386, 394 (1989).

80. Farmer v. Brennan, 511 U.S. 825, 832–33 (1994).

81. *Hudson*, 503 U.S. at 9.

82. Helling v. McKinney, 509 U.S. 25, 32–33 (1993).

83. Rowe v. Wall, Case No. 15-C-1006, 2016 WL 11695974, at *2 (E.D. Wis. July 12, 2016); Wilkerson v. Stalder, 639 F. Supp. 2d 654, 677 (M.D. La. 2007).

84. Coker v. Georgia, 433 U.S. 584, 593, 596 (1977) (plurality opinion); Kennedy v. Louisiana, 554 U.S. 407, 420 (2008).

85. Ford v. Wainwright, 477 U.S. 399, 406 (1986).

86. Atkins v. Virginia, 536 U.S. 304, 311–12 (2002); Hall v. Florida, 572 U.S. 701, 708 (2014).

87. Thompson v. Oklahoma, 487 U.S. 815, 821 (1988); Roper v. Simmons, 543 U.S. 551, 560–61 (2005).

88. Enmund v. Florida, 458 U.S. 782, 797 (1982).

89. *Maynard*, 486 U.S. at 362.

90. Kansas v. Marsh, 548 U.S. 163, 175 (2006); Brown v. Sanders, 546 U.S. 212, 215 (2006).

91. Baze v. Rees, 553 U.S. 35 (2008); Glossip v. Gross, 576 U.S. 863 (2015); Bucklew v. Precythe, 139 S. Ct. 1112 (2019).

92. Nance v. Ward, 142 S. Ct. 2214, 2219–20 (2022).

93. Brown v. Plata, 563 U.S. 493, 503–45 (2011); *Farmer*, 511 U.S. at 852–53 (Blackmun, J., concurring); *Hudson*, 503 U.S. at 16 (Blackmun, J., concurring); Apodaca v. Raemisch, 139 S. Ct. 5, 6 (2018) (statement of Sotomayor, J., respecting denial of cert.).

94. Peter Baumann, note, "'Waiting on Death': Nathan Dunlap and the Cruel Effect of Uncertainty," *Georgetown Law Journal* 106, no. 3 (2018): 878; Diane P. Wood, "Our 18th Century Constitution in the 21st Century World," *New York University Law Review* 80, no. 4 (2005): 1100.

95. *Trop*, 356 U.S. at 101; Estelle v. Gamble, 429 U.S. 97, 102 (1976); Gardner v. Florida, 430 U.S. 349, 357 (1977); Rhodes v. Chapman, 452 U.S. 337, 346 (1981); *Hudson*, 503 U.S. at 8; *Farmer*, 511 U.S. at 833.

96. *Furman*, 408 U.S. at 242 (Douglas, J., concurring); *id.* at 269–70 (Brennan, J., concurring); *id.* at 327, 329 (Marshall, J., concurring).

97. *Woodson*, 428 U.S. at 293; *Roberts*, 428 U.S. at 336.

98. Graham v. Florida, 560 U.S. 48, 58 (2010).

99. *Bucklew*, 139 S. Ct. at 1123; see also *Glossip*, 576 U.S. at 899 (Scalia, J., concurring).

100. Trozzi v. Lake County, Ohio, 29 F.4th 745, 751 (6th Cir. 2022).

101. Jones v. Mississippi, 141 S. Ct. 1307, 1336n4 (2021) (Sotomayor, J., dissenting).

102. United States v. Briggs, 141 S. Ct. 467, 472 (2020).

103. Fawn M. Brodie, *Thomas Jefferson: An Intimate History* (New York: W. W. Norton, 1974), 244.

104. McGautha v. California, 402 U.S. 183 (1971).

105. Jeffrey L. Kirchmeier, *Imprisoned by the Past: Warren McCleskey and the American Death Penalty* (Oxford: Oxford University Press, 2015).

106. *Furman*, 408 U.S. at 309–10 (Stewart, J., concurring).

107. *Furman*, 408 U.S. at 310 (Stewart, J., concurring); Linda Hirshman, *Sisters in Law: How Sandra Day O'Connor and Ruth Bader Ginsburg Went to the Supreme Court and Changed the World* (New York: HarperCollins, 2015).

108. *Furman*, 408 U.S. at 315–22, 364 (Marshall, J., concurring).

109. E.g., Mark V. Tushnet, *Making Civil Rights Law: Thurgood Marshall and the Supreme Court, 1936–1961* (Oxford: Oxford University Press, 1994); Juan Williams, *Thurgood Marshall: American Revolutionary* (New York: Three Rivers, 1998).

110. *Furman*, 408 U.S. at 364–66 (Marshall, J., concurring).

111. Brandon L. Garrett, *End of Its Rope: How Killing the Death Penalty Can Revive Criminal Justice* (Cambridge, MA: Harvard University Press, 2017), chap. 1.

112. *Furman*, 408 U.S. at 260, 263–65, 271–73, 279, 281, 288 (Brennan, J., concurring); *id.* at 316, 318–23, 345 (Marshall, J., concurring); *id.* at 377–78, 380, 391–92 (Burger, C.J., dissenting); *id.* at 422 (Powell, J., dissenting).

113. *Gregg*, 428 U.S. at 179–80; *Proffitt*, 428 U.S. at 247; *Jurek*, 428 U.S. at 268.

114. The "Baldus study"—two sophisticated statistical studies examining more than two thousand Georgia murder cases—was performed by three professors. David C. Baldus, George Woodworth, and Charles Pulaski, "Comparative Review of Death Sentences: An Empirical Study of the Georgia Experience," *Journal of Criminal Law and Criminology* 74, no. 3 (1983): 661.

115. McCleskey v. Kemp, 481 U.S. 279 (1987).

116. Mark V. Tushnet, ed., *Thurgood Marshall: His Speeches, Writings, Arguments, Opinions, and Reminiscences* (Chicago: Lawrence Hill Books, 2001), 293, 295.

117. *McCleskey*, 481 U.S. at 287, 291–92, 299–309; see also John H. Blume, Theodore Eisenberg and Sheri Lynn Johnson, "Post-*McCleskey* Racial Discrimination Claims in Capital Cases," *Cornell Law Review* 83, no. 6 (1998): 1776 (discussing the findings of the Baldus study).

118. State v. Santiago, 122 A.3d 1, 97 (Conn. 2015) (Norcott and McDonald, JJ., concurring).

119. Jack Greenberg, "Capital Punishment as a System," *Yale Law Journal* 91, no. 5 (1982): 915.

120. Peggy M. Tobolowsky and Chad R. Trulson, "What Happens after Commutation? An Examination of Institutional Misconduct by Previously Death-Sentenced Intellectually Disabled Capital Offenders," *Criminal Law Bulletin* 51, no. 5, art. 2 (2015): 1074.

121. Deborah W. Denno, "Getting to Death: Are Executions Constitutional?," *Iowa Law Review* 82, no. 2 (1997): 412n498.

122. DPIC, *The DPIC Death Penalty Census*, https://deathpenaltyinfo.org/facts-and-research/death-penalty-census (noting that "more than 9,700 death sentences" were imposed in the United States "between 1972 and January 1, 2021").

123. DPIC, *Facts about the Death Penalty*, October 11, 2023, https://dpic-cdn.org/production/documents/pdf/FactSheet.pdf.

124. Albert E. Scherr, "Ineffective Assistance of Counsel in DNA Cases: A Re-appraisal of the Effectiveness of *Strickland v. Washington Judges*," *Loyola of Los Angeles Law Review* 55 (2022): 577; Conservatives Concerned About the Death Penalty, "Innocent Lives in the Balance: The Real Risk of Executing the Innocent," ScheerPost, October 10, 2023, https://scheerpost.com/2023/10/10/innocent-lives-in-the-balance-the-real-risk-of-executing-the-innocent/. The Innocence Database of the Death Penalty Information Center identifies each case in which DNA played a role in the exoneration. DPIC, *Innocence Database*, accessed October 16, 2023, https://deathpenaltyinfo.org/database/innocence.

125. *Furman*, 408 U.S. at 292 (Brennan, J., concurring).

126. Lee Kovarsky, "The Trump Executions," *Texas Law Review* 100 (2022): 629n61.

127. Meredith Martin Rountree, "Volunteers for Execution: Directions for Further Research into Grief, Culpability, and Legal Structures," *UMKC Law Review* 82 (2014): 322n119.

128. Nino C. Monea, "The Reprieve Power: May the Uniform Code of Military Justice Limit Executive Clemency?," *West Virginia Law Review* 123 (2020): 575.

129. James S. Liebman et al., *A Broken System: Error Rates in Capital Cases, 1973–1995* (Columbia Law School, Paper No. 15, 2000), Columbia Law School Scholarship Archive, https://scholarship.law.columbia.edu/faculty_scholarship/1219/.

130. David R. Dow and Jeffrey R. Newberry, "Reversal Rates in Capital Cases in Texas, 2000–2020," *UCLA Law Review Discourse* 68 (2020): 4–5.

131. "The World Coalition against the Death Penalty Turns 20 Years," Sant'Egidio, May 13, 2022, https://www.santegidio.org/pageID/30284/langID/en/itemID/48161/The-World-Coalition-against-the-Death-Penalty-turns-20-years.html.

132. DPIC, "U.S. Votes No, as Record Number of Nations Adopt UN Resolution for Global Moratorium on Death Penalty," December 20, 2022, https://deathpenaltyinfo.org/news/u-s-votes-no-as-record-number-of-nations-adopt-un-resolution-for-global-moratorium-on-the-death-penalty.

133. State v. Alvogen, Inc., 450 P.3d 390, 2019 WL 5390459, at *1 (Nev. Oct. 21, 2019); Brent E. Newton, "A Case Study in Systemic Unfairness: The Texas Death Penalty, 1973–1994," *Texas Forum on Civil Liberties and Civil Rights* 1, no. 2 (1994): 25.

134. *Santiago*, 122 A.3d at 58; Kathleen A. O'Shea, *Women and the Death Penalty in the United States, 1990–1998* (Westport, CT: Praeger, 1999), 113; Michael Johnson, "Fifteen Years and Death: Double Jeopardy, Multiple Punishments, and Extended Stays on Death Row," *Boston University Public Interest Law Journal* 23, no. 1 (2014): 95.

135. Founding-era executions were carried out in a matter of weeks or months after sentencing. Jacob Leon, "*Bucklew v. Precythe*'s Return to the Original Meaning of 'Unusual': Prohibiting Extensive Delays on Death Row," *Cleveland State Law Review* 68, no. 3 (2020): 489–99.

136. Virginia Marso, "Should Dead Men Walk Forever? A Look into Indiana's Execution Dilemma, the Constitutionality of Indefinite Death Sentences, and What Comes Next for Indiana," *Indiana Law Review* 54, no. 2 (2021): 482–83; Lee Kovarsky, "Delay in the Shadow of Death," *New York University Law Review* 95, no. 5 (2020): 1322n7; Lawrence M. Friedman, "The Same Only Different: Reflections on Robert Kagan's *Adversarial Legalism*," *Law and Social Inquiry* 45, no. 4 (2020): 1176.

137. Some people have spent close to—or more than—forty years on death row. Jordan v. State, 224 So. 3d 1252, 1253 (Miss. 2017); Ana M. Otero, "A Murder of Crows: The Politics of Death in Texas—the Bobby James Moore Story," *Gonzaga Law Review* 57, no. 3 (2022): 494.

138. Bharat Malkani, "Dignity and the Death Penalty in the United States Supreme Court," *Hastings Constitutional Law Quarterly* 44, no. 2 (2017): 149; Alkotmánybíróság (AB) [Constitutional Court of Hungary] Oct. 31, 1990, MK 23/1990 (X.31) (Hung.); State v. Makwanyane, 1995 (3) SA391 (CC) (S. Afr.).

139. Roger Hood and Carolyn Hoyle, "Abolishing the Death Penalty Worldwide: The Impact of a 'New Dynamic,'" *Crime and Justice* 38 (2009): 10–11.

140. Soria v. Leninger, No. 2:20-cv-1741 AC P, 2020 WL 6146388, at *3 (E.D. Cal. Oct. 20, 2020); Abram v. Rackley, No. 2:16-cv-2004 MCE KJN P, 2016 WL 6038172, at *2 (E.D. Cal. Oct. 14, 2016).

141. John D. Bessler, "Torture and Trauma: Why the Death Penalty Is Wrong and Should Be Strictly Prohibited by American and International Law," *Washburn Law Jour-*

nal 58 (2019): 1; United States v. Carignan, 342 U.S. 36, 41 (1951); Upshaw v. United States, 335 U.S. 410, 413 (1948); Irvine v. People of California, 347 U.S. 128, 141 (Black, J., dissenting).

142. Burton v. Livingston, 791 F.2d 97, 100 (8th Cir. 1986).

143. Northington v. Jackson, 973 F.2d 1518, 1520, 1522–24 (10th Cir. 1992).

144. Bessler, "Taking Psychological Torture Seriously," 79–80, 87.

145. Taylor v. Riojas, 141 S. Ct. 52, 53 (2020).

146. State v. Griffin, 262 A.3d 44, 65n20 (Conn. 2021); *id.* at 101 (Ecker, J., concurring in part and dissenting in part); Days v. Eastchester Police Dep't, 18-CV-11538 (NSR), 2020 WL 5504433, at *3 (S.D. N.Y. Sept. 9, 2020); Villegas v. City of El Paso, EP-15-CV-00386-FM, 2020 WL 981878, at *2 (W.D. Tex. Feb. 28, 2020); Thomas v. City of Philadelphia, 290 F. Supp. 3d 371, 375 (E.D. Pa. 2018); State v. Rettenberger, 984 P.2d 1009, 1012 (Utah 1999).

147. Lauren Morehouse, note, "Confess or Die: Why Threatening a Suspect with the Death Penalty Should Render Confessions Involuntary," *American Criminal Law Review* 56, no. 2 (2019): 531; Richard A. Leo and Richard J. Ofshe, "The Consequences of False Confessions: Deprivations of Liberty and Miscarriages of Justice in the Age of Psychological Interrogation," *Journal of Criminal Law and Criminology* 88 (1998): 477–79.

148. United States v. Rodgers, 186 F. Supp. 2d 971, 975 (E.D. Wis. 2002).

149. E.g., DPIC, "DPIC Analysis: At Least a Dozen Exonerations in 2021 Involved the Wrongful Threat or Pursuit of the Death Penalty," August 26, 2022, https://death penaltyinfo.org/news/dpic-analysis-at-least-a-dozen-exonerations-in-2021-involved-the -wrongful-threat-or-pursuit-of-the-death-penalty; DPIC, "Idaho Falls Will Pay $11.7 Million to Exoneree Coerced into False Confession by Threat of the Death Penalty," June 24, 2022, https://deathpenaltyinfo.org/news/idaho-falls-will-pay-11-7-million-to -exoneree-coerced-into-false-confession-by-threat-of-the-death-penalty; DPIC, "DPIC Analysis: 13 Exonerated in 2020 from Convictions Obtained by Wrongful Threat or Pursuit of the Death Penalty," August 6, 2021, https://deathpenaltyinfo.org/news/dpic -analysis-13-exonerated-in-2020-from-convictions-obtained-by-wrongful-threat-or -pursuit-of-the-death-penalty; DPIC, "DPIC Analysis: Use or Threat of Death Penalty Implicated in 19 Exoneration Cases in 2019," October 23, 2020, https://deathpenaltyinfo .org/facts-and-research/dpic-reports/dpic-special-reports/dpic-analysis-2019-exoner ation-report-implicates-use-or-threat-of-death-penalty-in-19-wrongful-convictions; DPIC, "False Confessions and Threats of the Death Penalty," August 8, 2013, https:// deathpenaltyinfo.org/news/false-confessions-and-threats-of-the-death-penalty.

150. Kara Sharkey, comment, "Delay in Considering the Constitutionality of Inordinate Delay: The Death Row Phenomenon and the Eighth Amendment," *University of Pennsylvania Law Review* 161, no. 3 (2013): 874.

151. Thompson v. McNeil, 556 U.S. 1114 (2009) (Stevens, J., statement respecting denial of cert.); Lackey v. Texas, 541 U.S. 1045 (1995) (Stevens, J., statement respecting denial of cert.).

152. Bessler, "Taking Psychological Torture Seriously," 72–80.

153. E.g., *Ex parte* Deardorff, 6 So. 3d 1235, 1240 (Ala. 2008); State v. Bell, 603 S.E.2d 93, 121 (N.C. 2004).

154. Feltrop v. Missouri, 501 U.S. 1262, 1263 (1991) (Marshall, J., dissenting from cert. denial).

155. E.g., Susan F. Sharp, *Hidden Victims: The Effects of the Death Penalty on Families of the Accused* (New Brunswick, NJ: Rutgers University Press, 2005), 158; Johnson v. Levy, No. M2009-02596-COA-R3-CV, 2010 WL 119288 (Tenn. Ct. App. Jan. 14, 2010).

156. Branden v. F.H. Paschen, S.N. Nielsen, Inc., No. CV 19-2406, 2019 WL 1760694, at *3–5 (E.D. La. Apr. 22, 2019) (threats of adverse employment action and physical harm, including a death threat, sufficient to support an intentional infliction of emotional distress claim).

157. See generally Bessler, "Taking Psychological Torture Seriously."

158. Faulder v. Johnson, 99 F. Supp. 2d 774, 775–77 (S.D. Tex. 1999).

159. E.g., Jennifer Hansler and Nectar Gan, "US 'Disappointed' by Chinese Court's Decision to Uphold Death Sentence for American Citizen," CNN, April 14, 2023, https://www.cnn.com/2023/04/14/china/us-citizen-death-sentence-upheld-china-intl-hnk/index.html; David Brennan, "Biden Aides Condemn 'Horrifying' Iran Execution Despite Nuclear Deal Hopes," Newsweek, December 14, 2020, https://www.newsweek.com/biden-aides-sullivan-blinken-condemn-horrifying-iran-execution-despite-nuclear-deal-hopes-1554459.

160. Elena De Santis, note, "'Life with the Imposition or Exacerbation of Severe Mental Illness and Chance of Death': Why This Distinct Punishment Violates the Eighth Amendment," American Criminal Law Review 56, no. 1 (2018): 247–49.

161. Kenneth Williams, "The Death Penalty and Race and How the Ultimate Punishment Highlights the Flaws in Our Criminal Justice System," Southwestern Law Review 50 (2022): 414. The National Registry of Exonerations, which tracks exonerations in capital and noncapital cases, has documented 3,299 exonerations, including in 1,280 homicide cases. National Registry of Exonerations, Exonerations by Year and Type of Crime, accessed October 16, 2023, https://www.law.umich.edu/special/exoneration/Pages/Exoneration-by-Year-Crime-Type.aspx.

162. Ashlynd Huffman, "One Oklahoma Lawmaker Says Richard Glossip's Claim of Innocence Should Be Enough to Halt Executions," The Frontier, October 3, 2023, https://www.readfrontier.org/stories/one-oklahoma-lawmaker-says-richard-glossips-claim-of-innocence-should-be-enough-to-halt-executions/; Jodi S. Cohen, "Richard Glossip Has Eaten Three Last Meals on Death Row," Pro Publica, July 27, 2022, https://patch.com/oklahoma/across-ok/richard-glossip-has-eaten-three-last-meals-death-row#; Reed Smith, "Reed Smith Investigation into Glossip Death Row Case Raises Grave Concerns," June 15, 2022, https://www.reedsmith.com/en/news/2022/06/reed-smith-investigation-into-glossip-death-row-case-raises-grave-concerns#:~:text=OKLAHOMA%20CITY%20–%20Today%2C%20global%20law,case%20and%20his%20murder%20conviction. Ahead of a later canceled May 2023 execution date, Glossip's murder conviction and death sentence were affirmed even though Oklahoma's attorney general had joined Glossip in a joint motion asking that Glossip's execution be stayed until August 2024. Glossip v. State of Oklahoma, Case No. PCD-2023-267, D-2005-310, 2023 WL 3012463, at *1 (Okla. Ct. Crim. App. Apr. 20, 2023).

163. Rachel King, "No Due Process: How the Death Penalty Violates the Constitutional Rights of the Family Members of Death Row Prisoners," Boston University Public Interest Law Journal 16, no. 2 (2007): 195; Rachel King, "The Impact of Capital Punishment on Families of Defendants and Murder Victims' Family Members," Judicature 89, no. 5 (2006): 292.

164. Wilkerson, 99 U.S. at 136; Estelle, 429 U.S. at 102; Furman, 408 U.S. at 319 (Marshall, J., concurring).

165. Erin Huntington, "Torture and Cruel, Inhuman or Degrading Treatment: A Definitional Approach," U.C. Davis Journal of International Law and Policy 21 (2015): 287.

166. Filártiga v. Peña-Irala, 630 F.2d 876, 880 (2d Cir. 1980).

167. Declaration on the Protection of All Persons from Being Subjected to Torture, G.A. Resolution 3452, 30 U.N. GAOR Supp. (No. 34) 91, U.N.Doc. A/1034 (1975), art. 1.

168. CAT, art. 1.

169. GC III, art. 17.

170. Al Shimari v. CACI Premier Technology, Inc., 840 F.3d 147, 157n5 (4th Cir. 2016).

171. Flores Molina v. Garland, 37 F.4th 626, 633–36 (9th Cir. 2022); Rogel Lopez v. Garland, 861 Fed. Appx. 130, 133–34 (9th Cir. 2021); Doe v. Attorney General of the United States, 956 F.3d 135, 144 (3d Cir. 2020).

172. E.g., Kathleen G. McAnaney, Laura A. Curliss, and C. Elizabeth Abeyta-Price, note, "From Imprudence to Crime: Anti-stalking Law," *Notre Dame Law Review* 68 (1993): 886.

173. E.g., Bathen v. Allison, Case No. 20-cv-2063-MMA (MSB), 2021 WL 4554589, at *5, 8 (S.D. Cal. Oct. 5, 2021).

174. 8 C.F.R. § 1208.18; see also Habtemicael v. Ashcroft, 370 F.3d 774, 782 (8th Cir. 2004).

175. Austin Sarat et al., "The Face of Lethal Injection: Decomposition of the Paradigm and Its Consequences," *British Journal of American Legal Studies* 11 (2022): 97.

176. Estate of Lockett by and through Lockett v. Fallin, 841 F.3d 1098, 1105–10, 1113 (10th Cir. 2016). Other courts have held that qualified immunity does not shield someone from liability who is personally involved in acts of torture. Wilson v. Estate of Burge, No. 21-cv-03487, 2023 WL 2750946, at *22, 24 (N.D. Ill. Mar. 31, 2023); Tillman v. Burge, 813 F. Supp. 2d 946, 966n12 (N.D. Ill. 2011); Escobar v. Reid, 668 F. Supp.2d 1260, 1294–95 (D. Colo. 2009).

177. William W. Berry III, "Individualized Executions," *U.C. Davis Law Review* 52 (2019): 1791.

178. Helen Prejean, *The Death of Innocents: An Eyewitness Account of Wrongful Executions* (New York: Random House, 2005), 258; Helen Prejean, *Dead Man Walking: An Eyewitness Account of the Death Penalty in the United States* (New York: Random House, 1993), 124; Vicki Quade, "The Voice of Dead Men: Interview with Sister Helen Prejean," *Human Rights*, summer 1996, 12, 14.

179. E.g., Austin Sarat, *Gruesome Spectacles: Botched Executions and America's Death Penalty* (Stanford, CA: Stanford Law Books, 2014); Austin Sarat, *Lethal Injection and the False Promise of Humane Execution* (Stanford, CA: Stanford University Press, 2022).

180. Henry Mascia, comment, "A Reconsideration of Haitian Claims for Withholding of Removal under the Convention against Torture," *Pace International Law Review* 19, no. 2 (2007): 288.

181. Luban and Shue, "Mental Torture," 824; Amanda C. Pustilnik, "Pain as Fact and Heuristic: How Pain Neuroimaging Illuminates Moral Dimensions of Law," *Cornell Law Review* 97, no. 4 (2012): 828.

182. 18 U.S.C. § 2340(1)-(2)(A)-(D).

183. A total of 108 countries had completely abolished the death penalty by the end of 2021, with only a small fraction of the world's countries—18 nations—carrying out executions in 2021. Amnesty International, *Death Sentences and Executions 2021* (2022). In 2022, Amnesty International recorded executions in 20 countries. Amnesty International, *Death Sentences and Executions 2022* (2023). In the United States, while 23 states and the District of Columbia have outlawed capital punishment, 27 states and the U.S. government and the U.S. military still authorize death sentences. DPIC, *Facts about the Death Penalty*, October 16, 2023, https://dpic-cdn.org/production/documents/pdf /FactSheet.pdf.

184. John D. Bessler, "Tinkering around the Edges: The Supreme Court's Death Penalty Jurisprudence," *American Criminal Law Review* 49, no. 4 (2012): 1918–19, 1928.

185. 18 U.S.C. § 2340(2)(C) (2004); Department of the Army, *Field Manual 34-52: Intelligence Interrogation* (Washington, DC, September 28, 1992), 1–8; Orantes-Hernandez v. Meese, 685 F. Supp. 1488, 1492 (C.D. Cal. 1988); Acree v. Republic of Iraq, 271 F. Supp. 2d 179, 185, 210, 218 (D. D.C. 2003), *vacated on other grounds*, 370 F.3d 41 (D.C. Cir. 2004); Pau Pérez-Sales, *Psychological Torture: Definition, Evaluation and Measurement* (New York: Routledge, 2017).

186. Metin Başoğlu and Ebru Şalcıoğlu, *A Mental Healthcare Model for Mass Trauma Survivors: Control-Focused Behavioral Treatment of Earthquake, War, and Torture Trauma* (Cambridge: Cambridge University Press, 2011), 41.

187. John D. Bessler, "What I Think About When I Think About the Death Penalty," *St. Louis University Law Journal* 62 (2018): 789–802.

188. Robert M. Bohm, *The Ultimate Sanction, Understanding the Death Penalty through Its Many Voices and Many Sides* (New York: Kaplan, 2010).

189. Jeanne Fogle, *Washington, D.C.: A Pictorial Celebration* (New York: Sterling, 2005), 22.

190. Kenneth S. Greenberg, ed., *Nat Turner: A Slave Rebellion in History and Memory* (Oxford: Oxford University Press, 2003), xi; Harry M. Ward, *Public Executions in Richmond, Virginia: A History, 1782–1907* (Jefferson, NC: McFarland, 2012), 22–28.

191. John D. Bessler, "The Inequality of America's Death Penalty: A Crossroads for Capital Punishment at the Intersection of the Eighth and Fourteenth Amendments," *Washington and Lee Law Review Online* 73, no. 1 (2016): 515, 526–27.

192. Robert J. Smith, "The Geography of the Death Penalty and Its Ramifications," *Boston University Law Review* 92, no. 1 (2012): 227.

193. Richard C. Dieter, *The 2% Death Penalty: How a Minority of Counties Produce Most Death Cases at Enormous Costs to All* (Washington, DC: DPIC, 2013).

194. Universal Declaration of Human Rights, art. 5; International Covenant on Civil and Political Rights, art. 7.

195. See, e.g., Roger Hood, "Capital Punishment," in *The Handbook of Crime and Punishment*, ed. Michael Tonry (Oxford: Oxford University Press, 1998), 765.

196. Tom Wicker, "The Death Penalty Again in California: Proposition Limits Powers of Courts," *Decatur Herald* (Decatur, IL), November 15, 1972, 6.

197. *Gregg*, 428 U.S. at 179–80; Carolyn Young, "Death Penalty Re-examined," *Daily Utah Chronicle* (Salt Lake City, UT), May 15, 1975, 3.

198. HRW and ACLU, *Human Rights Violations in the United States: A Report on U.S. Compliance with the International Covenant on Civil and Political Rights* (1993), ix, 132.

199. Equal Justice Initiative, *Lynching in America: Confronting the Legacy of Racial Terror*, 3rd ed. (2017), 4. ("EJI has documented 4084 racial terror lynchings in twelve Southern states between the end of Reconstruction in 1877 and 1950.")

200. DPIC, *Facts about the Death Penalty*, October 16, 2023, https://dpic-cdn.org /production/documents/pdf/FactSheet.pdf (noting that of the 1,577 executions that have taken place in the United States, 1,287 of them were carried out in the South).

201. McDonald v. City of Chicago, 561 U.S. 742, 857 (2010) (Thomas, J., concurring); Press-Enterprise Co. v. Superior Court of California for the County of Riverside, 478 U.S. 1, 8 (1986).

202. Kate Sullivan and Maegan Vazquez, "Biden Signs Bill Making Lynching a Federal Hate Crime into Law," CNN, March 30, 2022, https://www.cnn.com/2022/03/29 /politics/biden-emmett-till-antilynching-act/index.html#:~:text=President%20Joe%20 Biden%20signed%20a,relic%20of%20a%20bygone%20era.

203. Al Shimari v. CACI Premier Technology, Inc., 368 F. Supp. 3d 935, 956 (E.D. Va. 2019).

204. Weissbrodt and Heilman, "Defining Torture," 343; Camilla Amato, comment, "*Salim v. Mitchell*: A First in Accountability for Victims of the United States Torture Program," *Santa Clara Journal of International Law* 18, no. 2 (2020): 230.

205. *Filártiga*, 630 F.2d at 882, 884; 28 U.S.C. § 1350.

206. Michaela P. Sewall, note, "Pushing Execution over the Constitutional Law: Forcible Medication of Condemned Inmates and the Eighth and Fourteenth Amendments," *Boston College Law Review* 51, no. 4 (2010): 1285.

207. See, e.g., Declaration on the Protection of All Persons from Being Subjected to Torture, G.A. Resolution 3452, 30 U.N. GAOR Supp. (No. 34) 91, U.N.Doc. A/1034 (1975), art. 1; GC III, art. 17.

208. Restatement (Third) of the Foreign Relations Law of the United States § 702 and cmt. N. (1987); United States v. Bellaizac-Hurtado, 700 F.3d 1245, 1261 (11th Cir. 2012) (Barkett, J., concurring).

209. E.g., Nuru v. Gonzales, 404 F.3d 1207, 1222 (9th Cir. 2005).

210. E.g., Michael Mello, *Against the Death Penalty: The Relentless Dissents of Justices Brennan and Marshall* (Boston: Northeastern University Press, 1996).

211. In *Glossip*, Justice Breyer—joined by Justice Ginsburg—sought a "full briefing" on "whether the death penalty violates the Constitution." *Glossip*, 576 U.S. at 908 (Breyer, J., dissenting).

212. H.H. v. Garland, Nos. 21-1150 and 21-1230, 2022 WL 12360158 (1st Cir. Oct. 21, 2022); Saint Fort v. Ashcroft, 329 F.3d 191, 196 (1st Cir. 2003).

213. Jackson v. Bishop, 404 F.2d 571, 579–80 (8th Cir. 1968).

214. John D. Bessler, "The Rule of Law: A Necessary Pillar of Free and Democratic Societies for Protecting Human Rights," *Santa Clara Law Review* 61, no. 2 (2021): 467.

215. John D. Bessler, "The Concept of 'Unusual Punishments' in Anglo-American Law: The Death Penalty as Arbitrary, Discriminatory, and Cruel and Unusual," *Northwestern Journal of Law and Social Policy* 13, no. 4 (2018): 2.

216. Hope v. Pelzer, 536 U.S. 730, 731, 735n2 (2002).

217. Douglas L. Simon, "Making Sense of Cruel and Unusual Punishment: A New Approach to Reconciling Military and Civilian Eighth Amendment Law," *Military Law Review* 184 (2005): 104–5.

218. 10 U.S.C. § 855; United States v. Willman, No. ACM 39642, 2020 WL 5269775, at *7 (A.F. Ct. Crim. App. Dec. 2, 2020); United States v. Matthews, 16 M.J. 354, 368 (U.S. Ct. Mil. App. 1983); United States v. St. Croix, 18 C.M.R. 465, 466 (U.S. Coast Guard Bd. of Rev. 1955).

219. Martinez-Davalos v. Garland, 846 Fed. Appx. 630, 631 (9th Cir. 2021).

220. CAT.

221. BMW of North America, Inc. v. Gore, 517 U.S. 559, 576–77 (1996).

222. Ex parte Key, 891 So. 2d 384, 390 (Ala. 2004).

223. In August 2023, a federal judge in Idaho—refusing to dismiss an Eighth Amendment claim—acknowledged the significance of intense psychological suffering in a case brought by Gerald Pizzuto, a death row inmate in that state. Austin Sarat, "Idaho Judge Opens the Door for an Exploration of the Psychological Cruelty of Capital Punishment," Justica, August 18, 2023, https://verdict.justia.com/2023/08/18/idaho-judge-opens-the-door-for-an-exploration-of-the-psychological-cruelty-of-capital-punishment. In denying a motion to dismiss brought by the defendants, the Idaho Department of Correction and various state officials, U.S. District Court Judge B. Lynn Winmill ruled that "Defen-

dants' repeated rescheduling of his execution is like dry firing in a mock execution or a game of Russian roulette" and that "[w]ith each new death warrant comes another spin of the revolver's cylinder, restarting the thirty-day countdown until the trigger pulls." Memorandum Decision and Order, *Pizzuto v. Tewalt*, et al., Case No. 1:23-cv-00081-BLW (D. Idaho, Aug. 1, 2023), https://reason.com/wp-content/uploads/2023/08/06312784217 .pdf, p. 9. In December 2023, the U.S. Department of Justice also unsealed war crimes charges against four Russia-affiliated military personnel in the Eastern District of Virginia. Among the charges: torture, threatening to kill the victim, and conducting a mock execution. Press Release, "Four Russia-Affiliated Military Personnel Charged with War Crimes in Connection with Russia's Invasion of Ukraine," U.S. Department of Justice, Dec. 6, 2023, https://www.justice.gov/opa/pr/four-russia-affiliated-military-personnel -charged-war-crimes-connection-russias-invasion.

224. Albert Camus, "Reflections on the Guillotine," in *Resistance, Rebellion, and Death*, trans. J. O'Brien (New York: Alfred A. Knopf, 1961), 199–200; *Furman*, 408 U.S. at 288n36 (Brennan, J., concurring).

2

What Was "Unusual" in *Furman*?

LINDA ROSS MEYER

The Eighth Amendment forbids "cruel and unusual" punishments. What does that mean? On their face, "cruel" and "unusual" are meaningfully different standards. The language seems to suggest that a punishment could be cruel, but not unconstitutional.[1] Though many Supreme Court opinions elide the two words, in the context of the stubborn persistence of the death penalty, this distinction seems important, because otherwise, it is hard to understand how punishing someone with death could not be ipso facto cruel and therefore forbidden. What more can the state take from me than the rest of my life? So if the death penalty persists, one imagines, perhaps it is because the death penalty is not unusual, not because the death penalty is not cruel. As in many areas of the law, legal recognition of cruelty is occluded by the usual cruelties to which we have become accustomed.[2]

Yet for a brief time fifty years ago, the Supreme Court disagreed.[3] In *Furman v. Georgia*, the Court did decide that the "cruel" punishment of death, still in common use,[4] was nonetheless "cruel and unusual," and the Court declared the death penalty a violation of the Constitution. I propose to focus on how the various *Furman* justices interpreted "unusual" in reaching this result. Thinking about what "unusual" means may also help unpack our current Eighth Amendment interpretive stalemate between Chief Justice Earl Warren's "evolving standards of decency" approach and Justice Clarence Thomas's originalist "any execution no more painful than hanging is still constitutional" test. Here's my suggestion: If one understands "unusual" in a normative vein rather than a descriptive vein, as Justice William Brennan did in *Furman*, the death penalty is not only cruel but unusual. Death as a punishment is unusual because it treats criminal defendants as things, excepting and excluding them unusually (and permanently) from the human community. And death is an unusual penalty because it demands an unusual (and ultimately contradictory and judicially unattainable) level of precision. The essay concludes that a penalty so unusual as to be beyond judicial competence to apply should require abstention of the sort demanded by Justice Harry Blackmun's *Callins v. Collins* dissent, akin to that exercised by the Court for political questions and unconstitutional statutory grants of jurisdiction. Judges should refuse to enforce the penalty of death as an unconstitutional grant of judicial power.

Evolving Standards and Usual Cruelties

The Supreme Court's first detailed discussion of the Eighth Amendment was in 1910 in *Weems v. United States* (217 U.S. 349). The case held that a fifteen-year sentence of hard labor and permanent outlawry was cruel and unusual punishment for a minor fraud. While the death penalty was not at issue, it did come up. The *Weems* Court, distinguishing *Wilkerson v. Utah* (99 U.S. 130), explained that "death was an usual punishment for murder, that it prevailed in the Territory [of Utah] for many years, and was inflicted by shooting; also that that mode of execution was usual under military law" (370–71). The Court then cited part of the analysis in Thomas Cooley's 1871 constitutional treatise.[5] Following Cooley, the *Weems* Court noted that while some states found the whipping post "odious, but not unusual" (377), and therefore not constitutionally "cruel *and* unusual," "to establish the whipping post and the pillory in states where they were never recognized as instruments of punishment, or in states whose constitutions, revised since public opinion had banished them" would be both cruel and unusual (378). In this passage, the *Weems* Court seemed to consider "unusual" as a separate limitation from cruel. If a common-law-era penalty were cruel but not unusual, it would not be a constitutional violation, but the same penalty could not be reinstituted if it had become unusual over time.[6]

Mutatis mutandis, in *In re Kemmler*, 136 U.S. 436 (1890), the Court considered whether the Eighth Amendment should apply to the states, and if so, whether electrocution, then a new (and therefore unusual) method of execution, violated the Eighth Amendment. While the Court found it unnecessary to decide at that time whether the Eighth Amendment applied by its terms to a state execution, it did find that Fourteenth Amendment due process had been provided. (In 1890, the Eighth Amendment had not yet been fully "incorporated" in the Fourteenth Amendment due process clause or applied to restrict the states to the same extent that it restricted federal

66 / Linda Ross Meyer

power.) In reviewing whether New York had given Mr. Kemmler due process, the Court noted that the "courts of New York held that the mode adopted in this instance might be said to be unusual because it was new, but that it could not be assumed to be cruel" because the legislature had adopted electrocution to provide a more humane alternative to the "usual" methods of execution (447). Taken together, the reasoning of *Weems* and *Kemmler* becomes circular: In *Kemmler* the punishment is unusual, but it is not cruel, because it is more humane than usual forms of execution.[7] Yet, according to the Court's later analysis in *Weems*, execution itself was permissible only because it was not unusual, not because it was not cruel. Nonetheless, the *Kemmler* Court gave an endorsement of the death penalty often quoted in later opinions: "Punishments are cruel when they involve torture or a lingering death; but the punishment of death is not cruel within the meaning of that word as used in the constitution. It implies there something inhuman and barbarous,—something more than the mere extinguishment of life" (447). At this point in doctrinal history, the Court stated that the death penalty was neither cruel nor unusual. After all, the state was merely going to take your life.

Kemmler and *Wilkerson* were both preincorporation cases construing the Fourteenth Amendment, not the Eighth Amendment directly, and, as Justice Felix Frankfurter put it in his concurrence in *Louisiana ex rel Francis v. Resweber*, 329 U.S. 459 (1947), during that era the guarantees of the Fourteenth Amendment "neither contain[ed] the particularities of the first eight amendments nor [were] they confined to them" (468). The Fourteenth Amendment, at the time of *Kemmler* in 1890, protected state citizens only to the extent that state conduct "violate[d] standards of decency more or less universally accepted" (469).[8] Hence, applying the Eighth Amendment through the lens of the Fourteenth, as the Court did before incorporation, blurs the difference between cruel and unusual, because cruelty, to violate due process, had to be assessed through "consensus of society's opinion" (471). A practice can be considered to violate due process only if it is unusual. "Cruel" essentially drops out of the preincorporation due process analysis; all that matters is whether the penalty is "unusual."

The blurring of cruel with unusual continued in *Trop v. Dulles*, 356 U.S. 86 (1958), even though *Trop*, like *Weems*, was a federal case, and so the Eighth Amendment issue was not clouded by the Fourteenth Amendment analysis. The *Trop* Court held that stripping a person of U.S. citizenship was "cruel and unusual" punishment. In dicta distinguishing denationalization from the death penalty, the *Trop* Court elided cruel with unusual, noting that "the death penalty has been employed throughout our history, and, in a day when it is still widely accepted, it cannot be said to violate the constitutional concept of cruelty" (99). But in a footnote the Court also confronted the distinction between "cruel" and "unusual" directly:

Whether the word "unusual" has any qualitative meaning different from "cruel" is not clear. On the few occasions this Court has had to consider the meaning of the phrase, precise distinctions between cruelty and unusualness do not seem to have been drawn. . . . These cases indicate that the Court simply examines the particular punishment involved in light of the basic prohibition against inhuman treatment, without regard to any subtleties of meaning that might be latent in the word "unusual." . . . If the word "unusual" is to have any meaning apart from the word "cruel," however, the meaning should be the ordinary one, signifying something different from that which is generally done. Denationalization as a punishment certainly meets this test. It was never explicitly san[c]tioned by this Government until 1940 and never tested against the Constitution until this day. (100n32)

Without further ado, the *Trop* Court then articulated the blended "cruel and unusual" Eighth Amendment standard that has been used ever since: "The words of the [Eighth] Amendment are not precise and their scope is not static. The Amendment must draw its meaning from the evolving standards of decency that mark the progress of a maturing society" (100–101).

Though *Trop* blends "cruel" with "unusual" as a general prohibition against "inhuman treatment," it is perhaps because of the inflection "unusual" has alongside "cruel" that the standard of cruelty "evolves." The Court's formulation in *Trop*, then, is still congruent with the Court's statement in *Weems* that the desuetude of a "cruel but once usual" punishment might result in a violation of the Eighth Amendment. In other words, decency evolves, and the Eighth Amendment is not limited to forbidding those punishments already forbidden at the time of the founding.

The *Trop* standard was further refined by the Court's trio of opinions in the juvenile sentencing cases. There, Justice Anthony Kennedy held that the "evolving standards of decency" test required a two-part inquiry: (1) "Objective indicia of national consensus." Kennedy looked at both state legislation and actual sentencing practices. Implicitly, this inquiry seems to test whether or not a type or application of a penalty is unusual—or on its way to becoming so. (2) "Independent" judicial review of the match between the culpability of offenders, the severity of the crimes and punishments, and whether the challenged sentencing practice is justified by "legitimate penological goals." In effect, this second inquiry seems more attuned to whether the sentencing practice is excessive, unnecessarily harsh, or cruel.[9]

More recently, several justices have tacked the other way, advocating for eliminating any independent judicial evaluation of cruelty and ignoring whether a punishment is (now) unusual. They have called into question *Trop*'s

68 / Linda Ross Meyer

"evolving standards of decency" standard in favor of an unevolving application-originalism. For example, Justices Thomas and Antonin Scalia have long intoned that "the Eighth Amendment's prohibition . . . must be understood in light of the historical practices that led the Framers to include it in the Bill of Rights."[10] "The evil the Eighth Amendment targets is intentional infliction of gratuitous pain, and that is the standard our method-of-execution cases have explicitly or implicitly invoked. [102] . . . To the extent that there is any comparative element to the inquiry, it should be limited to whether the challenged method inherently inflicts significantly more pain than traditional modes of execution such as hanging and the firing squad" (106). With originalist interpretive approaches now accepted by a majority of the Court, "cruel" threatens to become statically confined to its purportedly original applications to torture and mutilation.[11]

So perhaps it is a good time to reconsider the term *unusual*. After all, if *Weems* was right that the Eighth Amendment's "unusual" language might prohibit a long-abandoned penalty from being reinstated, that understanding would at least prevent states from returning to founding-era practices of pillories, whippings, brandings, and ear-clippings. More importantly, perhaps there are other ways to think about the Eighth Amendment's "unusual" prohibition that might go farther still. How did the Supreme Court hear "unusual" in *Furman*, when it decided to prohibit a death penalty that was not, at the time, unusual at all? As the rest of this essay lays out, the *Furman* opinions seem to read "unusual" in various ways: infrequent now, infrequent at the founding, unlawful, unruly, and "simply not done."

Infrequent Now

As explained earlier, Chief Justice Warren articulated the current[12] Eighth Amendment "evolving standards of decency" test in *Trop v. Dulles*. Though he did not treat "cruel and unusual" as separate standards, he read "unusual" as requiring the Court to consider whether or not a punishment is "generally not done." Infrequency may confirm a view that a harsh penalty violates "evolving standards of decency," as he held was the case with denationalization.

In *Furman*, likewise, Justice Thurgood Marshall's analysis of *Trop* emphasized that looking to "evolving standards of decency" does not merely prohibit punishments that were unusual at the time of the founding but also may prohibit a penalty "if popular sentiment [now] abhors it" (325). He noted that even before *Trop*, the Court had looked to contemporary punishments "inflicted for other crimes and to those imposed in other jurisdictions, and concluded that the punishment was excessive" (325, citing *Weems*). Marshall concluded that the death penalty, though an accepted practice in the eighteenth century, may "be unconstitutional if citizens [now] found it to be morally unacceptable" (332). Again, Marshall's analysis accords with the *Weems* Court's view that a punishment once cruel but usual may become unconstitutional if it falls out of common practice.

We are all by now familiar with the nose-counting of the state statutes that is done in many Eighth Amendment opinions to determine whether a challenged practice conforms to "evolving standards of decency." Indeed, in the juvenile death and life-without-parole (LWOP) cases, the nose-counting developed subrules allowing the Court to overrule the once-acceptable juvenile death penalty because of "trends" in state legislation (*Roper v. Simmons*), and in the juvenile LWOP cases, because of trends in how states imposed the penalty in practice—figures that were highly contested (*Graham v. Florida* and *Miller v. Alabama*).

But this interpretation of "unusual" as merely "infrequent" always seemed unsatisfying—after all, why should one state have to bow to the "majority choice" of other states? Why should the Supreme Court serve as a superlegislature to require rogue states to conform to a majority-of-states rule? The federalism constructed by constitutional law that encourages state experimentation runs against this rule of conformism, and as numerous Scalia dissents scathingly pointed out, there's no principle here to determine when a "majority" of states becomes a "consensus" or a "trend." And, of course, there's no guarantee that state legislative trends will be toward "decency" at all or even that "decency" will be interpreted as requiring less cruel rather than more cruel punishments. (See *Graham*, Thomas, J., dissenting at 109, noting that "states over the past 20 years have consistently increased the severity of punishments for juvenile offenders.") The search for "contemporary standards of decency" too often devolves into a weird deference to "trends" and "culture" that doesn't have the ring of constitutional principle, and it ignores the fact that trends can lead to harsher as well as kinder approaches to punishment.

Marshall tried to solve this puzzle in *Furman* by arguing that there are no rational reasons for maintaining capital punishment: "I cannot believe that at this stage in our history, the American people would ever knowingly support purposeless vengeance. Thus, I believe that the great mass of citizens would conclude on the basis of the material already considered that the death penalty is immoral and therefore unconstitutional" (363). But Marshall gave little deference to legislative findings in reaching this conclusion, nor does his optimism ring true today, given the resurgence in the 1990s of a retributive philosophy and practice that led to longer sentences, more executions, more solitary confinement, and, eventually, mass incarceration.[13]

Warren Burger's dissent in *Furman*, while keeping to the letter of the *Trop* decision, nonetheless argued that courts owe deference to the moral

70 / Linda Ross Meyer

judgment of state legislatures, and courts are not the right institution to serve as a "trend identifier" or a "frequency evaluator":

> The Court up to now has never actually held that a punishment has become impermissibly cruel due to a shift in the weight of accepted social values; nor has the Court suggested judicially manageable criteria for measuring such a shift in moral consensus.
>
> The Court's quiescence in this area can be attributed to the fact that in a democratic society legislatures, not courts, are constituted to respond to the will and consequently the moral values of the people. (383)

Justice Lewis Powell's dissent put it more succinctly: "The assessment of popular opinion is essentially a legislative, not a judicial, function" (443).

Infrequent Then

The Court these days is moving away from an examination of contemporary frequency to an examination of historical frequency, as it begins to disavow the faith of *Trop v. Dulles* that "standards of decency" evolve rather than devolve. An application-originalist version of "unusual" would refer us to the frequency with which a punishment was used at the time of the founding. Justices Scalia and Thomas have argued that the phrase "cruel and unusual" forbids only punishments considered to be so at the time of constitutional framing. Since capital punishment was "ubiquit[ous] . . . in the Founding Era" (Thomas, *Baze v. Rees*, concurring) (or, if the execution is in a state criminal justice system, at the time of the ratification of the Fourteenth Amendment), on an application-originalist interpretation, capital punishment cannot be unusual or a violation of the Eighth Amendment, however cruel mere death may be.

There's also a serious problem with treating "unusual" as "infrequent then," of course. By this measure, a post-state-trial lynching would not be constitutionally unusual, as mob lynching was widespread in the states at the time of the Fourteenth Amendment's ratification.[14] Mob dismemberment as a sentence also would not be unusual, however cruel, and therefore, for a hard-nosed application-originalist, it would not be in itself a constitutional violation.

It's not even clear that the original application of the term *cruel and unusual* would forbid the tortures that Supreme Court originalists think it did. Anthony Granucci made this point in his famous law review article on the original meaning of "cruel and unusual." In that article, he demonstrates that the language "cruel and unusual" was first used in the 1689 English Bill of Rights. Granucci points out that the original phrase "illegal and cruel" slipped, in the course of drafting, to "cruel and unusual" without discussion and probably as a matter of "chance and sloppy draftsmanship" (855). Granucci then notes that the English Bill of Rights was invoked not against drawing and quartering and the like but against punishments that were imposed without statutory authorization or with too much judicial discretion, or that were disproportionate to the offense. Drawing, quartering, gibbeting, burning at the stake, and whipping continued after 1689, despite the statute. So, an application-originalist reading of the phrase from its origin in 1689 would perhaps not do the work of forbidding torture that our current originalists on the Court believe it did.[15]

This example further demonstrates the artificiality of originalism disputes. The application-originalism used at times by Justices Scalia and Thomas in their arguments for the constitutionality of capital punishment would result in an Eighth Amendment that would also allow the kinds of public vivisection (based on the practices cited by Granucci as still current post-1689) that the founders themselves clearly thought they were prohibiting ("framer's intent originalism"). I note that both Scalia and Thomas quickly move from application-originalism to framer's-intent arguments to make clear that drawing and quartering and other death-penalty-plus punishments should be ruled out (*Baze v. Rees*, Thomas, concurring; *Harmelin v. Michigan*, Scalia, plurality opinion). Most originalists agree that originalism based on contemporary public meaning is a more defensible approach to originalism than either application-originalism or framer's-intent originalism narrowly conceived. But the irony then is that we accept the 1787-era ahistorical "contemporary public meaning" interpretation of this 1689-era language but refuse to accept longer-standing and more well-accepted ahistorical public meaning interpretations of that same language, like the 1972 *Trop v. Dulles* formulation. And of course, in our originalist dive into the framers' nonoriginalist reading, we ignore the possibility that the framers themselves were not originalists, as Brennan argues in *Furman*, as well as ignoring the principles of justice themselves that the framers most likely wished us to attend to.

The purported reason for all this originalism, of course, is a "social contract" theory of the Constitution, which holds us to the terms of the contract at the time it was entered into in 1791 or 1868. But as many others have pointed out, social contract theories of the Constitution ignore the glaring problem that women, men of color, and most of those without real property were excluded from those contracts. And even the contract analogy is problematic, since normal contracts are interpreted to include the course of conduct and "usages of the parties," where a contractual relationship has, over time, been filled out and filled in by practice (U.C.C. § 1-303). So why should social contracts, intended to last for centuries, exclude subsequent usages and interpretations when regular contracts do not?

Moreover, social contract theory is not the only political theory of a constitution, as the immense literature on constitutional interpretation bears out. For example, a student of mine recently referred to our Constitution as a "mission statement."[16] Mission statements gain authority through a history of adherence and acceptance and application over time, not because of a contract analogy. In sum, while originalists purport to eschew normative, political, or philosophical positions, their "social contract" premises are based on a very specific, unrepresentative, and not very convincing normative political theory.

I note also that Justices Scalia and Thomas agreed with Granucci's account that the original 1689 "illegal and cruel" language ruled out punishments imposed "arbitrarily" or without statutory authorization, but they did not agree with Granucci's history with respect to whether the 1689 Bill of Rights ruled out disproportionate punishments. Granucci argues that the courts did strike down such punishments; Scalia argues that they did not (*Harmelin v. Michigan*, plurality opinion by Scalia, J.; *Baze v. Rees*, concurring opinion by Thomas, J.). The controversy among the justices over whether the Eighth Amendment includes a requirement that punishments not be "grossly disproportionate," as opposed to forbidding only certain "types" of particularly painful punishments, raged for decades, with majorities going back and forth from *Solem* to *Harmelin* to *Ewing*. A proportionality requirement did finally seem to gain a stable (6–3) majority in *Graham v. Florida*. Now, the new turn toward originalism on the Court may throw the question open once again, which would have the effect of deregulating (as a matter of constitutional law) all state and federal prison sentences. Even on an originalist interpretation, however, it seems counterintuitive that excessive fines should include a proportionality principle, but not cruel and unusual punishment, since the two prohibitions are joined in the same phrase and born from the same context and concerns.[17]

In any case, engaging in these arcane historical disputes seems like so much hand-waving, because the contemporary Court has not made clear its historical methodology or identified (and limited) the historical sources courts and advocates should consult. But more importantly, it just seems bizarre for originalist justices to be articulating constitutional rights by picking sides in debates among historians or trying to find scraps of constitutional certainty in incomplete seventeenth- or eighteenth-century archives. Originalist majority opinions never attempt to justify constitutional conclusions as humane, dignified, workable, honorable, consistent, fair, or good—because that kind of judgment of principle, they argue, must be left for legislatures alone.[18] Because constitutional law is no longer grounded in principle, the public meaning of these history-squabble opinions becomes itself hopelessly arcane, garbling the Court's institutional voice, which no longer even tries for grand or magisterial. And the littleness and pettiness of the Court's new voice threatens to undermine the authority of the Constitution itself. Public officials who swear to uphold the Constitution apparently swear to no normative principles but swear to squint and quibble at the fine gothic print in Bracton or to unearth the flaking remains of colonial broadsides.[19]

In both tone and substance, the originalist arguments of today differ dramatically from the approaches of all nine members of the *Furman* Court in 1972—or the *Gregg* Court in 1976. Even the dissenters in *Furman* agreed that an application-originalist version of the Eighth Amendment was wrongheaded, and they believed unanimously that the expansive language of the Constitution pointed forward as well as backward:

> The fundamental premise upon which either standard is based is that notions of what constitutes cruel and unusual punishment or due process do evolve. Neither the Congress nor any state legislature would today tolerate pillorying, branding, or cropping or nailing of the ears— punishments that were in existence during our colonial era. Should, however, any such punishment be prescribed, the courts would certainly enjoin its execution. (429–30, Powell, J., dissenting)[20]

Unlawful

Somewhat ironically, White's concurrence in *Furman* comes closest to defining "unusual" as "illegal" in the way that Granucci argues was the original meaning of the phrase in 1689. White's concurrence focuses on the lack of "rational basis" for the death penalty, arguing that its infrequent occurrence can create no deterrence. White's arguments that capital punishment is "unjustified" have been echoed in recent years by economists, who support White's intuition that an infrequently imposed death penalty is "irrational"—and possibly even counterproductive—from the standpoint of the purposes of general deterrence.[21] On this view, the death penalty would not satisfy a "rational basis" test under the due process clause, because the state has no good reason for its policy. The "no good reason" test goes to the basic requirement that governments must act according to reason—that is, that governments act legally—hence the original wording of "unusual" as "illegal." Justices Brennan and Marshall also argue in their concurrences that a penalty that has no policy justification is "irrational" and therefore "unusual" in this sense and thus violates the Eighth Amendment. Justice Mar-

74 / Linda Ross Meyer

shall goes further, declaring that retribution should never be a reason for the state to punish.

Justice Kennedy later carries this idea into the juvenile sentencing cases as well, testing each challenged penalty against the "purposes of punishment" to see whether there is a rational policy basis for it (*Graham v. Florida*). However, as Scalia's concurrence in *Ewing v. California*, 538 U.S. 11, 31 (2003), emphasizes, the deference to legislative judgment required by the Court's "rational basis" test allows nearly anything to be "legal" in this very minimalist sense, and there is bite to the argument that the Court should not be picking and choosing among otherwise-rational penal theories ("The plurality is not applying law but evaluating policy").

The return of retributive penal theory in the 1990s also makes the point here. While Marshall's concurrence in 1972 imagined that retribution was a moribund and cruel philosophy, "condemned by scholars for centuries," out of which we had now "evolved" (343), only ten years after *Furman* retributivism became not only acceptable but the dominant theory of punishment across the country. The *Anderson* decision in California, which seemed to Marshall in June 1972 the beginning of a trend to declare capital punishment unconstitutional in state courts, was decisively reversed in November 1972 when the electorate in California reinstated the death penalty by initiative (Proposition 17) and in 1986 threw their anti-death-penalty Supreme Court justices out of office (Chief Justice Rose Bird, Justice Cruz Reynoso, and Justice Joseph Grodin). And the remaining penal philosophies acceptable to Marshall, like deterrence[22] and incapacitation, came to justify sentences that even retributivists found to be cruel and disproportionate.[23]

Like the long sentences in *Ewing*, a death penalty can be rationally justified merely as incapacitating a dangerous (or inconvenient) person, even if it is not retributively proportionate to the crime. Allowing cruel punishments whenever there is a utilitarian reason for them leads us into a dark place. During the war on terror, courts and commentators justified even torture—a favorite originalist example of cruel and unusual punishment—as a necessary utilitarian evil.[24] But as Chief Justice Burger says in dissent in *Furman*, "Among those favoring the [Eighth] Amendment, no sentiment was expressed that a punishment of extreme cruelty could ever be justified by expediency" (392).

Unruly

Douglas's opinion in *Furman* (and more succinctly and obliquely, Stewart's opinion) takes "unusual" in a slightly different sense than White does. He takes it as "unprincipled." Douglas's deepest concern in *Furman* is that the death penalty is "unprincipled" and "unpatterned" and follows no guidance or rule. It is "unusual" in the sense of "arbitrary," "unpredictable," and "unruly."

Douglas expressly draws on Granucci's point that the English Bill of Rights, originally understood, forbids "illegal" cruelties, and Douglas emphasizes Blackstone's gloss that punishments must be authorized by statute so that penalties apply "without respect of persons" (863).[25] Therefore, Douglas argues, "it would seem to be incontestable that the death penalty inflicted on one defendant is 'unusual' if it discriminates against him by reason of his race, religion, wealth, social position, or class, or if it is imposed under a procedure that gives room for the play of such prejudices" (242). For Douglas, the death penalty is unconstitutional because legal actors have too much discretion to impose death disproportionately—and especially to impose death on poor Black men out of a peculiarly American history of racism and lynching.

And for Douglas, identifying racial and class bias is not just a matter of examining the "law on the books" but also a matter of examining the "law as applied." Douglas's opinion is one of the first to name the racism at play in the death penalty and to refer explicitly to the race of the defendants.[26] Before that period, "colorblindness" in constitutional criminal rights opinions meant that racism remained part of the unspoken background. Not naming race made the Court's reasons for more careful review of state criminal cases unclear from the face of their opinions, perhaps contributing to the federalism backlash of the 1980s.[27] Douglas, however, is explicit about the racism pervading punishment. He cites *Yick Wo*'s prohibition on racial discrimination in policing and prosecution to suggest that even a facially mandatory death penalty might be "unusual" in the sense of "unrule-bound" or "discriminatory," if, as is likely, it is applied only to the poor and those of color. Likewise, for Douglas, even a "frequent" death penalty would be "unusual" in this sense if it were applied "frequently" only to one caste or class or race.

Douglas's comments in 1972 sound strikingly contemporary, echoing the analysis of race and privilege found in far more recent books like Isabel Wilkerson's *Caste: The Origin of Our Discontents* (2020) or Michelle Alexander's *The New Jim Crow: Mass Incarceration in the Age of Colorblindness* (2012). Douglas writes,

> In a Nation committed to equal protection of the laws there is no permissible "caste" aspect of law enforcement. Yet we know that the discretion of judges and juries in imposing the death penalty enables the penalty to be selectively applied, feeding prejudices against the accused if he is poor and despised, and lacking political clout, or if

he is a member of a suspect or unpopular minority, and saving those who by social position may be in a more protected position. In ancient Hindu law, a Brahman was exempt from capital punishment, and, under that law, "[g]enerally, in the law books, punishment increased in severity as social status diminished." We have, I fear, taken in practice the same position, partially as a result of making the death penalty discretionary and partially as a result of the ability of the rich to purchase the services of the most respected and most resourceful legal talent in the Nation.

The high service rendered by the "cruel and unusual" punishment clause of the Eighth Amendment is to require legislatures to write penal laws that are evenhanded, nonselective, and nonarbitrary, and to require judges to see to it that general laws are not applied sparsely, selectively, and spottily to unpopular groups.

A law that stated that anyone making more than $50,000 would be exempt from the death penalty would plainly fall, as would a law that in terms said that blacks, those who never went beyond the fifth grade in school, those who made less than $3,000 a year, or those who were unpopular or unstable should be the only people executed. A law which, in the overall view, reaches that result in practice has no more sanctity than a law which in terms provides the same.

Thus, these discretionary statutes are unconstitutional in their operation. They are pregnant with discrimination, and discrimination is an ingredient not compatible with the idea of equal protection of the laws that is implicit in the ban on "cruel and unusual" punishments. (255–57)

Powell's rejoinder to Douglas, that it is a "sad truth" that the people who commit crimes "happen to be underprivileged" (447), seems especially tone-deaf in 2022, as it fails to engage the core problem of institutional racism. Powell argues that the case for an equal protection violation on the basis of racial discrimination was not made here, because the defendant did not prove racial discrimination in his case (449–50). Powell's position, that evidence of racial bias in the system cannot invalidate a particular death sentence, prefigured the Court's 1987 ruling in *McCleskey v. Kemp*, 481 U.S. 279 (1987). *McCleskey*'s holding—that racial discrimination "in the background" is not relevant to the case at bar—means that the Court never considers the problem Douglas poses: whether pervasive racial discrimination in its application should invalidate the death penalty. Powell's reasoning precludes and occludes any investigation of institutional racism as a reason for declaring the death penalty unusual: If you show racial discrimination in your case, then you may receive a new trial, but the death penalty remains untouchable. If you show systemic racism but cannot prove racial discrimination in your case, the death penalty still remains untouchable. To make things worse, Powell argues that "evolving standards of decency" work against removing the death penalty on racial discrimination grounds, because "the segregation of our society in decades past, which contributed substantially to the severity of punishment for interracial crimes, is now no longer prevalent in this country. Likewise, the day is past when juries do not represent the minority group elements of the community" (450). This is quite a stunning pronouncement for 1972, less than a decade after the Civil Rights Act was enacted.

But Douglas's approach has its own flaws. If all we demand is a hard and fast rule equally applied, then the mandatory death penalty should not be unusual in the sense of unprincipled, as long as both the rule and the application are procrustean. As Justice Sandra Day O'Connor said in her concurrence in *Lawrence v. Texas*, in some circumstances, an equal protection orientation may make the need for federal court substantive review less crucial, because if a rule is imposed (and enforced) on everyone, legislatures are less likely to enact harsh laws in the first place.

A mandatory, procrustean death penalty might soon be eliminated by democratic processes, if its application were truly universal. If our substantive criminal law required the death penalty for every death—accidental or intentional—then perhaps democratic self-interest would keep the death penalty at bay. But the very decisions the substantive criminal law requires around intention and self-defense also inject the exercise of discretion and judgment. Jurors' judgments about defendants' intentions or about their reasonable grounds for self-defense open up the potential for race and class discrimination, as we have seen in countless police-shooting and stand-your-ground self-defense cases.

A procrustean death penalty would also eliminate the discretion we value in allowing juries to consider the very kinds of social inequality Douglas decries. If we read "unusual" as "not fitting, or not according to desert," as Granucci and to some extent Brennan would suggest, then we must allow consideration of mitigating evidence. And in death penalty cases, mitigating evidence abounds: horrific child abuse and abandonment, racialized bias and lack of basic opportunity, sexual assault, extreme poverty, inattention to mental illness, trauma, environmental toxicity, and addiction. A mandatory version of the death penalty would require us to ignore these factors, but these are the very factors that reveal the need for compassion toward those who suffer poverty and discrimination in America. Equity and "fitting the punishment to the case" require precisely what Douglas will not tolerate—"a procedure that gives play" to prejudice. Discretion to be merciful is the bright side of discretion to be racist. Yet the answer cannot be, for humans, the elimination of discretion (per Douglas) or the demand of retributive perfection (per Kennedy and Marshall), for those are both human impossibilities.

Twenty-two years after *Furman*, in *Callins v. Collins*, 510 U.S. 1141 (1994), Justice Blackmun, who dissented in *Furman*, came to agree with Douglas's assessment that the death penalty is not "lawful" and is fraught with arbitrariness. But while Douglas never suggests that the death penalty is unfixable, Blackmun does: "The problem is that the inevitability of factual, legal, and moral error gives us a system we know must wrongly kill some defendants, a system that fails to deliver the fair, consistent, and reliable sentences of death required by the Constitution" (1145–46). Though Blackmun had struggled to uphold and apply capital punishment for more than two decades, he came to believe that its internal contradictions are insuperable. Not only is there inevitable "error," as he describes earlier, but he understands that the perfect justice demanded by the final penalty is not possible: the need to be fair to the myriad circumstances of the individual case cannot be reconciled with the need to eliminate discrimination. Requiring juries to abide by neutral rules and, at the same time, give effect to "any and all mitigating evidence" creates an internal contradiction in the Court's doctrine that makes its application impossible. Yet, eliminating jury discretion completely in order to "'identify before the fact those characteristics of criminal homicides and their perpetrators which call for the death penalty, and to express these characteristics in language which can be fairly understood and applied by the sentencing authority, appear to be tasks which are beyond present human ability'" (1146, Blackmun, quoting Harlan). Blackmun concludes, famously, that "from this day forward, I no longer shall tinker with the machinery of death. . . . Rather than continue to coddle the Court's delusion that the desired level of fairness has been achieved and the need for regulation eviscerated, I feel morally and intellectually obligated simply to concede that the death penalty experiment has failed" (1130).

"Simply Not Done"

Another possibility is to read "unusual" with a normative valance, as Brennan's opinion in *Furman* does. As the archetypal *Downton Abbey* Granny Violet might say, "That simply isn't done." What she means, of course, is not that it really isn't done but that it isn't done in polite society or *should* not be done at all. Little girls might pick their noses at the dinner table frequently, but nonetheless, it is "unusual" in that it "isn't done." The claim is one of identity: our own dignity would be lost were we to engage in such practices, so *we* don't do that; it is not fitting, it is im-pro-per—literally, "not one's own." *Unusual* has a similar etymology—not "for use, of common use, customary."

Certainly, such normative usages of "unusual" were more common in the seventeenth and eighteenth centuries—hence the odd slippage from "illegal" to "unusual" in the 1689 English Bill of Rights drafting process that Granucci points out. Like the word *normal*, unusual can have both normative and nonnormative valances—both norm-as-aim and norm-as-average. So, while lynching might have been frequent at the time of the Fourteenth Amendment's ratification, one may still argue that such an act was "unusual" in this normative sense—mob abuse and dismemberment is not the way we do things here, not our custom, not sanctioned by law, and those horrifying practices, even if routinized, were and are not in accord with our values as a nation.

Justice Brennan's concurrence in *Furman* helps us out of the trap of "infrequent now" or "infrequent then" and gives normative bite to the word *unusual*. First, he emphasizes the breadth and uncertainty of the phrase "cruel and unusual." He notes that Mr. Livermore opposed it in congressional ratification debates on that ground—and was concerned that the amendment might outlaw punishments well accepted at the time, like hanging, whipping, and "perhaps having their ears cut off" (262). This ratification debate demonstrates, for Justice Brennan, that the framers "were well aware that the reach of the Clause was not limited to the proscription of unspeakable atrocities. Nor did they intend simply to forbid punishments considered 'cruel and unusual' at the time. The 'import' of the Clause is, indeed, 'indefinite,' and for good reason," so that it could "be capable of wider application than the mischief which gave it birth" (263, quoting *Weems*). Hence, Brennan concludes, the "unusual" must be judged not only by contemporary frequency at the time of the founding but by "evolving standards of decency that mark the progress of a maturing society" (269–70, quoting *Trop v. Dulles*).

Yet somehow, these "evolving standards" must not be merely those chosen by a majority of state legislatures. As is his consistent understanding of the Bill of Rights, Brennan reads the Eighth Amendment as intended to thwart majority tyranny and protect political underdogs—particularly those reviled as criminals. But the *Trop v. Dulles* "evolving standards" doctrine, which seems to read "unusual" as "infrequent-as-of-now," pulls in two directions—a factual inquiry in which one evaluates what contemporary legislatures are doing but also a normative inquiry into what is cruel. In the end, as we know, Justice Kennedy tried to operationalize this doctrine by looking both at contemporary frequency (what majorities of voters thought was acceptable) and at what judges judged was cruel. Yet Justices Scalia and Thomas vilified Kennedy's "independent analysis" as elitist and antidemocratic.

Brennan's approach (at least in the first half of his opinion) more straightforwardly injects normative constraints into "unusual" and sets up the judiciary to determine, based on these criteria, which punishments are forbidden, however frequent or popular or "justified" on policy grounds they might be. Brennan himself refers to "the dignity of man" and "civilized standards"—echoing (but not relying on) language drawn from international human rights, the then-still-young United Nations, and the Nuremberg (1945–46) and Eichmann (1963) trials.

Brennan, then, points not only to "severe pain" (as Thomas and Scalia do) as the measure of cruelty but also to "dignity"—the hallmark of which is that human beings are not to be treated "as objects to be toyed with and then discarded" (272–73). For example, he draws on prior cases for the proposition that punishment for illness is a violation of dignity, as it treats human beings' will (mens rea) as irrelevant, and he repeats *Trop*'s stricture that expatriation completely excludes a person from "the human community" (274, citing *Trop*). Unequally distributed punishments or disproportionate punishments—those not "serving any penal purpose more effectively than a less severe punishment"—would also be an offense to dignity, according to Brennan. Brennan's test is articulated this way:

> The test, then, will ordinarily be a cumulative one: if a punishment is unusually severe, if there is a strong probability that it is inflicted arbitrarily, if it is substantially rejected by contemporary society, and if there is no reason to believe that it serves any penal purpose more effectively than some less severe punishment, then the continued infliction of that punishment violates the command of the Clause that the State may not inflict inhuman and uncivilized punishments upon those convicted of crimes. (282)

The heavy lift for Brennan is to explain why the death penalty—widely practiced and approved by most states (and by the framers)—nonetheless counts as unusual. Part of his answer is that even when practiced, it is treated as unusual and ringed around with safeguards and qualifications. Its rarity itself creates an "inference" "that the punishment is not being regularly and fairly applied" (293). It is also unusual in its severity and inevitable pain and suffering, both physical and mental, and in its irreversibility.

But in my view, Brennan's strongest point here is that the annihilation of an individual is the final expatriation from the human community, hence the final and complete indignity and "thingifying" act. Unlike some of his other arguments, which echo those made by other members of the Court, here Brennan relies on a normative understanding of "unusual," not merely on contemporary frequency. Unusual here means "not treating human beings as human beings." Unusual is a violation of the imperative to treat humans alike as part of the human community in two senses: Expunging a person permanently from the human community is making them unusual, "an exception." And for judges to judge that another person is or should be a thing, they must themselves be standing outside the constraints of human understanding in time—an unusual, indeed impossible, Archimedean point of view. Therefore, it is normatively unusual to treat humans as things; it is simply not done. Brennan's normative understanding of "unusual" as what "isn't done" would thus focus on the defendant's continuing and usual place in the community of humanity, not merely on whether a state legislature had facts to back up a policy of retributive justice or deterrence. Brennan's reference to human dignity was an attempt to find in "unusual" a normative universal.

But today, perhaps, we no longer share a post–World War II consensus or experience that would ground such a gesture to universal law. Justice John Paul Stevens, the last Supreme Court World War II veteran, passed away in 2019, and Justice Kennedy, the last Supreme Court justice to speak in such ringing universals, retired in 2018. "Human dignity" and "evolving norms of civilized nations" no longer point us to a satisfying consensus, as they perhaps did for Brennan's Greatest Generation. Our critique of those phrases today comes from both the left (they are colonialist, presuming a hierarchy of civilization that "matures" into Western standards) and the right (they are un-American, globalist, elitist, and subjective). The right's critique stings: why should nine old, mostly white, privileged lawyers from elite law schools set moral standards instead of voters? Why is their moral vision any clearer or better than the legislators who demand death for murder (felony murder, or rape, for that matter)? As then-justice Rehnquist puts it in dissent in *Furman*, "Rigorous attention to the limits of this Court's authority is likewise enjoined because of the natural desire that beguiles judges along with other human beings into imposing their own views of goodness, truth, and justice upon others" (467). As Justice Thomas puts it more stridently in *Graham v. Florida*,

> The Court does not conclude that life without parole itself is a cruel and unusual punishment. It instead rejects the judgments of those legislatures, judges, and juries regarding what the Court describes as the "moral" question of whether this sentence can ever be "proportionat[e]" when applied to the category of offenders at issue here. . . . I am unwilling to assume that we, as members of this Court, are any more capable of making such moral judgments than our fellow citizens. Nothing in our training as judges qualifies us for that task, and nothing in Article III gives us that authority. (*Graham*, at 97)

This judicial handoff to legislatures to establish standards of "cruel and unusual" assumes that democratic majorities will protect those convicted of crimes. This assumption seems hard to square with (1) the existence of the Fourth, Fifth, Sixth, and Eighth Amendments, which demonstrate that the founders, at least, did not believe that assumption to be true; (2) the drug-sentencing frenzy of 1976–2008,[28] which stopped only when a global recession made prisons too expensive; (3) felon disenfranchisement, which silences the political voices that have experienced punishment firsthand and distorts the democratic process; and (4) the reality of democratic politics, which often in our history has rewarded bigotry and cruelty rather than upheld probity and virtue, making it necessary "to guard one part of the society against the injustice of the other part."[29] The wisdom of *Carolene Products*'s famous footnote 4,[30] that democratic majorities cannot be expected to protect vilified minorities—especially those accused of crimes—is lost in Justice Thomas's appeal to the wisdom of "our fellow citizens."

My own response to the "judicial elitism" critique draws from Brennan's emphasis on the "finality" of death and its affinity with expatriation, but I would answer from Blackmun's place of humility, not from Brennan's place of certainty about universal norms of human dignity. Judges in this dispute over the death penalty can call on legislatures to recognize their own limitations as legislators and remind them of the limitations of judging. Death is a perfect and final punishment, but humans are never perfect and always in progress (until death). Judges and juries cannot claim to predict, once and for all, the future dangerousness or importance of a human life, when they are bound at the same time to assume free will—they cannot know the future. Judges and juries also cannot know everything about the facts of crime and mitigation to construct a perfectly retributive death penalty, free of bias. Judges are not in a position to determine, as Brennan puts it, who may stay in the human community, because judges don't have a standpoint outside time, or beyond that community, from which to judge a life still in progress. Hence, unrevisable punishments like the death penalty and life without parole should be off the table, for judges who acknowledge their own limitations.

Brennan's opinion, with Blackmun's gloss, thus comes closest to the heart of the matter. Judges should strike down death penalty statutes not because they know more than—or are morally superior to—state legislators but because they, as Socrates once said, are wise enough only to know that they don't know, and can't know, the full and mysterious worth of a human life. Judges don't have better judgment; they have the experience of judgment. As Justice Blackmun's opinion in *Callins v. Collins* explains, from the legislative perspective, it is not obvious that a fair death penalty is impossible: "On their face, these goals of individual fairness, reasonable consistency, and absence of error appear to be attainable" (1144). But once you try to harmonize these goals, once you see them in action, you realize that human institutions cannot achieve them. So, part of this Socratic wisdom comes from swimming in the stream of cases that constantly show judges the fuzzy edges of law, the hard choices, the "misfit" cases, the unintended consequences of rules, the areas of uncertainty. Judges are experts in facing uncertainty at the vanishing edges of words and doctrines and the contradictions of evidence. More than voters and more than legislators, judges understand the inevitable imperfection of all law, as it is applied in individual cases. More than voters and more than legislators, judges bear the responsibility for making decisions under this kind of imperfect uncertainty. They should therefore bear the authority to say that demanding a life requires an unusual level of certainty that judges cannot attain—a level of certainty that would be unusual for all humans.

Even when factual guilt is undisputed, there are questions of mental illness and desert. U.S. district judge Robert Chatigny faced such a case in 2005, when he demanded that Michael Ross's attorney investigate claims that his client was not competent to agree to execution or to waive challenges to his death sentence. On the one hand, Michael Ross, who had confessed to and was convicted of multiple rape-murders of young women, was, after years of litigation, apparently willing to be executed. He had retained new counsel to make this argument to the court. But Ross's father and the public defenders who had represented Ross in prior proceedings provided evidence that Ross was making this choice out of despair and illness caused by conditions of solitary confinement, not with a clear mind and a free will. They filed a petition for a stay of execution with Judge Chatigny.

Judge Chatigny had only a few hours to make up his mind whether to allow the execution to go forward. Ross's lawyer had not had an expert evaluate Ross's competence to make this life-ending decision. Chatigny refused to allow the execution to go forward in these conditions of uncertainty about Ross's competence to "agree" to execution[31] (though Chatigny's stays were overturned on appeal). Chatigny's refusal provoked vicious accusations of "judicial activism,"[32] and critics called him a "conniving bully" who threatened Ross's lawyer's license. These accusations also subjected Chatigny to a hearing for judicial misconduct[33] and lost him the opportunity to serve on the Second Circuit.[34]

Yet, Chatigny's own statements at the hearing demonstrate how the death penalty demands superhuman perfection under time-pressured conditions of uncertainty—a perfection unattainable by human institutions. A last-minute phone call with the lawyers about whether a stay was necessary in order to hold an evidentiary hearing into Ross's competency reveals the judge's agonizing and anxiety. Chatigny urges Ross's lawyer to reconsider, to wait, to interview the fellow prisoners who claim Ross is suicidal, to have Ross examined by a psychiatrist, to counsel his client to reconsider: "But I'm not going to stand by here and take it upon myself to watch you go to your death when all these questions have been raised. I cannot do it as an officer of the court. I cannot do it. That's what I would tell him."[35] Repeatedly, the judge excoriates Ross's lawyer, telling him that he is "terribly, terribly, wrong" and could be making "the worst mistake of his life": "No matter how well motivated you are, you have a client whose competence is in serious doubt and you don't know what you're talking about." The judge mentions that his own blood pressure is rising and that he will not be leaving his chambers that evening: "I'll be here. I'll be here. And if I'm not here, somebody will be here who knows how to get me. But I'm not going anywhere.... This is more important than whatever other plans I might have made."

The human moment recorded by this phone call shows the real pressure that judges and lawyers face when there are no second chances, when motions for reconsideration are laughable. And the process of trying to achieve perfect justice created expanding waves of cruelty: it tortured Michael Ross, his lawyers, his witnesses, his executioners, and his victims' families, who all had to try to emotionally prepare themselves for impending executions multiple times.[36] One official witness wrote,

> From any perspective, this story is an American tragedy. It is the story of the waste of at least nine lives—the lives of the eight women whom Ross brutally raped and murdered, and his own. It is the story of a destructive mental illness. And it is the story of an imperfect justice system given the responsibility of deciding the ultimate punishment—a system that not only metes out punishment on the condemned, but also leaves the surviving families twisting in the wind as they wait for closure.[37]

This particular example of the death penalty's inevitable conflict between finite judicial capacity and unreviewable punishment is just one of many. In every death case, there is uncertainty—sometimes of guilt, but always of the precise contours of mitigation and desert, competence and sanity. Uncertainty is the consequence of courts' good-faith efforts to apply a death penalty fairly and lawfully, in last-ditch, last-minute circumstances when there are no second chances to get it right. These are moments not faced by legislators or by voters, who never see the abstractions of policy become concrete in the courtroom and fatal in the execution chamber, as all those involved agonize and "twist in the wind." Yet this is the world that judges and lawyers and the people trying to live on or in the shadow of death row inhabit daily.

Hence, to Justice Thomas's point that judges shouldn't pretend to know more than legislators, I would point out that judges do know something about the death penalty that legislators (as legislators) cannot know: how messy, undignified, torturous, unfair, uncertain, and inhumane it is to try to apply.[38] It should be possible for judges to lay claim to their own incompetence, as they often do in other contexts, and to recognize that perfect infinite judgments cannot be made by finite humans in even more finite time, and that, consequently, the death penalty cannot be administered in a way that approaches, let alone guarantees, justice or dignity for anyone. Death is not only cruel; it is unusual.

Refusing to enforce legislative mandates in court is nothing new. Judges refuse to hear cases on quasi-humility grounds in a range of cases. When Congress has given the courts more power than the Constitution allows, the Court refuses jurisdiction (as in *Marbury v. Madison* and *United States v. Morrison*). And courts have exercised great discretion to refuse cases even squarely within their constitutional jurisdiction in "political question" cases, when they determine that a case requires normative or political judgment beyond core judicial competence or demands grayscale nuance that cannot be couched in black-and-white doctrine (*Rucho v. Common Cause*). Courts also exercise the authority to abstain from deciding cases in a score of other areas where they argue that judicial humility should be invoked (cases involving national security, state secrets, or abstention doctrines). In these cases, the Court frequently invokes the limitations of its competence, the limitations of its judicial toolkit, and the limits of its wisdom. Chief Justice John Roberts's expression of judicial humility in *Rucho* is even more appropriate in the context of death penalty application:

> Deciding among . . . different visions of fairness . . . poses basic questions that are political, not legal. There are no legal standards discernible in the Constitution for making such judgments, let alone limited and precise standards that are clear, manageable, and politically neutral. Any judicial decision on what is "fair" in this context would be an "unmoored determination" of the sort characteristic of a political question beyond the competence of the federal courts. (588 U.S. ___, 139 S. Ct. 2485, 2500 [2019])

Just as judges, out of humility, refuse to tinker with legislative redistricting, national security, and even state water rights, state and federal judges should follow Justice Blackmun's lead in *Callins v. Collins* and refuse to "tinker with the machinery of death." Judges lack the capacity to make infinite decisions in finite time. Judges and juries lack the capacity to give effect to all mitigating factors while still treating like cases alike. They lack the capacity to, for once and all, predict the future of a human soul. And they lack the superhuman jurisdiction to order the unusual: to exclude humans from the human community. As in other contexts where judges accept the limitations of legal judgment, judges ought to acknowledge that the death penalty cannot be applied with dignity and legal justice, given the limited knowledge and competence of courts of law.[39]

ACKNOWLEDGMENTS

I am grateful to Austin Sarat for as-always insightful comments and suggestions and for inviting me to participate with the illustrious scholars in this volume. I am also grateful to Carol and Jordan Steiker for their careful read and corrections of an earlier draft and, generally, for keeping me from making a fool of myself. But see note 34. Remaining mistakes, of course, are all on me. Thanks are also due to all of the thoughtful contributors to this volume for their robust discussion of a much earlier draft of this essay, and to my daughter, Cara Ross Meyer, who kindly commented, and commented kindly, on the penultimate version. With all their help, this essay is better than I could have made it on my own, though still finite and imperfect, and a product of its time. I am grateful that no lives depend on the accuracy of my words or the quality of my judgment.

NOTES

1. For this reason, state supreme courts may construe a state constitutional ban on "cruel *or* unusual" punishments differently. See, e.g., "State Constitutions. Cruel or Unusual Punishment. Michigan Supreme Court Casts Doubt on its Commitment to Adhere to Federal Interpretations of Parallel Constitutional Provisions. *People v. Bullock*, 485 N.W. 2d 866 (Mich. 1992)," *Harvard Law Review* 106, no. 5 (1993): 1230–35.

2. For an argument that our legal understanding of pain and suffering is deeply influenced by what we are used to, see Linda Ross Meyer, "Suffering the Loss of Suffering: How Law Shapes and Occludes Pain," in *Knowing the Suffering of Others: Legal Perspectives on Pain and Its Meanings*, ed. Austin Sarat (Tuscaloosa: University of Alabama Press, 2014): 14–25.

3. The Court struck down the death penalty in *Furman v. Georgia* (1972) only to reinstate it with more procedural due process regulation in *Gregg v. Georgia* (1976).

4. Far more usual than today—see Steiker and Steiker, this volume. See also Carol S. Steiker and Jordan M. Steiker, *Courting Death: The Supreme Court and Capital Punishment* (Boston: Harvard University Press, 2016) (documenting how the Court's snarled regulation of the death penalty post–*Gregg v. Georgia* has reduced the number of executions but not reduced their basic unfairness).

5. Thomas M. Cooley, *A Treatise on the Constitutional Limitations Which Rest upon the Legislative Power of the States of the American Union* (Boston: Little, Brown, 1871) 329–30: "It is certainly difficult to determine precisely what is meant by cruel and unusual punishments. Probably any punishment declared by statute for an offence which was punishable in the same way at the common law, could not be regarded as cruel or unusual in the constitutional sense. And probably any new statutory offence may be punished to the extent and in the mode permitted by the common law for offences of a similar nature. But those degrading punishments which in any State had become obsolete before its existing constitution was adopted, we think may well be held forbidden by it as cruel and unusual. We may well doubt the right to establish the whipping-post and the pillory in States where they were never recognized as instruments of punishment, or in States whose constitutions, revised since public opinion had banished them, have forbidden cruel and unusual punishments. In such States the public sentiment must be regarded as

having condemned them as 'cruel,' and any punishment which, if ever employed at all, has become altogether obsolete, must certainly be looked upon as 'unusual.'" Cooley's treatise is available here: https://repository.law.umich.edu/books/10/.

6. This argument is also made in John F. Stinneford, "The Original Meaning of 'Unusual': The Eighth Amendment as a Bar to Cruel Innovation," *Northwestern University Law Review* 102 (2008): 1739.

7. I note that Thomas Cooley's treatise, often invoked by Eighth Amendment originalists, disagrees with this idea that "less cruel" punishments could be substituted. He would instead discharge a defendant: "A defendant, however, in any case is entitled to have the precise punishment meted out to him which the law provides, and no other. A different punishment cannot be substituted on the ground of its being less in severity. Sentence to transportation for a capital offence would be void; and as the error in such a case would be in the judgment itself, the prisoner would be entitled to his discharge, and could not be tried again." Cooley, *Treatise on Constitutional Limitations*, 330.

8. The Eighth Amendment's cruel and unusual clause was finally fully "incorporated" as part of the Fourteenth Amendment's definition of due process, in Robinson v. California, 370 U.S. 660 (1962) (overturning a California statute that criminalized "being addicted" to narcotics as "cruel and unusual"). The excessive fines clause was "officially" incorporated in Timbs v. Indiana, 586 U.S. ___, 139 S.Ct. 682 (2019).

9. Graham v. Florida, 560 U.S. 48, 62–68 (2009).

10. Baze v. Rees, 553 U.S. 35, 94 (2008) (Thomas, J., concurring in the judgment).

11. See also Harmelin v. Michigan, 501 U.S. 957, 957–94 (1991) (plurality opinion of Scalia, J.).

12. I'm not sure, really, what the current test is. But this one is still on the bar exam, for the moment. See Jacob Leon, "*Bucklew v. Precythe*'s Return to the Original Meaning of 'Unusual': Prohibiting Extensive Delays on Death Row," *Cleveland State Law Review* 68 (2020): 485–519. ("Two principles have been established in the U.S. Supreme Court's Eighth Amendment jurisprudence for approximately sixty years. First, to decide whether a punishment is 'cruel and unusual,' the Court analyzes whether the punishment corresponds with a maturing society's 'evolving standards of decency.' Second the Court's application of the 'evolving standards of decency' test has remained inconsistent for sixty years. Surprisingly, the Supreme Court appeared to erase both principles in its 2019 capital punishment opinion, *Bucklew v. Precythe*, by not once mentioning the evolving-standards test . . . instead . . . interpreting the phrase 'cruel and usual' with originalist methods. *Bucklew* bifurcated 'cruel and unusual' into two distinct requirements and interpreted each term by turning back the clock to the eighteenth century." 487.)

13. See, e.g., Jeffrie Murphy, "The State's Interest in Retribution," *Journal of Contemporary Legal Issues* 5 (1994): 283; Michelle Alexander, *The New Jim Crow: Mass Incarceration in the Era of Color-Blindness* (New York: New Press, 2010). See also Bessler, this volume.

14. Equal Justice Initiative, *Lynching in America: Confronting the Legacy of Racial Terror* (2017).

15. Anthony F. Granucci, "'Nor Cruel and Unusual Punishments Inflicted': The Original Meaning," *California Law Review* 57, no. 4 (1969): 859. All the traditional punishments for treason—burning, drawing and quartering, etc.—continued after the 1689 statute was enacted. Granucci argues that the American founders, however, read the phrase to forbid such punishments.

16. Something of this "mission statement" idea is captured by Jed Rubenfeld's *Freedom and Time: A Theory of Constitutional Self-Government* (New Haven, CT: Yale University Press, 2001).

17. See Cooley, *Treatise on Constitutional Limitations*, 328–29: "By Magna Charta a freeman was not to be amerced for a small fault, but according to the degree of the fault, and for a great crime in proportion to the heinousness of it, *saving to him his contenement*; . . . The merciful spirit of these provisions addresses itself to the criminal courts of the American States through the provisions of their constitutions." Cooley then cites State v. Danforth, 3 Conn. 112, 115–16 (1819), for the proposition that "imprisonment without limitation" or "imprisonment for life" was an "extravagance" that the common law "can never require." 329. Hence, it's not at all clear that the common law or colonial antecedents made any distinction between restrictions on disproportionate fines and restrictions on disproportionate imprisonment; rather, the two seem to be linked together. Moreover, as Justice Stevens pointed out in his dissent in *Ewing v. California*, it is hardly consistent with the aspirations of our constitutional culture to protect people's money more than we protect their liberty.

18. See New York State Rifle and Pistol Ass'n v. Bruen, 597 U.S. ___, 142 S.Ct. 2111 (2022) (compare majority opinion with Breyer dissent, part III B and C).

19. For a thoroughgoing critique of originalism, see Erwin Chemerinsky, *Worse Than Nothing: The Dangerous Fallacy of Originalism* (New Haven, CT: Yale University Press, 2022).

20. A variation on application-originalist interpretations is to argue, as John Stinneford has, that "unusual" includes not only punishments that were infrequent at some historical point of reference but also new or innovative punishments. Stinneford, "Original Meaning of 'Unusual,'" 1745. He draws on dicta in In re *Kemmler* in which the Court noted that electrocution in 1890 "might be said to be unusual because it was new." *In re* Kemmler, 136 U.S. 436, 447 (1890) (deferring to the New York legislature's judgment that electrocution was a more humane method than hanging and therefore not cruel). Under this interpretation, any new punishment, as well as any punishment not used frequently in the founding period, must be evaluated as to its cruelty before it may be used. However, being "unusual" cannot in itself be enough for a constitutional ban; in *Furman*, Justice Marshall asserts that an "unusual" punishment that is no crueler than previous punishments might still be constitutional (331). Stinneford argues that, because lethal injection is an innovation since the founding period, it cannot be used if it is cruel. Because lethal injection is an innovation (already "unusual"), no evaluation of its contemporary or historical frequency or widespread use is relevant. Even if it were used daily in every state, it could be "cruel and unusual" as long as it were simply "cruel."

21. John J. Donohue III, "Estimating the Impact of the Death Penalty on Murder," *American Law and Economics Review* 11, no. 2 (2009): 249–309.

22. One of the curious features of Marshall's opinion is that he believes abolitionists have provided "clear and convincing" evidence that capital punishment is not justified by deterrence or incapacitation, and therefore, the state may not justify capital punishment on this ground (354). He concludes by asserting that there is "no rational basis" for capital punishment, and it therefore violates the Eighth Amendment (359). This statement fits into a much larger and more contentious debate about what burden a plaintiff must meet to overturn a statute. Generally, due process doctrine requires the government to provide only a "plausible rational basis" to fend off even extremely strong evidence that the legislature's policy justifications are not borne out in fact (see, e.g., Nordlinger v. Hahn, 505 U.S. 1 [1992]). Somewhat "heightened scrutiny," which does allow evaluation of the legislature's evidence against evidence presented at trial, is officially available for sex discrimination, though it has also been applied "under the radar" as "rational basis with bite" in cases involving nonracial discrimination against a vulnerable group.

What Was "Unusual" in *Furman*? / 89

"Strict scrutiny," which would require the government to have strong evidence that the legislation is necessary to achieve the government's compelling policy goal, does allow a plaintiff to overcome a statute's legislative evidence based on evidence presented at trial, but that more searching review is available only for legislation that infringes fundamental rights (including, one would suppose, one's right to life) or is facially discriminatory. Even in the strict scrutiny context, however, the Court has been inconsistent in its willingness to defer to congressional fact-finding rather than to facts proved at trial (as in partial-birth abortion cases). In Commerce Clause cases, by contrast, the Court has come to demand some hard evidence from Congress that the activity it is regulating "affects" interstate commerce, and the Court has not deferred to congressional fact-finding on that point, let alone made vague gestures toward "plausibly true."

The cruel and unusual punishment clause has never been explicitly connected to this due process "levels of scrutiny" framework, though the evaluation of a state's "reasons" for the challenged punishment has become part of the Court's analysis. Comparing the Court's very deferential discussion of legislative reasons in Ewing v. California, 538 U.S. 11 (2003), to other due process cases, however, shows that there is a lot unsettled about exactly what standard of review the Court is applying with regard to whether the state is actually justified in enforcing a penalty. The most recent lethal injection cases put the burden on the capital defendant, not the state, to demonstrate a more humane alternative, and they defer greatly to state legislative fact-finding. *Baze*, 553 U.S. 35 (2008); Glossip v. Gross, 576 U.S. 863 (2015). One would think that life and physical liberty, explicitly mentioned in the Bill of Rights, would count as fundamental rights. If so, under the traditional due process analysis, strict scrutiny should apply to any state attempt to take it away, and the Court should require the state to prove its "compelling interest" and "narrow tailoring" and not defer to legislative fact-finding. See Sherry Colb, "Freedom from Incarceration: Why Is This Right Different from All Other Rights?," *New York University Law Review* 69 (1994): 781. However, the Court has refused invitations to evaluate punishments via due process doctrine rather than Eighth Amendment doctrine. And recent cases have called into doubt whether the Court will even continue to use its "levels of scrutiny" approach in fundamental rights cases. Instead, the Court has signaled that, going forward, application-originalism may determine the legitimacy of state legislation in any constitutional right case—i.e., any exercise of a fundamental right is permitted if not forbidden by laws extant in 1791 (or, maybe, for states, 1868). *Bruen*, 597 U.S. ___, 142 S.Ct. 2111 (2022). Justice Thomas in particular has repeatedly and explicitly eschewed the substantive due process balancing tests that have been in use for the last century. Under a *Bruen*-like analysis, the state would have the burden of demonstrating the historical bona fides of its regulation, and the Court would scrutinize its account of history with excruciatingly strict scrutiny and give it absolutely no deference. *Id.*

23. See, e.g., Dan Markel, "State, Be Not Proud: A Retributivist Defense of the Commutation of Death Row and the Abolition of the Death Penalty," *Harvard Civil Rights and Civil Liberties Review* 49 (2005): 407–80.

24. See, e.g., Alan M. Dershowitz, *Why Terrorism Works: Understanding the Threat, Responding to the Challenge* (New Haven, CT: Yale University Press, 2002).

25. Citing William Blackstone, 4 Commentaries on the Law of England, 369–72 (Oxford: 1769).

26. Marshall's opinion expands on this theme as well, also citing evidence of discrimination against Black Americans, but it is not Marshall's central argument. Marshall is also the only one to mention the disparity in death sentences for men and women, though he does not examine the background frequency of men versus women committing murder.

Nica Siegel kindly directed me to Tony Amsterdam's powerful oral history about litigating *Furman*. Amsterdam makes clear the connection for the advocates between capital punishment abolition and race: "Don't assume that we were abolitionists from the beginning because that is simply not true.... We got into [death penalty litigation] because of race, not because of the death penalty.... It was about unjust lynchings, legal lynchings of African Americans for crimes against whites" (55). Moreover, Douglas's focus on the "evolving" and discriminatory implementation of punishment, and not just on the text of state statutes, was another brainchild of Amsterdam's and the LDF lawyers' (98). Interview with Anthony G. Amsterdam, by Myron Farber, April 1, 2, 8, and 9, 2009, http://www.columbia.edu/cu/libraries/inside/ccoh_assets/ccoh_8616918_transcript.pdf.

27. See, e.g., Mark Curriden and Leroy Phillips, *Contempt of Court: The Turn-of-the-Century Lynching That Launched a Hundred Years of Federalism* (New York: Anchor Books, 2001) (giving a powerful example of the racial injustice that moved the Supreme Court toward incorporation and federal habeas review of state court convictions); Paul M. Bator, "Finality in Criminal Law and Federal Habeas Corpus for State Prisoners," *Harvard Law Review* 76, no. 3 (1963): 441–528 (powerful article that began the backlash against federal review of state criminal convictions). The only mention of a history of race discrimination in Bator's article was in a discussion of a case that held that the exclusion of Black jurors in state court did not give federal courts habeas jurisdiction—supporting Bator's view that habeas review by lower federal courts should be severely limited to cases in which state courts had "no jurisdiction." Bator also never mentions the Reconstruction background of Congress's 1867 expansion of the writ. And Bator asserts that state high court review should be sufficient to correct any claims of racial discrimination without resort to collateral challenges in federal court. Nothing could be further apart than Bator's "race-blind" account of the history of federal habeas corpus and Douglas's opinion about why federal court intervention was crucial to curb lynching and discriminatory application of criminal laws to Black citizens.

28. Jonathan Simon, *Governing through Crime: How the War on Crime Transformed American Democracy and Created a Culture of Fear* (Oxford: Oxford University Press, 2009).

29. *The Federalist* no. 51 (James Madison) (1788).

30. United States v. Carolene Products Co., 304 U.S. 144, 152n4 (1938).

31. Ross ex. rel. Dunham v. Lantz, 2005 WL 1539020 (D.Conn.)(2005)(unpublished opinion), https://ctd.uscourts.gov/sites/default/files/opinions/012504.RNC_.Ross_.pdf.

32. Robert Blecker, "God Love Him?," *Hartford Courant*, February 5, 2005, https://www.cjlf.org/deathpenalty/BleckerComment.htm.

33. In re Charges of Judicial Misconduct, 465 F.3d 532 (2d Cir. Jud. Council 2006), https://casetext.com/case/in-re-charges-of-judicial-misconduct-2. See also, Report to the Judicial Council of the Second Circuit from the Special Committee re. 05-8512, 05-8513, 05-8514, 05-8516, 05-8517, and 05-8519, July 11, 2006. https://ww3.ca2.uscourts.gov/Docs/CE/Spec%20Cmte%20Report.pdf.

34. Jonathan M. Kirshbaum, "Habeas Corpus—'Controversy,'" *Habeas Corpus Blog*, March 10, 2010, https://habeascorpusblog.typepad.com/habeas_corpus_blog/2010/03/habeas-corpus-controversy.html.

35. Transcript of hearing on motion to stay execution in Ross ex rel. Dunham v. Lantz, 05-CV-0116 (D. Conn), January 24, 2005, 28–29, 30.

36. Martha J. H. Elliott, "At Ross' Side While Death Comes Closer," *Connecticut Law Tribune*, February 7, 2005, https://www.law.com/ctlawtribune/almID/900005423060/.

37. *Id.*

38. Serious kudos here should go to Austin Sarat, who in a series of powerful op-eds, tweets, and excellent monographs has tried to bring the concrete cruelty and indignity of the death penalty's application to the attention of legislators and voters. See, e.g., Austin Sarat, *When the State Kills: Capital Punishment and the American Condition* (Princeton, NJ: Princeton University Press, 2018); *Gruesome Spectacles: Botched Executions and America's Death Penalty* (Stanford, CA: Stanford University Press, 2014); *Lethal Injection and the False Promise of Humane Execution* (Stanford, CA: Stanford University Press, 2022); and the op-eds posted on his Twitter feed @ljstprof.

39. Both Martel and Lain, this volume, explain why this is a fool's hope, because (1) capital punishment will likely remain, in some form, in order to exhibit and reinforce state sovereign power, and (2) the current Supreme Court is clearly an opponent, not a proponent, of capital punishment abolition. But a fool I am. We used to think that juvenile LWOP was inviolate and that crack and powder cocaine would forever be sentenced at ridiculously different rates. But judicial minds and hearts can change, even as can the minds and hearts of those sitting on death row. Humans are never perfect, but they can get better.

3
The Foreignness of *Furman*

CAROL S. STEIKER AND JORDAN M. STEIKER

Introduction

Reading *Furman v. Georgia*[1] today can be a jarring experience. In some ways, the landmark decision feels contemporary. It happened in our lifetimes. Although none of the justices who decided the case is still alive, many of the other major players in the case are still around, including Tony Amsterdam, who argued *Furman* and one of its companion cases, as well as his two opponents at the Supreme Court lectern, Dorothy Beasley from Georgia and Ronald George from California. Michael Meltsner, who was on the NAACP Legal Defense Fund (LDF) team and wrote an insider's account of the litigation in 1973,[2] published a second edition of his book in 2011 and is still active as a senior statesman in the anti-death-penalty community. But in other ways, *Furman* feels profoundly foreign, an illustration of the adage that "the past is another country." Both the jurisprudential landscape and the shape of capital practices have changed dramatically over the past fifty years, to the point that much of *Furman*'s framing, analysis, and politics fails to track contemporary circumstances or understandings.

This paper explores several discontinuities between *Furman*'s constitutional engagement with the American death penalty and present approaches. Most notably, *Furman*'s account of what was wrong with the death penalty in 1972 is not congruent with the chief concerns that courts and others are most likely to raise about the practice of capital punishment today. This central discontinuity is in large part the product of *Furman* itself. The decision and its progeny changed capital practices and influenced the shape of constitutional and wider discourse about the death penalty. In addition to tracking the discontinuity of the central concerns about capital punishment, we highlight a number of other differences in constitutional methodology and political context that demarcate the gulf between Furman and today. With regard to changing constitutional methodology, we explore differences in the Court's reliance on international comparisons, its use of empirical evidence, and its reliance on social-scientific experts in its Eighth Amendment jurisprudence. With regard to changing political context, we explore the increasingly dynamic environment of capital punishment practices in the states, the influence of late-stage litigation on the Court's current approach to capital issues, and the changed nature of what constitutes a "liberal" versus a "conservative" justice on the Supreme Court.

We also identify the (fewer) continuities between Furman's context and the present time, such as the dramatic decline in the use of capital punishment in the years immediately preceding Furman and in the present day, as well as the shadow of race discrimination that influenced the Court then and influences it now. For a period of several years prior to the 2016 presidential election, many predicted that the enormous withering of capital practices on the ground would lead to a modern-day Furman decision from the Supreme Court abolishing the death penalty. Although prospects for a "next" Furman in the near future have diminished substantially in the past few years, such a decision, were it written today, would look much different from its predecessor.

What Was/Is Wrong with Capital Punishment in America?

Much of what is in the five solo opinions of the Furman majority sounds a bit odd today—not completely bonkers but also not completely congruent with contemporary practice or discourse. Consider the two concurring opinions that are taken to be the heart of the majority—those by Justices Potter Stewart and Byron White. Stewart and White had joined the majority opinion the previous year in McGautha v. California,[3] which rejected the claim that standardless sentencing discretion in capital cases violated the due process clause of the Fourteenth Amendment. Furman posed the very same claim, but under the cruel and unusual punishments clause of the Eighth Amendment. Hence, Stewart's and White's votes were crucial to the slim five-justice Furman majority and were widely understood, both then and now, as voicing the central concerns of the decision. Stewart's concurrence contains what is probably the most famous line in the lengthy set of opinions—his conclusion that "these death sentences are cruel and unusual in the same way that being struck by lightning is cruel and unusual."[4] In support of this striking analogy (pun intended!), Stewart describes the operation of the Georgia and Texas rape statutes, both of which gave sentencing juries unbridled discretion to choose among a broad range of punishments that included death, life imprisonment, or a term of years not less than five (Texas) or between one to twenty (Georgia).[5]

Stewart's concurrence references a system that is so foreign today that current students are often incredulous when they learn the details of its operation. Capital statutes in the pre-*Furman* era often included a variety of crimes beyond murder—not only rape but also kidnapping, armed robbery, burglary, arson, and more.[6] Despite this breadth of eligibility for death, executions in the 1960s had declined from a few dozen a year to a handful to zero in the years leading up to *Furman*, a product of the NAACP LDF's successful nationwide "moratorium" strategy.[7] The combination of the extreme breadth of capital statutes, the lack of any attempt to guide jury discretion among a wide range of sentencing options, and the dramatic decline in the actual practice of capital punishment led Stewart to describe the imposition of the death penalty in language that might otherwise seem hyperbolic: "capricious[]," "random," "wanton[]," "freakish[]," and "lightning"-like.[8] Of course, critics today continue to decry the arbitrary imposition of death sentences and executions,[9] and we ourselves would be among the last to claim that the problem of arbitrariness has been fixed in the post-*Furman* era.[10] But the nature of the underlying system has significantly changed. The Supreme Court has constitutionally limited the death penalty for interpersonal crimes to murder,[11] and all of the 1,500-plus executions in the modern era have been for that offense. The mechanisms by which discretion flows through the system have been hidden by the structures that states built in response to *Furman*. Broad eligibility for death is generated today by the proliferation of aggravating factors in complex capital sentencing schemes,[12] and jury discretion is amplified by the constitutional requirement of individualized sentencing through mitigating evidence presented at a separate capital sentencing proceeding.[13] Stewart's critique in *Furman* is still apt—but for a system that would be unrecognizable to the *Furman* Court.

White's concurrence raises a related concern that is more directly applicable today. The dramatically declining use of capital punishment despite its broad authorization raises the possibility that, in White's words, "the death penalty could so seldom be imposed that it would cease to be a credible deterrent or measurably to contribute to any other end of punishment in the criminal justice system."[14] In the current moment of dramatic diminution of capital punishment, White's warning seems compelling—so much so that a federal judge declared California's death penalty unconstitutional on exactly such grounds, though the decision was reversed on appeal.[15] But it is White's analysis of the "end[s] of punishment" that rings oddly in the current moment. His focus in the quoted passage, which is consistent with the focus of other justices in their opinions, is on deterrence as the primary penological goal of capital punishment. The question of whether the death penalty deters murder better than other possible punishments remains a potent issue today, but it is overshadowed by what many take to be an article of faith—that the death penalty is necessary to give the most heinous criminals their just deserts. Starting in the 1970s, the United States experienced a "retributive movement" in punishment policy that lasted for at least a quarter century and was embraced by both Republican and Democratic politicians.[16] Although the last two decades have seen some modest retrenchment from the ferocity of tough-on-crime retributive rhetoric, current debates about capital punishment seem always to begin (and for many, end) with invocation of the most heinous offenders—the 9/11 hijackers, the Boston Marathon bombers, the Charleston church shooter, or the Parkland school shooter. How could any punishment less than death be just for such offenders? Yet retribution as an "end of punishment" gets only a single, dismissive line from White.[17] ·

In contrast, Stewart devotes an entire paragraph to defending retributivism, but in what today seems an odd position of rebutting the claim that "retribution is a constitutionally impermissible ingredient in the imposition of punishment."[18] Such a claim would be an almost laughable nonstarter today; why does Stewart give it such serious attention? The answer is that Justice Thurgood Marshall's concurrence makes the claim at length, concluding that "Retaliation, vengeance, and retribution have been roundly condemned as intolerable aspirations for government in a free society . . . and the Eighth Amendment itself was adopted to prevent punishment from becoming synonymous with vengeance."[19] From the vantage point of an era in which it is often assumed that retribution *requires* capital punishment, it is incongruous to read a debate in the Supreme Court about whether the constitution *permits* consideration of retribution as one possible purpose of the death penalty.

But the opinion most out of sync with present political and constitutional debates about the death penalty is that of Justice William Brennan, who argued that the death penalty was per se "cruel and unusual" because it was "uncivilized" and "inhuman" owing to its failure to comport with "human dignity."[20] Marshall's opinion, too, has some of this flavor, concluding by echoing former attorney general Ramsey Clark's view that abolition of the death penalty would constitute "a major milestone in the long road up from barbarism."[21] Clark's moral rejection of the death penalty as an atavistic practice reflected the dominant critique of capital punishment at the time. Capital punishment, according to its critics in the *Furman* era, was the "last of the dark ages,"[22] a "disgusting indecency,"[23] a "retreat to the law of the jungle,"[24] a "primitive form of justice,"[25] a "barbarous practice,"[26] a "relic of an age when punishment was an act of vengeance,"[27] and a "cancer."[28] To be sure, critics of the death penalty also challenged its failures in practice rather than in essence, such as its discriminatory application and its failure as a deterrent, but the dominant register of critical public discourse at the time was profoundly moral.

The tone and substance of public discourse found its way into the *Furman* briefs, especially in the main brief in *Aikens v. California*, which was the lead case in the *Furman* litigation until it was mooted out when the California Supreme Court declared the state's death penalty unconstitutional under the state constitution.[29] Brennan's opinion draws heavily on the petitioner's arguments in the *Aikens* brief, which argued that capital punishment "has been progressively rejected in the course of an ideological and moral debate resonant with concerns that are intimately connected with the 'principle of civilized treatment' and 'the dignity of man.'"[30] Indeed, "uncivilized" is one of the nicer terms used in the *Aikens* brief to describe the death penalty; alternatively, the brief characterizes capital punishment as an "atavistic horror,"[31] "inhuman[] and indecen[t],"[32] "horrible,"[33] "disgust[ing],"[34] and "brutally degrading."[35] The *Aikens* brief quotes at length from Albert Camus's famous midcentury diatribe against the death penalty, *Reflections on the Guillotine*, to argue that "repugnance" is the only answer to the question why the state performs executions in secret behind prison walls if their purpose is to deter others from committing crimes.[36]

Camus's impassioned moralism became the dominant strain in European abolition of the death penalty—from Minister of Justice Robert Badinter's successful efforts in the French parliament in 1981 to the more general adoption of the view that capital punishment constitutes a violation of basic human rights.[37] But over the past half century, as abolition through a human rights lens became firmly entrenched in Europe, American legal and political abolitionist discourse shifted away from the type of vivid, high-flown rhetoric of the *Aikens* brief and the opinions of Brennan and Marshall in *Furman*. As Mugambi Jouet wryly observes, "Nowadays, one could imagine a senior litigator scolding a junior attorney for quoting Camus in the draft of a legal brief."[38] Instead of attacking the death penalty as a repulsive and atavistic practice, current legal and political critiques focus on deficiencies in the process by which capital punishment is applied, noting lengthy delays, high cost, risk of error, and arbitrary or discriminatory patterns of imposition. In 2015, Justice Stephen Breyer penned a lengthy dissent, joined by Justice Ruth Bader Ginsburg, calling on the Supreme Court to reconsider the constitutionality of capital punishment.[39] Breyer's opinion, which

The Foreignness of *Furman* / 97

he also took the unusual step of publishing separately as a book,[40] argued that the death penalty was "cruel" under the Eighth Amendment—but based this conclusion on its unreliability, arbitrariness, and long delays, not on its "atavistic horror" as the *Aikens* brief had done.

One sees a similar pivot in the political realm. When Governor Gavin Newsom in 2019 imposed a moratorium on executions in California, the state with the country's largest death row, he explained that the punishment was "unfair, unjust and wasteful" and listed discrimination, unreliability, and cost as the central problems with California's death penalty.[41] Similar arguments predominated in the legislative debates that led to the most recent state abolition of the death penalty in Virginia, the state that has executed the most people in the course of American history. State Senator Scott Surovell introduced the abolition bill by emphasizing a litany of procedural problems with the state's death penalty, including the risk of executing the innocent, the impossibility of having a fair trial when capital punishment is in play, the striking of the majority of jurors who are opposed to the death penalty, inequitable application, cost, and lack of transparency.[42] And when Virginia governor Ralph Northam signed the bill into law, he emphasized that "the death penalty comes down to one fundamental question, one question: Is it fair?"[43] Northam went on to explain that "fair" meant equally applied and not in error.

Of course, many current abolitionists harbor fundamental moral objections to the death penalty, objections that still surface in both legal and public discourse on the topic. But while it may be hard to say whether or to what degree abolitionists' subjective motivations have changed in the past fifty years, it is much easier to see how the center of gravity of legal and public discourse has shifted from substance to procedure, from essence to practice, from morality to pragmatism. This profound shift is what renders so incongruous much of the argumentation in the *Aikens* brief and the categorical opinions of Justices Brennan and Marshall.

But the foreignness of *Furman* to the modern reader is as much a product of what is *not* in the opinions as of what is included. Many of what current observers would describe as the most significant problems with capital punishment today are either absent or marginal in the Court's varied critiques of the death penalty at the time of *Furman*—most notably problems relating to innocence, cost, delay, and execution methods. The risk of executing the innocent is the single issue that has had the most influence on public opinion about the death penalty in the modern era, especially after DNA evidence catalyzed the "innocence revolution" of the late 1990s.[44] This concern led a Republican governor to grant commutation to the entire death row of the state of Illinois in 2003 in response to a series of exonerations of condemned prisoners.[45] It led a federal judge to declare the federal death penalty to be unconstitutional in 2002, although that decision was reversed on appeal,[46] and it played a central role in Justice Breyer's 2015 dissent in *Glossip v. Gross*.[47] It has received prominent attention in decisions by governors issuing moratoria on executions and by legislators voting to abolish the death penalty, including the most recent abolition in the state of Virginia.[48]

The problem of wrongful conviction and execution of the innocent, however, gets barely a mention in the hundreds of pages of *Furman* opinions. Only Justice Marshall gives the issue sustained attention, arguing that if members of the public were aware "of the potential dangers of executing an innocent man," they would find the death penalty unacceptable.[49] Although Marshall cites the available literature on wrongful convictions, he acknowledges that "proving one's innocence after a jury finding of guilt is almost impossible" and that "we have no way of judging how many innocent persons have been executed," though he argues "we can be certain that there were some."[50] Marshall's arguments ring weakly to the modern ear, when today we have scientific means by which condemned prisoners can challenge their convictions, a national registry of exonerations,[51] and plausible attempts by scholars to quantify the error rate in capital cases.[52]

Marshall is similarly the only justice to give any attention to the high cost of the death penalty, arguing again that if members of the public were aware that "the costs of executing a capital offender exceed the costs of imprisoning him for life," they would find the death penalty unacceptable.[53] Today, the high cost of the death penalty is tremendously salient in public discussions about the death penalty. Many death penalty states have done self-studies demonstrating the much higher costs of capital convictions relative to noncapital convictions.[54] This disparity is driven by the costs of capital prosecutions and appeals as well as lengthy incarceration on death row, both of which have increased dramatically since 1972. Had the disparity in cost been similar at the time of *Furman*, one would have expected more mention of it, especially in the lengthy discussions the justices engage in about the death penalty's purported deterrent effect. Surely, had the costs of the death penalty been anything like what they are today, at least one of the majority justices might have thought to suggest that the tremendous financial resources required to administer the death penalty would provide for much greater deterrence or prevention of crime if applied in some other way.

The death penalty's high cost today is partly driven by the ever-lengthening time that that condemned prisoners spend on death row. Between 1984 and 2017, the average time between sentence and execution more than tripled, rising from six years to twenty years.[55] And it has continued to increase beyond that. For the twenty-two people executed in 2019, the average time that elapsed between their sentence and execution was twenty-two years—"by far the longest time between sentence and execution since capital punishment resumed in the U.S. in the 1970s."[56] Lengthy time on death row was not an issue addressed by any of the justices in *Furman*, but had such stunning delays been in existence then, they would have bolstered Justice White's argument that the death penalty as then administered was unlikely to make measurable contributions to its penological ends, especially deterrence. Not surprisingly, Justice Breyer made exactly this argument in his *Glossip* dissent in 2015: "Lengthy delays . . . undermine the death penalty's penological rationale, perhaps irreparably so."[57]

Finally, it is distinctly odd to modern sensibilities that the *Furman* opinions make no mention of the potentially unconstitutional cruelty of the electric chair, the dominant execution method in 1972. Today, concerns about the potential for cruelty in lethal injection, which was adopted as a more humane and less disfiguring alternative to the electric chair and other authorized modes of execution,[58] are central to both public debates about the death penalty and legal challenges to executions. After European and American manufacturers of some common lethal injection drugs stopped providing them for executions, many states scrambled to find alternatives, turning to new drug combinations or single-drug protocols or seeking assistance from lightly regulated compounding pharmacies.[59] These new drugs and protocols led both to protracted legal battles and to a number of botched executions.[60] Numerous justices on the Supreme Court have penned or joined opinions decrying as unconstitutionally cruel the risk of suffering inherent in lethal injection, using language like "excruciating pain,"[61] "slow asphyxiation,"[62] "burning, searing pain,"[63] and "the chemical equivalent of being burned at the stake."[64] Although these objections have been rejected (sometimes narrowly) by a majority of the Court, the issue has been joined numerous times in recent years. It is thus jarring for a modern reader to find no whisper of constitutional concern in *Furman* about an execution method like electrocution, which had famously malfunctioned in Louisiana only twenty-five years previously.[65] The modern reader will no doubt remember the more recent episode in 2000, when Florida's electric chair ("Old Sparky") was hastily abandoned by the state legislature after the Supreme Court granted review following "two highly publicized incidents in which a malfunctioning chair resulted in particularly gruesome deaths."

The Supreme Court's Role in Transforming the American Death Penalty

The changed landscape since *Furman* is unsurprising given the sheer number of years—a half century—separating the present moment from that landmark decision. But the changed circumstances are not simply the product of the passage of time: *Furman* itself and the Court's subsequent decisions have greatly influenced prevailing capital practices and discourse. The Court's choice to invalidate capital statutes in 1972, to uphold new statutes in 1976, and to embark on a path of extensive top-down constitutional regulation of the death penalty has significantly influenced the distinctively American version of capital punishment in place today. Some of the changes linked to *Furman* and its progeny are entirely predictable. For example, *Furman's* condemnation of standardless discretion naturally prodded states toward their embrace of Model Penal Code–styled statutes limiting the death penalty to aggravated murder, in contrast to the breadth of the pre-*Furman* schemes permitting its imposition for some nonhomicidal offenses and practically all murders. Though there are reasons to be skeptical about the extent to which aggravating factors today are actually successful in narrowing the class of death-eligible offenders to a genuinely smaller subset of the "worst of the worst" murderers, the change wrought by *Furman* (and its progeny) in jettisoning virtually all nonhomicidal offenses and simple murder from the list of capital offenses has substantially shifted and to some extent limited the concerns surrounding the "wanton," "freakish," and "arbitrary" administration of the death penalty in the United States.

Changing Discourse

More surprising is the extent to which *Furman* has contributed to the muting of human dignity discourse, which by the 1960s had become the dominant framework for anti-death-penalty advocacy in the United States and especially around the world. As far back as the early nineteenth century, opponents of the death penalty in the United States emphasized its "uncivilized" character. Antigallows societies built on Enlightenment ideas about the inherent worth of individuals and the necessity of restraints on state power. The claim that the death penalty constituted an unjust and uncivilized punishment accelerated in the wake of World War II and the experience of the Holocaust. Postwar abolition in Germany and Italy was fueled by an emerging insistence on universal human rights, including the right to life and the prohibition on torture (though the death penalty was not yet widely understood to invariably violate either of these commands). By the 1960s, the belief that the death penalty was wrong not just as a matter of public policy but as a violation of basic rights was ascendant, motivating much of the abolitionist advocacy of that period, as evident in the *Aiken* briefing described earlier. Justice Brennan's appeal to human dignity in *Furman* as a ground for invalidating the death penalty reflected the emerging appeal of that argument as the basis for abolition.

But the other opinions supporting the *Furman* result did not urge this ground (apart from Justice Marshall's concurrence), focusing less on the death penalty as a punishment than on its manner of administration. When the Court upheld new capital statutes in *Gregg v. Georgia* and its accompanying cases in 1976, the Court decisively rejected the claim that the death penalty was inconsistent with "evolving standards of decency" given states' widespread adoption of new statutes in the wake of *Furman* and the willingness of juries to return death sentences in the four intervening years.[66] Over the next several decades, the Court continued to focus on the administration rather than the ultimate morality of the death penalty, requiring states, among other things, to facilitate the consideration of mitigating evidence in the death penalty decision,[67] to guide sentencer discretion in determining which offenders are "death eligible,"[68] and to limit "excessive" applications of the death penalty for certain offenses (e.g., rape) and against certain offenders (e.g., juveniles and persons with intellectual disabilities).[69]

The Court's opinions in *Furman* and *Gregg* decisively changed the legal as well as public debate surrounding American capital punishment. In the wake of those decisions, legal advocates no longer addressed the moral standing of capital punishment and instead challenged particular state practices as contrary to the Court's emerging complex rules for its administration. Outside of the Court, these foundational decisions undercut the claim that the death penalty should be rejected as an uncivilized practice in three interrelated ways. First, *Furman*'s invalidation of prevailing statutes mobilized political support for the death penalty, as politicians loudly seized on capital punishment as a promising wedge issue, emphasizing the Court's extraordinary intervention at a time of rising crime and deep skepticism about the Court's perceived overreaching in the criminal justice domain. The backlash effect of *Furman* is reflected in the remarkable *increase* in support for capital punishment following the decision, from 50 percent in March 1972 (just prior to the decision) to 57 percent in November 1972 (just a few months after the decision), with support rising to 66 percent in the Gallup poll taken after the argument in *Gregg* but before the decision in 1976.[70] The dramatic shift in numbers in such a short span suggests that *Furman* (and the reaction it engendered) likely influenced public support for the death penalty in the early to mid-1970s.

Second, *Furman*'s condemnation of the rarity of death sentences and executions, particularly in Justice White's opinion, meant that increased recourse to capital punishment was now an essential part of a post-*Furman* state strategy. In the run-up to Furman, the American death penalty was in substantial decline, with marginal numbers of new death sentences and a five-year period without executions. The LDF had argued to the Court that the rarity of the death penalty was doubly fatal: it suggested that the American people had turned their back on the punishment (especially given its wide availability under prevailing statutes), and it also suggested that the death penalty could not possibly secure much deterrent or retributive value (essentially Justice White's argument). *Furman* thus incentivized states that wanted to preserve the death penalty to err on the side of aggressive use; modest use would likely not survive constitutional scrutiny. Ironically, then, *Furman's* seeming death blow to the American death penalty seems to have revived the practice, with far more death sentences secured in the two decades post-*Furman* than the decades preceding the decision. By the mid-1990s, the country was producing over three hundred death sentences a year, as well as dramatically increasing the number of executions.[71] In this environment, opponents of the death penalty were inclined to emphasize pragmatic reasons for restricting or abolishing the punishment; it was much harder to win the hearts and minds of state political actors and the general public by insisting that they had moved the country down an immoral path of violating human rights.

Third, the Court's decision in *Gregg* affirming the constitutionality of the death penalty weakened the claim that the death penalty violates basic human rights. While it is of course true that the U.S. Constitution does not prohibit every immoral practice, the Supreme Court has played an outsized role in American political and public discourse. Its pronouncement that states had the prerogative to retain or abolish the practice, on the ground that it plausibly serves deterrence or retributive purposes, was an important and defining moment for the American death penalty. *Gregg* remains the first and only time that the Court directly addressed whether the death penalty constitutes "cruel and unusual" punishment, and its negative answer to that question not only shifted litigation strategy in the capital defense bar but also marginalized the moral claim that the death penalty is a barbaric, atavistic practice with no legitimate place in a constitutional democracy. The fact that the Court's reasoning focused on its perception of "evolving standards of decency" rather than relying on American history and tradition, or the seeming textual support for capital punishment in the Constitution, underscored the Court's view that the death penalty could still play an important role in "civilized" criminal justice systems.

Overall, then, had the Court not entered the constitutional fray in *Furman*, the American death penalty might well have continued to wither, and states would not have felt the need to revive or expand the practice. Without the Court's intervention as a target, the death penalty's value as a wedge issue would have been weakened. And the Court would not have been pressed to decisively declare the practice a permissible tool of criminal justice policy. Instead, the backlash to *Furman* pushed the United States off its path toward de jure or de facto abolition in much of the country and inspired its widespread frenzied embrace, culminating with the Court granting its imprimatur regarding the basic decency of the practice in 1976. Whereas the justices supporting the result in *Furman* likely thought they were setting the terms for the end of the American death penalty, they instead transformed the politics on the ground and shifted momentum toward broader acceptance.

New Problems in the Administration of the Death Penalty

At the same time that *Furman* and its progeny diminished the prospects for total abolition and sidelined discourse regarding the basic morality of capital punishment, it radically restructured capital practices in ways that generated and highlighted other problems with the practice. Most fundamentally, *Furman*'s "constitutionalization" of the death penalty—subjecting the death penalty to continuing regulatory oversight by the federal courts—dramatically increased the costs of its administration.[72] The proliferation of new statutes post-*Furman* generated extensive litigation regarding a host of new issues, including the adequacy of new "aggravating" factors triggering death penalty eligibility, the ability of defendants to present and have considered "mitigating" factors calling for leniency, and the administration of "proportionality" review required in some state schemes. The new legalism surrounding the death penalty required a better-trained and more specialized capital defense bar, something that simply did not exist prior to *Furman*. The Court's insistence on individualized sentencing, in particular, with its recognition of the importance of evidence regarding a defendant's character and background and the circumstances of the offense, prompted a dramatically different approach to capital representation. Prior to *Furman*, capital trials focused primarily on the guilt of the accused, and lawyers in capital cases generally had no special expertise regarding death penalty advocacy.[73] The new 1976 statutes approved by the Court, however, mandated bifurcated proceedings with a special punishment phase devoted entirely to the question of the appropriateness of the death penalty; by the 1980s, state-of-art representation of capital defendants no longer involved advocacy by a single attorney but representation by a capital defense "team," including a new role for "mitigation specialists" dedicated to uncovering and presenting a wide range of facts about the defendant's life circumstances. The change in capital trial practices was reflected in the American Bar Association's promulgation of special guidelines for capital trial representation, first in 1989[74] and with greater detail in 2003,[75] followed by supplementary guidelines elaborating on the mitigation function in 2008.[76]

Cost

The costs of capital trials pre-*Furman* were comparable to those of other serious felony cases, but post-*Furman* the costs began to rise significantly as emerging norms of capital trial representation, reflected in the new American Bar Association guidelines, started to take hold. The new legalism also bolstered resources for collateral litigation to "audit" the adequacy of capital trials. Prior to *Furman*, states by and large had ad hoc mechanisms of post-conviction review and spotty assistance to indigent inmates seeking such review.[77] By the 1990s, most states had modernized their previous writ systems into comprehensive proceedings of postconviction review, and most provided indigent death-sentenced inmates (but not other inmates) access to counsel.[78] In the late 1980s, Congress authorized representation for indigent death-sentenced inmates seeking federal habeas review of their state convictions and sentences.[79] Federal constitutional regulation of the death penalty also had the collateral effect of increasing state scrutiny of the death penalty under state constitutional law. The U.S. Supreme Court's endorsement of the principle that "death is different"—not in the sense that it is invariably cruel but rather in deserving special procedural safeguards—was echoed by many state supreme courts as they elaborated their own, newly demanding legal requirements for the administration of the punishment.[80]

The promulgation of new constitutional rules for capital punishment initiated a cycle that dramatically raised the cost of capital trials, appeals, postconviction review, and incarceration: new legal rules established the need for increased professionalization of the capital defense bar, and the professionalization of the capital defense bar led to innovative challenges to capital practices, necessitating more resources for capital representation. In the decades following *Furman*, new nonprofit organizations emerged litigating on behalf of capital defendants and death-sentenced inmates. Specialized federal habeas units within federal public defender offices (capital habeas units or CHUs) were established to provide expert representation to death-sentenced inmates.[81] States created their own offices for capital representation at all levels—trial, appeal, and state postconviction.[82] The presence of a professionalized capital bar and the guarantee of representation for indigent defendants and death-sentenced inmates ensured that capital litigation would be more time-consuming and resource-consuming than its pre-*Furman* counterpart. These developments also dramatically lengthened the time between the commission of an offense and execution. In the pre-*Furman* years, there were few delays between the arrest of a suspect and his trial; appeals and postconviction proceedings were relatively short, and execution would occur within months or perhaps a year or two of conviction. Today, a capital trial might occur years after arrest (to facilitate a comprehensive mitigation investigation); capital appeals often involve dozens of issues and can take years to resolve; and the complexity of state postconviction (which also requires extensive mitigation investigation to assess whether there was adequate mitigation advocacy at trial) has in many states created a shortage of lawyers able or willing to undertake such representation, leading to very lengthy delays. Federal habeas litigation is likewise extraordinarily complex, often requiring many years to resolve.

Apart from the sheer cost of these multilayered proceedings is the added cost of lengthy incarceration. In the years prior to *Furman*, the death penalty was seen as a cost-saver, because an execution would end a state's expenses. Post-*Furman*, the litigation costs are not offset by lower incarceration costs, because death-sentenced inmates spend years on death row after conviction, and the costs of contemporary death-row incarceration are dramatically higher than previously. By the late 1990s, most states gravitated toward solitary-style death row incarceration, which imposes significantly greater costs than housing inmates in the general prison population (as well as other problems, discussed later).[83]

Thus, even as *Furman* and *Gregg* muted claims that the death penalty was uncivilized and immoral, they transformed the practice in ways that made it extravagantly inefficient and expensive.[84] The increased inefficiency and expense in turn diminished the appetite of prosecutors to seek the death penalty, because mitigation investigation and trial costs could be avoided or lessened by accepting a plea or waiving death as a penalty. As death sentences have declined, the death penalty has become even less efficient and more costly, because the fixed costs (e.g., maintaining capital defense offices and operating a death row and a death chamber) are spread over fewer cases. As states began to focus on the burgeoning costs of the newly regulated American death penalty, a novel metric emerged—cost per execution—which highlights the absurd figure generated by dividing public expenditures on the capital system by the (decreasing) number of executions states consummate.[85] Unsurprisingly, concerns about the death penalty's cost—more than reservations about its ultimate morality—have figured prominently in the choice by numerous states to repeal their capital statutes in the past fifteen years. In this way, the choice of constitutional regulation rather than abolition shifted the debate about the death penalty to its usefulness as a public policy rather than its morality in the abstract, and the Court had a strong hand in decimating the pragmatic case for retaining the punishment.

Extended Death Row Incarceration
One caveat is necessary to the point that the Court's regulation generally lessened the focus on the human rights dimensions of the death penalty and

shifted to its pragmatic appeal. The Court's regulation contributed to the rise of two human rights concerns surrounding the contemporary American death penalty: the cruelty of lengthy death row incarceration and the risk of botched executions. As the time separating the pronouncement of sentence and execution grew, and the conditions of America's death row became more harsh (mandated solitary confinement without human contact or opportunity to work), more attention was directed to the inhumanity surrounding the "death row phenomenon," a term that captures a series of related critiques. One critique focuses on the ethical dilemma posed by executing someone for a crime committed decades earlier, given the possibility of maturation and change. Is the state really punishing the "same" person after decades have elapsed? Another critique focuses on the psychological trauma of living under a sentence of death for so long—the unending uncertainty of when death will finally be imposed (and the possibility of enduring numerous execution dates). Still another critique focuses on the cruelty of "double punishment" in the prevailing system, which consists of decades of extraordinary deprivation (solitary confinement) followed by the administration of the death penalty. Finally, lengthy delays undercut the ability of the death penalty to serve deterrent or retributive purposes, rendering the death penalty excessive given its diminishing penological value. It is worth noting that none of these critiques challenges the inhumanity of the death penalty itself; rather, it is the present aggravated form of the death penalty characterized by lengthy delays and harsh conditions of confinement that creates a separate concern of excessive cruelty.

This human dignity argument found a home on the Court with Justice Stevens and Justice Breyer lamenting in a series of opinions respecting denial of certiorari the "double punishment" of lengthy incarceration followed by execution as well as the limited penological value of the death penalty under such circumstances.[86] Justice Breyer subsequently made this concern about the death row phenomenon a centerpiece of his dissent in *Glossip* calling for reconsideration of the death penalty as a punishment.[87] In his view, the extensive constitutional regulation of the death penalty is a feature of the American system that cannot be withdrawn, such that the present American version of the death penalty is unconstitutionally cruel, even if the death penalty by itself, in some other criminal system, is not. He memorably captured this view in his declaration that in "this world, or at least in this Nation, we can have a death penalty that at least arguably serves legitimate penological purposes or we can have a procedural system that at least arguably seeks reliability and fairness in the death penalty's application. We cannot have both."[88] Thus, even as *Furman* and *Gregg* ultimately sustained the death penalty as a humane punishment, they paved the way for a new version of the death penalty that is vulnerable to the charge of inhumanity.

Lethal Injection Woes

Another distinctive feature of the contemporary death penalty is concern about the central means of execution—lethal injection. Lethal injection became the dominant mode of execution post-*Gregg*, replacing the electric chair, as states sought a less painful process for the inmate and a less disturbing one for participating prison personnel and observing witnesses. But the turn to lethal injection was complicated by the risks posed by the three-drug protocol that states uniformly adopted after it was first designed and adopted (in an ad hoc manner) in Oklahoma. The first drug is administered as a sedative to prevent the condemned from experiencing pain, and the second drug is administered to paralyze the inmate to shield witnesses from observing involuntary movements. The third drug causes death. But prison officials administering the protocol lack the expertise of doctors (who are precluded from participating in executions given their Hippocratic oath), creating a risk that insufficiently anaesthetized inmates might experience terrible pain that would go unnoticed because of the paralyzing agent.[89] Apart from these risks, pharmaceutical producers of the drug used as a sedative in most states' lethal injection protocols sought to prohibit their use in executions (to the point of withdrawing some drugs from the market),[90] which caused states to experiment with other, less reliable, means of sedating inmates. Resulting litigation over states' lethal injection practices has significantly impaired the ability of states to consummate executions over the past twenty years.[91]

The Court's regulation of the death penalty contributed to this development in a powerful, albeit indirect, way. In the first fifteen years or so post-*Furman*, it was still not an extraordinary event for a death-sentenced inmate to be without counsel as his execution approached; there were also few resources apart from appointed counsel to raise claims regarding "end-stage" issues, such as challenges to execution methods. The lethal injection issue began to have traction after the turn of the millennium, at a point when few death-sentenced inmates were without counsel or supporting resources as they approached execution. Constitutional regulation of the death penalty produced a death penalty defense community, with increased sophistication, specialization, and training. Whereas pre-*Furman* there were few death penalty attorneys of any sort, by 2008, when the U.S. Supreme Court addressed its first challenge to the three-drug protocol in *Baze v. Rees*,[92] there were a significant number of attorneys who had developed particular expertise on lethal injection issues; these lawyers shared information and pleadings with capital defense lawyers and teams around the country. As states sought to avoid problems associated with the three-drug protocol, death penalty lawyers challenged the adoption of new protocols under state administrative procedure provisions;[93] as states tried to secure alternative supplies of sodium thiopental in response to suppliers' withdrawal from the market, lawyers challenged their efforts on numerous grounds, including whether alternative suppliers followed appropriate safeguards regarding drug potency and even challenges based on illegal trafficking under federal drug laws. Death penalty teams also identified special risks that lethal injection might pose for their particular clients, including inadequate vein access caused by prior drug use;[94] they also highlighted the failures in particular states to have reliably trained personnel administer the protocols. Apart from these broad and targeted legal challenges, death penalty defense advocates participated in state processes for adopting new lethal injection protocols, in many cases successfully defeating recourse to untried and untested execution methods.

One striking aspect of the lethal injection saga is its disruptive power on execution efforts despite the Supreme Court's consistent rejection of any significant Eighth Amendment protection in this area. In the three major cases it addressed,[95] the Court adopted an extremely permissive standard for states, insisting that even a significant risk of pain would not condemn the application of a challenged protocol unless a death-sentenced petitioner identified a readily available, less problematic protocol (which presumably the petitioner would accept as a means of execution).[96] Lethal injection challenges delayed or defeated executions not because federal courts frequently found state protocols deficient under the Eighth Amendment—lawsuits almost never succeeded along these lines. Rather, defense lawyers and allied actors devoted considerable energy to learning the science (in many cases pseudoscience) of various protocol options and uncovering the deficiencies in state prison administration of those protocols (including the sourcing of inadequately vetted drugs and the use of poorly trained executioners). These efforts often bore fruit outside of the courts—by persuading state actors to decline to adopt new protocols, by shining light on the problematic ethics of using medicines designed to improve health in the execution process, and by educating institutional actors and the general public about the genuine hazards associated with a mode of killing previously heralded as a painless, modern alternative to outdated modes of execution. None of this could have happened in the pre-*Furman* era, because death-sentenced inmates were essentially on their own and those who had representation could not expect their lawyers to have the knowledge, time, or resources to bring any real scrutiny to prevailing execution practices. *Furman*, *Gregg*, and the embrace of constitutional regulation created the institutional structures necessary for systemic engagement of state execution practices.

Concerns about Wrongful Executions
A similar dynamic is at play in the emergence of risk of error as perhaps the dominant concern in the present era of the American death penalty. Fear of

executing innocents is likely as old as the death penalty. Moreover, well-publicized wrongful executions have frequently spearheaded abolitionist efforts around the world, notably in England, where the wrongful execution of Timothy Evans in 1950 was a powerful impetus for parliamentary review and eventual repeal of capital punishment in the 1960s.[97] In the United States, though, concerns about executing the innocent did not occupy a central role in the LDF's abolitionist campaign in the 1960s and received relatively slight attention in the *Furman* opinions supporting the invalidation of prevailing statutes. But the discovery of numerous wrongfully convicted death-sentenced inmates in Illinois in the late 1990s catapulted the issue to the forefront of the American death penalty debate, decreasing public appetite for the punishment and contributing to its repeal in numerous jurisdictions.

As in the lethal execution context, the Court's constitutional regulation of the death penalty has not directly highlighted, or expressed particular solicitude for, concern about executing innocents. In fact, in the early 1990s, prior to the experience in Illinois, the Court displayed a notable indifference to the problem: it declined an invitation to declare that the Constitution prohibits the execution of an innocent person, insisting instead that long-standing principles do not appear to require a judicial forum to address an inmate's newly discovered evidence of actual innocence, even where that inmate is condemned to death.[98] But constitutional regulation indirectly changed the conditions on the ground to make them more hospitable to a focus on innocence. First, constitutional regulation increased the likelihood of uncovering error in capital cases, by uniformly providing counsel to death-sentenced (but not other) inmates in state and federal postconviction proceedings and, relatedly, by substantially extending the time between sentence and execution. In a previous era, many of the inmates exonerated in Illinois would almost certainly have been executed prior to the discovery of error (even with the delays of the modern era, at least one of those exonerated, Anthony Porter, came within hours of execution before he received a stay on grounds unrelated to his claim of innocence).[99] Second, constitutional regulation of the death penalty contributed to the development of the type of "cause" lawyering and advocacy that has been critical to the success of the innocence movement. The Court's constitutional supervision of capital punishment produced a new and virtually unprecedented form of advocacy in the criminal justice realm—a team approach bringing together lawyers, mitigation specialists, and a variety of experts (forensic, mental health, and others). Of course, such resources were not present in all or even most cases in the early years following *Furman* and *Gregg*. But the institutional structures created in the wake of those decisions raised expectations for capital advocacy, and the American Bar Association guidelines reflected the new norms for representation and advocacy.

The newly heightened concern about wrongful convictions was led in large part by the tenacious advocacy of founders of innocence-focused centers, including Barry Scheck and Peter Neufeld (who established the Innocence Project at Cardozo Law School) and Rob Warden (who launched the Center for Wrongful Convictions at Northwestern Law School). Their work built on the capital model, with the development of increasingly sophisticated legal and policy strategies to highlight the risk of error in criminal (not just capital) cases. As in the capital sphere, advocates for reducing wrongful convictions and exonerating the wrongly convicted built broader networks for disseminating strategies and increasing public awareness of the extent of the problem (including the National Registry of Exonerations, now operated by a consortium of universities).[100] Overall, constitutional regulation provided the infrastructure to make litigating innocence claims possible and the blueprint for aggressive, multitiered political and policy efforts to make the underlying problems visible and to motivate change.

Changes in Constitutional Methodology and Political Context

Widening the lens beyond *Furman*'s framing of the failures of capital punishment and the changed circumstances that render that framing inapposite to the current moment, the foreignness of reading the case today also resides in changed aspects of capital and constitutional jurisprudence and in changed political context. A great deal has changed in the past fifty years along both these dimensions, far too much even to be briefly surveyed. Here, we sketch changes in each dimension that seem most salient to understanding how *Furman*'s legal and political contexts differ from the current moment.

Constitutional Methodology

The Court's decision in *Furman*, contrary to what many believed at the time, marked a beginning more than an end. It was the beginning of fifty years of what is now known as the Supreme Court's Eighth Amendment capital jurisprudence—a complex body of law growing out of the Court's decision to take on a continuing regulatory stance regarding the practice of capital punishment across the country. During this half century of constitutional regulation, the Court has adjudicated issues regarding the scope and shape of capital statutes, the conduct of capital trials, the specific duties of capital defense counsel, and the rights of the condemned on death row and during the execution process. This comprehensive regulatory approach led the Court to develop new approaches to resolving constitutional issues similar

The Foreignness of *Furman* / 111

to the ones presented in *Furman*. Reading *Furman* today highlights the absence of what are today standard methodological approaches.

First, consider the relevance of international comparisons. The petitioners in the *Furman* litigation repeatedly and vociferously urged the Court to consider the international movement away from the death penalty as evidence of "the basic standard of decency of contemporary society."[101] Their brief noted that "most of the nations of Western Europe and the Western Hemisphere have legally abolished capital punishment as a penalty for civilian crime" and that the "majority of nations in the world retain the death penalty on the books but use it relatively infrequently."[102] The relevance of this trend, urged petitioners, is its illumination of American constitutional values: "The values which have been most consistently opposed to capital punishment, and which have largely extirpated it in the western world over the course of the last two centuries, lie very close to the root of the Anglo-American conception of a free and civilized society."[103] The petitioners included a separate appendix to their brief that "describes the world trend toward abolition of the death penalty during the past two centuries."[104]

But even the justices in the *Furman* majority most sympathetic to the petitioners' framing of the issues refused to bite. Justice Brennan, whose overall approach most closely tracked that of the petitioners, framed a central part of his inquiry as "whether there are objective indicators from which a court can conclude that contemporary society considers a severe punishment unacceptable."[105] In answering this question, however, Brennan makes no mention of the rest of the world; rather, he concludes that his "examination of the history and present operation of the *American practice* of punishing criminals by death reveals that this punishment has been almost totally rejected by contemporary society."[106] Justice Marshall as well, after offering a lengthy history exegesis, concludes that "the foregoing history demonstrates that capital punishment was carried from Europe to America but, *once here*, was tempered considerably."[107] Like Brennan, he relies entirely on American, not international, experience.[108]

In the modern era, however, the Court has embraced international comparisons as central to its Eighth Amendment analysis in capital cases. Starting as early as 1977, the Court began consulting international practice and opinion in its Eighth Amendment capital cases. In *Coker v. Georgia*, which held unconstitutional the imposition of death for the rape of an adult woman, the Court observed that "in the light of the legislative decisions in almost all of the States and *in most of the countries around the world*, it would be difficult to support a claim that the death penalty for rape is an indispensable part of the States' criminal justice system."[109] Soon thereafter, in *Enmund v. Florida*, which held unconstitutional the imposition of death for some of the least culpable felony murders, the Court reiterated that its Eighth

Amendment analysis called on it to look to "international opinion."[110] In *Atkins v. Virginia*, which held unconstitutional the execution of offenders with intellectual disability, the Court held (in a footnote) that the views of the "world community" supported its Eighth Amendment conclusion, citing an amicus brief filed in the case by European Union.[111] But the Court gave its most full-throated endorsement to the relevance of international comparisons in *Roper v. Simmons*, which held unconstitutional the execution of juvenile offenders.[112] The Court stated, "It is proper that we acknowledge the overwhelming weight of international opinion against the juvenile death penalty, resting in large part on the understanding that the instability and emotional imbalance of young people may often be a factor in the crime. The opinion of the world community, while not controlling our outcome, does provide respected and significant confirmation for our own conclusions."[113] The Court then concluded its opinion with ringing emphasis: "It does not lessen our fidelity to the Constitution or our pride in its origins to acknowledge that the express affirmation of certain fundamental rights by other nations and peoples simply underscores the centrality of those same rights within our own heritage of freedom."[114] The Court's use of international comparisons in its Eighth Amendment jurisprudence is not without its detractors—Justice Scalia even gave the practice a sarcastic "Prize for the Court's Most Feeble Effort to manufacture 'national consensus'" in his *Atkins* dissent[115]—but there can be no question that it is (for the moment) a long-settled feature of Eighth Amendment jurisprudence. Hence the modern reader's surprise at the *Furman* Court's total avoidance of the petitioners' arguments along these lines.

Second, the *Furman* Court's approach to empirical questions seems positively antiquated to a modern reader. The justices in *Furman* addressed two questions that required the analysis of empirical data—whether the death penalty was applied in a racially discriminatory manner, and whether the death penalty was a better deterrent than other possible penalties. Each discussion would clearly go very differently today because the technique of statistical analysis has changed so drastically since the time of *Furman*, requiring the Court to change the way that it approaches empirical questions in its constitutional analysis.

Justice William O. Douglas is the only justice in *Furman* to give sustained attention to the question of whether the death penalty was applied in a racially discriminatory manner. He cited a variety of studies finding an association between the Black race of defendants and the frequency of executions, as well as a reverse association between the Black race of condemned prisoners and the exercise of executive clemency.[116] But Douglas also quoted approvingly one study's conclusion that "it is not possible to indict the judicial and other public processes [for these associations]. Too many unknown or presently immeasurable factors prevent our making definitive statements about the relationship."[117] Because of the impossibility of what we today would call "controlling for confounding variables," Douglas rested his conclusion of discriminatory application of the death penalty on the way in which the standardless discretion given to capital sentencers allowed free play to their biases: "We deal with a system of law and of justice that leaves to the uncontrolled discretion of judges or juries the determination whether defendants committing these crimes should live or die. . . . People live or die, dependent on the whim of one man or of 12."[118] To Douglas, it was not necessary to offer statistical proof of discrimination; rather, he could conclude that "these discretionary statutes . . . are *pregnant* with discrimination."[119]

We know that such a discussion would go very differently today because it in fact *did* go very differently when the Court finally directly addressed the question of whether racially discriminatory patterns in the imposition of the death penalty violated the Constitution. In its 1987 decision in *McCleskey v. Kemp*, the Court considered a very different type of study from the ones collected by Douglas only fifteen years earlier.[120] The Baldus study used multiple regression analysis to control for the influence of 230 potentially confounding variables on the raw racial disparities that his data revealed, so as to isolate the influence of race.[121] Ultimately, the Court held that even if the study's conclusions were sound (which it assumed for the sake of argument), a constitutional violation could not be established in the absence of proof of intentional discrimination in McCleskey's individual case. Justice Powell, who penned the Court's opinion in *McCleskey*, privately admitted to discomfort with the sophisticated statistical techniques used in the study before the Court.[122] But *McCleskey* demonstrated that multiple regression analysis was by then the new normal in statistical proof and could not be avoided by the Court—except by assuming the validity of a contested statistical study but dismissing it as not relevant to the question at issue.[123]

Similarly, multiple regression analysis transformed the debate about the deterrent effect of the death penalty. In *Furman*, Marshall was the justice who gave the most sustained attention to disproving the purported deterrent effect of capital punishment. He devoted nearly ten pages of his opinion to reviewing the empirical evidence on the topic before concluding that "abolitionists . . . have succeeded in showing by clear and convincing evidence that capital punishment is not necessary as a deterrent to crime in our society."[124] Marshall gave pride of place to the work of Thorsten Sellin, who studied the deterrent effect of capital punishment by comparing the homicide rates of contiguous states with and without the death penalty, and the homicide rates within individual states before and after they abolished or reinstated the death penalty. This was state-of-the-art empirical research on deterrence in the mid-twentieth century, but the work of Isaac Erhlich, who introduced multiple regression analysis to deterrence studies, exploded the field. As Robert Weisberg has commented, "The death penalty deterrence debate might be said to be divisible in two eras: before Ehrlich (BE) and after Ehrlich (AE)."[125] Although Erhlich's findings were later discredited, his research was considered an important enough breakthrough to be submitted to the Court in draft form by the solicitor general when *Gregg v. Georgia*[126] was litigated, and it was cited by the 1976 *Gregg* plurality to conclude that there was a "scholarly standoff" on the issue of deterrence, rather than the "clear and convincing" proof of lack of deterrence that Marshall had found four years previously.[127] The debate about the deterrent effect of the death penalty has raged on through the present day—but overwhelmingly in the mode of multiple regression analysis. Hence the modern reader's bemused puzzlement at the much more low-tech mode of the deterrent discussion in *Furman* itself.

Political Context

When the LDF sought to persuade the Supreme Court of society's emerging rejection of the death penalty, it focused primarily on declining numbers of new death sentences and executions. The LDF focused on the diminished *practice* of the death penalty because there was little compelling evidence of the death penalty's *political* vulnerability, reflected in widespread efforts to significantly limit or abolish the punishment legislatively. The LDF insisted that prevailing statutes had fallen into desuetude, reflecting an outdated morality no longer embraced by the community but insulated from review because of states' exceedingly rare (and discriminatory) recourse to the punishment. Only two states, Iowa and West Virginia, had permanently abolished the death penalty in the four decades prior to *Furman*, both in 1965 (though Alaska and Hawaii entered the Union as abolitionist states in 1959, both having abolished the death penalty as territories in 1957).[128] When the Court confronted the claim that the death penalty violated contemporary standards of decency in 1972, fewer than ten states had fully abolished the death penalty.[129] Though *Furman* invalidated prevailing capital statutes, it did not reduce the footprint of the American death penalty, as the backlash to that decision ensured that roughly the same number of jurisdictions provided for capital punishment a decade after the decision as when *Furman* was decided.[130]

The past fifteen years, though, have seen an explosion of political efforts to abolish capital punishment. In some cases, like New Jersey in 2007, the state legislature jettisoned the death penalty after extensive public debate and scrutiny of its post-*Furman* experience.[131] In others, like New York, the legislature declined to fix its statute after the highest state court identified fatal but curable defects in the state scheme.[132] Eleven states have abolished the death penalty since 2007, the most dramatic era of repeal in our country's history.[133] Virginia, the most efficient executing state in the modern era (and the overall leader in executions dating back to colonial times), abolished the death penalty in 2021.[134] Governors have imposed moratoria on executions in three other capital jurisdictions (Oregon, Pennsylvania, and California), and several other states, including Kansas, Utah, and Montana, have experienced active repeal efforts in recent years.

The increased political attention to the death penalty by state political actors alters the dynamics of federal judicial review. On the one hand, the rapid and unprecedented jettisoning of capital punishment in eleven states, together with official and de facto moratoria on executions in many others, strengthens the case that the American death penalty no longer enjoys widespread support. The enormous decline in capital sentencing over the past two decades—a decline of more than 90 percent from 1995 to 2021[135]—reinforces the claim that the death penalty has become an exceedingly marginal practice, unlikely to secure much retributive or deterrent value in its current form. On the other hand, it can no longer be said that state statutes remain on the books because of legislative inattention. *Furman* initiated a dialogue with the states, and current capital practices are the product of an ongoing conversation between the Court and various political actors and constituencies within states.

A miniature version of this dynamic of inattention-intervention-reform played out on a subsidiary issue within the death penalty debate—whether to exempt persons with intellectual disabilities. Prior to 1986, states had paid essentially no attention to this issue, neither affirmatively choosing to allow the practice nor explicitly prohibiting it. The execution of a person with intellectual disability in Georgia was met with deep public disapproval, leading Georgia to become the first state to carve out a statutory exemption.[136] Three years later, the Supreme Court rejected the claim that the practice of executing offenders with intellectual disability violated evolving standards of decency, relying primarily on the fact that few jurisdictions had joined Georgia in prohibiting it.[137] Over the next decade or so, partly in response to the high visibility the Supreme Court litigation had brought to the issue, sixteen additional states barred such executions.[138] When the Court revisited the claim in 2002, it banned the practice, even though a majority of death penalty jurisdictions still tolerated it, emphasizing the speed and consistency of change toward prohibition.[139] Similarly, at the present moment, the Court faces a much different environment than *Furman*, one in which it cannot attribute prevailing statutes to inattention but also one in which engagement reveals radically diminishing support.

Another significant difference in the pre- and post-*Furman* world concerns the whirlwind of activity that accompanies virtually every execution.

The absence of any significant federal constitutional constraints on the death penalty in the pre-*Furman* era, together with the low level of resources allocated to death-sentenced inmates, ensured that executions by and large occurred without much drama or last-minute legal wrangling. The looming question in most cases was whether executive officials would grant clemency (which was substantially more likely than in the current moment, in part because of the absence of enforceable legal constraints or safeguards). After *Furman*, the Court's elaboration of novel constraining doctrines, the emergence of new and unprecedented state capital practices, and the increased availability of counsel to support end-stage litigation meant that executions increasingly produced a flurry of legal activity in state and federal courts. In the early post-*Furman* years, the contestation was heightened by the fact that both supporters and opponents of the death penalty viewed the performance or avoidance of particular executions as setting important precedents for the future of the death penalty. This dynamic was evident in the extraordinary end-stage litigation in Gary Gilmore's case, the first execution in the modern era, which raised a host of issues, most notably Gilmore's ability to waive his appeals.[140] The ACLU had obtained a stay in his case against his wishes, which was ultimately lifted, and the execution went forward.[141] Similar drama accompanied California's first execution in the post-*Furman* era (of Robert Alton Harris), when the U.S. Supreme Court repeatedly lifted stays granted by lower federal court judges in the Ninth Circuit and ultimately issued an astonishing order precluding any federal court from staying Harris's execution without its direct approval.[142]

End-stage litigation has heightened the political tensions on the Court around the death penalty. To some extent, end-state litigation is unavoidable because some issues—such as an inmate's competency to be executed or the appropriateness of a new lethal injection protocol—do not become ripe until an execution date approaches, ensuring that some last-minute litigation is inevitable. But some end-stage litigation is the product of capital defense triage strategies, in which lawyers and organizations devoted to defense-side capital representation do not focus on particular cases until an execution date seems likely (or has actually been announced). This is especially true in states such as Texas, where inmates often have received substandard representation at trial and in their initial postconviction proceedings, and yet their cases languish for many years before prosecutors and trial judges finally seek to schedule an execution. With literally dozens of cases in such a posture, lawyers in the defense community do not have the resources to do an audit in every one of these cases, and instead train scrutiny on them as they come closer to an actual execution. In many instances, the audit will reveal the presence of substantial, unresolved claims, often because of intervening case law (such as the Court's exemption of persons with intellectual

The Foreignness of *Furman* / 117

disability from the death penalty[143] or its willingness to excuse procedural default in cases of "double ineffectiveness"—ineffective representation at trial followed by ineffective representation on state habeas[144]).

In recent years, the tensions over end-stage litigation have boiled over, with both sides of the Court expressing their deep dissatisfaction with the status quo. On the conservative side, Justice Gorsuch has condemned what he regards as an obstructionist strategy by defense lawyers to delay and defeat the death penalty; writing for the Court in *Bucklew v. Precythe*,[145] which rejected an as-applied challenge to Missouri's lethal injection protocol, Justice Gorsuch lamented how Bucklew "managed to secure delay through lawsuit after lawsuit" despite unfavorable rulings and warned lower courts to "police carefully against attempts to use [method-of-execution] challenges as tools to interpose unjustified delay."[146] His opinion announced that "last minute stays" in capital litigation "should be the extreme exception, not the norm."[147]

On the liberal side, Justice Sotomayor condemned *Bucklew*'s insistence that lower courts review last-minute stay applications "with an especially jaundiced eye."[148] Her fear seemed to be born out when the Court vacated a stay of execution where Alabama had blatantly violated constitutional norms by permitting Christian chaplains, but not Muslim imams, to be present at an execution.[149] The Court did so not on the merits but because of the last-minute nature of the application,[150] even though Alabama had not clearly articulated its discriminatory policy until fifteen days before the execution (and the inmate had filed his complaint within five days of that notice).[151]

Even more troubling, from the liberal perspective, was the experience with the "Trump executions," in which the Court cleared the path for thirteen federal executions in the closing months of President Trump's presidency. The first four executions had been stayed by a federal district judge to consider an Eighth Amendment challenge to the new federal lethal injection protocol, with an explicit finding by that judge that the inmates had not been dilatory in raising the issue (and the DC Circuit Court of Appeals unanimously declined to vacate the stay).[152] Nonetheless, the Supreme Court vacated the stay in an unsigned five-to-four opinion allowing the executions to proceed, stating that the inmates had failed to make the requisite showing "to justify last-minute intervention" by a federal court.[153] Over the ensuing months, the Court repeatedly vacated stays or declined to issue stays despite the presence of substantial, unresolved constitutional and statutory claims.[154] Notably, the Court did so without opinion or explanation, even when lower courts had issued stays and made findings that the inmates had satisfied *Bucklew*'s "extreme exception" standard. These cases stand as perhaps the most troubling illustration of the emergence of the Court's "shadow docket," in which the Court rules on the rights of litigants without full briefing, oral argument, or any reasoned decision.[155] The overriding of stays, in particular, left the litigants and the public at large without any understanding of what was defective in the inmates' applications or in the lower court decisions putting the executions on hold. The last execution (of Dustin Higgs) was particularly troublesome because it seemed obvious that the Court's unusual behavior of granting certiorari before judgment (despite a lower court's schedule for expedited resolution) was designed to ensure that the execution was consummated before President Trump left office, given that executions would likely be paused in the next administration.[156] As Steven Vladeck argued in his illuminating book on the shadow docket, "the Court had not just enabled the Trump executions in general; it had invented a brand-new shadow docket procedure to allow the Trump Administration to execute one last prisoner on its way out the door."[157]

The firestorm around end-stage litigation seems predictable given that it is a microcosm of the death penalty writ large: death penalty supporters believe that the death penalty can and should be administered swiftly and that delays are the product of excessive gamesmanship on the part of anti-death-penalty "cause" lawyers. Opponents, on the other hand, insist that the death penalty cannot be administered in a reliable and fair way without keeping courts open to review substantial claims and that truncated consideration of those claims will inevitably produce inaccurate and unconstitutional results. For supporters, the obvious solution is to end or at least to significantly reduce federal constitutional oversight of the death penalty; for opponents, the solution is to recognize that an appropriately administered death penalty cannot serve penological goals because of inevitable, costly delays, and so the choice should be to jettison the death penalty (rather than its regulation).

An additional shift in the political climate on the Court is reflected in the difference in what it means to be a "liberal" and "conservative" justice at the time of *Furman* versus today. In *Furman*, the liberal position, associated with Justices Brennan and Marshall, regarded the death penalty as uncivilized and inhumane or, at a minimum, inconsistent with prevailing moral norms. They both voiced that view until their respective retirements, insisting in every case arriving at the Court that "the death penalty is in all cases cruel and unusual punishment."[158] With their departure, though, no justice has condemned the death penalty as essentially *immoral*. Instead, the liberal critique has focused exclusively on its inadequate administration: its arbitrariness, discrimination, error, and failure to achieve much in the way of social benefits. These pragmatic considerations led Justice Blackmun[159] and later Justice Stevens[160] to express doubts about the death penalty's constitutionality, with both insisting that the Court's constitutional regulation had failed to improve American capital practices. Justice Blackmun appeared to go further, insisting that no amount of regulation could cure the inherent obstacles to even-handed administration of the death penalty, but even he seemed to suggest that the problem was in *administering* the death penalty rather than in its inherent degradation. Justices Breyer and Ginsburg, too, near the end of their careers called for a reconsideration of the constitutionality of the death penalty.[161] Yet, they also declined to characterize the death penalty itself as barbaric or uncivilized. Like Justices Blackmun and Stevens, they focused on its arbitrary and inaccurate administration as well as its failure to secure meaningful penological goals. They lamented the inhumanity of prevailing death row incarceration, but of course such incarceration is not a necessary or essential feature of the death penalty, and some states have relaxed the harshness of death row confinement in the years following their call for reconsideration. The disappearance from the Court of any fundamental, deontological critique of the death penalty as inconsistent with human dignity is striking, especially given how powerfully that critique has motivated abolition around the world in the half century since *Furman*.

On the conservative side, the voices in dissent in *Furman* emphasized the values of federalism while at the same time voicing their own personal skepticism about the wisdom of the death penalty as a matter of public policy. At the outset of his opinion, Chief Justice Burger remarked that as a legislator, he would join the call to end the death penalty or at least to restrict it to very narrow categories of offenses.[162] Justice Blackmun went further, stating that he yielded to no one in the depth of his "distaste, antipathy, and indeed, abhorrence, for the death penalty."[163] Though the *Furman* dissenters adverted to the textual support for the death penalty in the Constitution and the historical support for the punishment, they conceded that the Eighth Amendment allowed for consideration in changes of public opinion. They did not deny that the appropriate framework for adjudicating the constitutionality of the death penalty was the "evolving standards of decency" approach announced in *Trop v. Dulles*. For the most part, they were simply deeply skeptical that the objective evidence of societal views supported the claim that the death penalty no longer comported with prevailing American values. In *Gregg*, this sentiment became the Court's holding, as the justices supporting the result rejected the claim that the death penalty violated existing moral commitments.

Over the past fifty years, though, the conservative position has become more unyielding in its support of the death penalty. None of the conservatives on the present Court express personal doubts or reservations about the wisdom of the death penalty. And when Justice Scalia joined the Court, a new voice emerged challenging the orthodoxy of *Trop*. In Justice Scalia's view, the Eighth Amendment does not authorize judicial invalidation of a punishment widely accepted and textually supported by the Constitution, regardless of intervening changes in public attitudes. Indeed, Justice Scalia's antipathy toward the *Trop* framework, elicited by Justice Breyer's call for reconsideration of the constitutionality of the death penalty in *Glossip v. Gross*, is remarkable in its severity: he described *Trop* not only as wrongly decided but as having "caused more mischief to our jurisprudence, to our federal system, and to our society than any other that comes to mind."[164] For a period of time, only Justice Thomas shared Justice Scalia's skepticism about *Trop* and the evolving-standards framework. But with the ascent of originalism as the defining philosophy of conservative judges in recent years, the Court now has a working originalist majority that denies the relevance of prevailing societal values to the constitutionality of the death penalty.[165] In *Bucklew*, Justice Gorsuch maintained that the death penalty is a constitutional punishment because it was the "standard penalty for all serious crimes at the time of the founding"; it is recognized in the text of the Fifth Amendment; and the First Congress, which proposed the Eighth Amendment, provided for numerous capital crimes.[166] Though the constitutionality of capital punishment was not before the Court in *Bucklew*, and Justice Gorsuch did not explicitly disavow *Trop* by name, it seems clear that his dicta about the unquestioned constitutional status of the death penalty is intended to forestall any further efforts to reconsider its constitutionality.

The shifting politics on the Court since *Furman*, with both conservative and liberal positions moving in some meaningful way to the right, seems odd given that outside of the Court, the politics have shifted decidedly in the other direction. Constituencies supporting the death penalty have declined remarkably over the past fifty years, with fewer vocal advocates for the death penalty and fewer politicians or interest groups committed to securing death sentences or executions; prosecutors, in particular, appear in many counties to have deep ambivalence about seeking death or working hard to consummate death sentences with executions. On the other side, opponents of the death penalty have a broader range of allies in their efforts to end or limit the death penalty, including some unlikely suspects, such as groups advocating for victims of crime, evangelical religious sects, and some prosecutor associations. The Court and the country appear to be moving in opposite directions, producing an increasingly deregulated yet declining practice.

Continuity and Change to Come

In reflecting on the half century separating *Furman* from the present era, we have highlighted the enormous chasm in underlying capital practices, changed perceptions about the most worrisome ills connected to those practices, and the foreignness of the various *Furman* opinions along many dimensions, including methodology and ideology. Despite these striking differences, some commonalities prevail. Most importantly, today's death penalty, like the death penalty of the 1960s and early 1970s, is in extraordinary decline. Now, as then, death sentences have dropped precipitously, polling data reveals relatively weak public support, executions are (comparatively) rare, and many observers predict the eventual end of the practice in the United States. Given the demonstrable wrongness of *Furman*-era prognostications of the death penalty's imminent demise, it is tempting to be cautious about viewing the present weakness of the American death penalty as a harbinger of abolition.

But even the weakness of the present death penalty is different from its weakness at the time of *Furman*. Today's weakness is more profound and encompassing. First and foremost, capital punishment is losing in the political arena, with eleven states having abandoned the death penalty during the past fifteen years, most through legislative repeal. These eleven jurisdictions amount to almost the same number of states (twelve) that had abandoned the death penalty as of 2007, before New Jersey's legislative repeal marked the beginning of the dramatic modern turn toward abolition. When the LDF sought judicial abolition in the 1960s, it was seeking such intervention in part because of the dim prospects of any broad success in the political arena; today, the political momentum is entirely toward abolition with no signs of any political will to reinstate or ramp up the death penalty in the jurisdictions that either have repealed or remain under a gubernatorial-mandated moratorium on executions. Those jurisdictions now constitute a majority of American states (and many other states are de facto abolitionist, having not carried out an execution in over a decade), reflecting the death penalty's new status as a minority practice.

The profoundness of the weakness of today's death penalty is illustrated as well in the lack of a visible constituency insisting on the death penalty's preservation. The death penalty has all but disappeared as a salient issue in elections, except in some notable local district attorney races in which opposition to the death penalty appears often to be a political asset rather than a liability. Even as conservative voices lament higher rates of violent crime, the absence of sustained advocacy in support of reinstating or accelerating use of capital punishment is telling.

Moreover, the weakness of the present death penalty comes on the heels of widespread skepticism about the ability of states or courts to limit its arbitrary or inaccurate administration. At the time of *Furman*, the death penalty was essentially unregulated, and concerns about its administration naturally led to calls for increased oversight. Today, few observers or participants in the capital system believe that increased regulatory efforts will cure persistent pathologies in its administration.

Finally, the isolation of the United States in retaining and using the death penalty makes it less likely that the decline in the practice will be reversed. States abandoning the death penalty find themselves linked to a broader international movement away from the practice. That movement is rooted in a view of the death penalty as incompatible with human dignity and democratic values (notwithstanding the fact that opposition in this country tends to focus on more prosaic concerns about the death penalty's administration). The broad rejection of the death penalty outside of the United States—unanimous among other developed Western democracies—creates an aura of inevitability regarding the end of the death penalty that blunts any momentum toward revitalizing the practice at home.

The only comparative strength of the American death penalty is in the current makeup of the U.S. Supreme Court, which boasts a strong majority that seems committed to unraveling constitutional regulation of the practice. This strength will preclude judicial abolition in the short term but will not generate the political enthusiasm necessary to revive a practice in extraordinary decline.

Another notable continuity between the present moment and *Furman* is the persistent concern about the role of race in the administration and distribution of the death penalty. The manifestly discriminatory application of the death penalty for rape prompted Justice Goldberg to dissent from denial of certiorari in *Rudolph v. Alabama* in 1963,[167] though he omitted any direct reference to race in his opinion at the urging of Chief Justice Warren.[168] That dissent inspired the LDF—the country's premier litigation nonprofit dedicated to racial justice—to devote substantial resources to its (successful) moratorium campaign. Its early efforts included amassing empirical data documenting the racially discriminatory distribution of death sentences for rape in Arkansas, a precursor to the more sophisticated study at issue in *McCleskey v. Kemp*.[169] When the U.S. Supreme Court responded to those efforts in *Furman* and other cases, it was extraordinarily reluctant to describe the problems of the American death penalty (or to craft its regulatory interventions) in racial terms, despite the urging of the LDF and other advocates.[170] But concerns about racial injustice no doubt loomed large in the Court's willingness to subject capital punishment to constitutional scrutiny, reflected in the Court's repeated euphemistic references to its "arbitrary" and "capricious" administration, as well as the Court's decision prohibiting the death penalty for rape—its first significant proportionality limit on the death penalty's reach.[171] Fifteen years after *Furman*, the Court finally confronted the claim of systemic racial discrimination in the distribution of the death penalty but declined in its 5–4 decision to extend relief under either the Eighth or Fourteenth Amendments.[172]

Today, race remains a salient aspect of the American death penalty. The decline of the death penalty has caused death sentences and executions to be concentrated to an even greater degree in states of the former Confederacy (and slave states bordering the Confederacy). Empirical studies link present-day risk of execution to a jurisdiction's prior experience with lynching.[173] Although the U.S. Supreme Court has never embraced broad challenges to the death penalty centered on racial discrimination, it has made a point of intervening in cases involving discrete instances of obvious (almost cartoonish) racial injustice, such as the transparent striking of Black prospective jurors in a capital case[174] and a defense lawyer's use of an expert who testified before a capital jury that Black defendants are more dangerous.[175] These interventions reflect anxiety about the persistent role of racial discrimination in the administration of the death penalty.

The absence of federal constitutional protection against racial discrimination has prompted a shift in litigation strategies to state courts, and strong evidence of racial discrimination in Washington State's death penalty recently led its Supreme Court to invalidate the prevailing use of the punishment on state constitutional grounds.[176] Outside of the courts, concerns about the racial dimensions of the death penalty have been heightened in recent years in part because of increased societal recognition of the extent of racialized violence in American policing and punishment, reflected in contemporary movements to address mass incarceration and to transform policing in ways that protect Black lives. Looking back at the arc of the American death penalty, race casts a dark shadow over the practice, and it seems unlikely that the United States would occupy its exceptional position among Western democratic nations in its retention without the disturbing continuity of race's outsized role.

The twin continuities between the period immediately preceding *Furman* and today—substantial diminution of the practice of capital punishment and concerns about racial discrimination in its application—might suggest that another *Furman*-type decision is on the horizon. Only a few years ago, many prognosticators (including ourselves) predicted just such a development.[177] But then Senate Republicans successfully blocked President Obama's nomination of Merrick Garland to replace Justice Scalia, who died in early 2016, and President Trump was able to replace Justices Scalia, Kennedy, and Ginsburg with Justices Gorsuch, Kavanaugh, and Barrett. The Court now has a conservative supermajority that has repeatedly indicated its skepticism of robust constitutional regulation of capital punishment. No "*Furman* II" decision will be forthcoming from this Court; indeed, the

Court may well move in the other direction to roll back some of the Eighth Amendment protections for capital defendants that have been imposed in the fifty years since *Furman*.

However, as history has shown, constitutional regulation of capital punishment is a long game—and it is still in play. A *Furman* II decision from the Supreme Court is almost certainly the only way to achieve complete, nationwide abolition of capital punishment, given our federal structure and the depth of support for the death penalty in some states. Despite the current Court's lack of enthusiasm for constitutional regulation of the death penalty (much less abolition), we remain convinced that we will eventually see another *Furman*. Why? The profound withering on the ground of the death penalty as a practice, even in states (like Texas) that are unlikely to formally abolish it, sets the stage for an eventual decision by the Court that capital punishment violates the "evolving standards of decency that mark the progress of a maturing society," which is the long-prevailing test for whether a punishment violates the Eighth Amendment.[178] The conditions that have produced this withering show no signs of reversing, so despite the currently hostile Court, we seem to be living in an era of "abolition in waiting."[179]

When a future, more progressive Court looks at the breadth (geographically) and length (in duration) of the death penalty's decline, it will be able to invoke (or reinstate, if necessary) a long Eighth Amendment tradition of evaluating punishment practices against "evolving standards of decency." Such a future analysis will likely differ from the approaches taken by the justices of the *Furman* Court. Justice Breyer's emphasis in his *Glossip* dissent on the problems of innocence and lengthy death row incarceration will likely be more central to a future Eighth Amendment decision than they were to the opinions in *Furman*. Moreover, the Court's intricately developed doctrinal framework for considering Eighth Amendment proportionality challenges to capital punishment encompasses not only objective evidence of declining use but also whether the challenged practice meaningfully contributes to its purported penological aims, whether it presents a special risk of wrongful conviction or disproportionate sentencing, whether the world community rejects the practice, and whether the views of expert organizations, religious leaders, and the public counsel against the practice.[180] This broad-ranging Eighth Amendment proportionality framework offers an encompassing and well-established doctrinal "blueprint" for a future constitutional abolition,[181] one that is more rooted in precedent than the varied approaches taken by the five justices of the *Furman* majority.

If—and we believe *when*—the Court rules that capital punishment is unconstitutional, that decision is likely to stick, contrary to the short-lived experience of *Furman*. In the half century since *Furman*, it has become increasingly clear that the Court's 1976 decision to change course, and to seek to mend rather than end the American death penalty, was a path doomed to failure. As state after state has abandoned capital punishment in light of its persistent pathologies, and as even retentionist states have stopped or dramatically reduced their use of the death penalty, there is little likelihood that a constitutional abolition will evoke the kind of outraged backlash that greeted *Furman* in 1972. It has been, and remains, a long and winding road, but the journey toward enduring constitutional abolition begun a half century ago will eventually arrive at the charted destination, albeit by means not fully imagined then.

NOTES

1. Furman v. Georgia, 408 U.S. 238 (1972).

2. Michael Meltsner, *Cruel and Unusual: The Supreme Court and Capital Punishment*, 2nd ed. (New York: Random House, 1973).

3. McGautha v. California, 402 U.S. 183 (1971).

4. *Furman*, 408 U.S. at 309 (Stewart, J., concurring).

5. *Id.* at 308, n.8.

6. See Hugo Adam Bedau, ed., *The Death Penalty in America: Current Controversies* (New York: Oxford, 1997), 7, table 1-1.

7. Meltsner, *Cruel and Unusual*, 78–92.

8. *Furman*, 408 U.S. at 309–10 (Stewart, J., concurring).

9. See, e.g., Richard C. Dieter, "The 2% Death Penalty: How a Minority of Counties Produce Most Death Cases at Enormous Costs to All," Death Penalty Information Center, October 1, 2013, https://deathpenaltyinfo.org/facts-and-research/dpic-reports/in-depth/the-2-death-penalty-how-a-minority-of-counties-produce-most-death-cases-at-enormous-costs-to-all; John J. Donohue III, "An Empirical Evaluation of the Connecticut Death Penalty System since 1973: Are There Unlawful Racial, Gender, and Geographic Disparities?," *Journal of Empirical Legal Studies* 11, no. 4 (2014): 637; Scott Phillips and Justin Marceau, "Whom the State Kills," *Harvard Civil Rights—Civil Liberties Law Review* 55, no. 2 (2020): 585.

10. Carol S. Steiker and Jordan M. Steiker, *Courting Death: The Supreme Court and Capital Punishment* (Cambridge, MA: Belknap Press of Harvard University Press, 2016), 155 ("In the end [constitutional] regulation has not solved or significantly ameliorated the problems it was designed to address").

11. See Kennedy v. Louisiana, 554 U.S. 407 (2008).

12. See Jonathan Simon and Cristina Spaulding, "Tokens of Our Esteem: Aggravating Factors in the Era of Deregulated Death Penalties," in *The Killing State: Capital Punishment in Law, Politics and Culture*, ed. Austin Sarat (New York: Oxford University Press, 1999), 81; Hidalgo v. Arizona, 138 S. Ct. 1054 (2018) (Breyer, J., statement respecting the denial of certiorari).

13. Steiker and Steiker, *Courting Death*, 167–68 ("Enshrining absolute, unaccountable discretion to withhold death based on any and all mitigating factors is difficult to reconcile with the *Furman* commitment to redressing the evils of 'standardless discretion'").

14. *Furman*, 408 U.S. at 311 (White, J., concurring).

15. Jones v. Chappell, 31 F. Supp. 3d 1050 (C.D. Cal. 2014), *rev'd*, Jones v. Davis, 806 F.3d 538 (9th Cir. 2015).

16. Daniel Small, "Too Much Justice: Questioning the United States' Pursuit of Retribution," *Social Justice and Equity Journal* 4, no. 1 (2020): 47, 60.

17. "When imposition of the penalty reaches a certain degree of infrequency, it would be very doubtful that any existing general need for retribution would be measurably satisfied." *Furman*, 408 U.S. at 311 (White, J., concurring).

18. *Furman*, 408 U.S. at 308 (Stewart, J., concurring).

19. *Id.* at 343 (Marshall, J., concurring).

20. *Id.* at 270 (Brennan, J., concurring).

21. *Id.* at 371 (Marshall, J., concurring) (citing Ramsey Clark, *Crime in America: Observations on Its Nature, Causes, Prevention, and Control* [New York: Simon & Schuster, 1970], 336).

22. Shirley Donnelly, opinion, "Death Penalty Doesn't Trim Crime Rates," *Beckley Post-Herald*, November 3, 1965, 4.

23. Vincent P. Carocci and James N. Riggio, "Speaker Orders Abolition of State Death Penalty; Electric Chair Removed," *Philadelphia Inquirer*, January 21, 1971, A1.

24. "Justice without Mercy," editorial, *New York Times*, April 24, 1969, 46.

25. *Id.*

26. "Britain Ends the Death Penalty," editorial, *New York Times*, December 20, 1969, 30.

27. "Abolishing the Death Penalty," editorial, *Des Moines Register*, February 6, 1965, 6.

28. "Overruled a Cancer," editorial, *New York Times*, July 3, 1972, 16.

29. People v. Anderson, 493 P.2d 880, 6 Cal. 3d 628 (Cal. 1972).

30. Brief for Petitioner, Aikens v. California, 406 U.S. 813 (1972), No. 68-5027 (1971), at 31.

31. *Id.* at 26.

32. *Id.* at 38.

33. *Id.* at 43.

34. *Id.* at 48.

35. *Id.* at 56 (citation omitted).

36. *Id.* at 46 (quoting at length from Albert Camus, *Reflections on the Guillotine*, in *Resistance, Rebellion and Death* [New York: Alfred A. Knopf, 1961]).

37. Badinter cited Camus in his impassioned speech to the French parliament. See Robert Badinter, "Histoire—grands discours parlementaires," Assemblée Nationale, September 17, 1981, https://www2.assemblee-nationale.fr/decouvrir-l-assemblee/histoire /grands-discours-parlementaires/robert-badinter-17-septembre-1981. Two years later, the Council of Europe promulgated Protocol 6 to the European Convention on Human Rights, prohibiting the use of the death penalty in peacetime. See Protocol No. 6 to the Convention for the Protection of Human Rights and Fundamental Freedoms concerning the Abolition of the Death Penalty, accessed October 25, 2023, Library_Collection_P6 _ETS114E_ENG.pdf, coe.int. https://70.coe.int/pdf/library_collection_p6_ets114e_eng .pdf. For an overview of the human rights lens that is applied to the death penalty in Europe and beyond, see William A. Schabas, *The Abolition of the Death Penalty in International Law*, 3rd ed. (Cambridge: Cambridge University Press, 2002).

38. Mugambi Jouet, "A Lost Chapter in Death Penalty History: Furman v. Georgia, Albert Camus, and the Normative Challenge to Capital Punishment," *American Journal of Criminal Law* 38, no. 49 (2022): 119–77.

39. Glossip v. Gross, 576 U.S. 863, 908 (2015) (Breyer, J., dissenting).

40. Stephen Breyer, *Against the Death Penalty*, ed. John D. Bessler (Washington, DC: Brookings, 2016).

The Foreignness of *Furman* / 127

41. Ca. Exec. Order No. N-09-19 (Mar. 13, 2019), https://www.gov.ca.gov/wp-content/uploads/2019/03/3.13.19-EO-N-09-19.pdf.

42. See Va. S.B. 1165 (Feb. 3, 2021), https://virginia-senate.granicus.com/MediaPlayer.php?view_id=3&clip_id=4033 (starting at 27:25).

43. Hailey Fuchs, "Virginia Becomes First Southern State to Abolish the Death Penalty," *New York Times*, March 24, 2021, https://www.nytimes.com/2021/03/24/us/politics/virginia-death-penalty.html.

44. See Daniel Medwed, *Wrongful Convictions and the DNA Revolution: Twenty-Five Years of Freeing the Innocent* (Cambridge: Cambridge University Press, 2017); Frank R. Baumgartner, Suzanna L. De Boef, and Amber E. Boydstun, *The Decline of the Death Penalty and the Discovery of Innocence* (Cambridge: Cambridge University Press, 2008).

45. George H. Ryan Sr., *Until I Can Be Sure: How I Stopped the Death Penalty in Illinois* (London: Rowman and Littlefield, 2020).

46. United States v. Quinones, 205 F. Supp. 2d 256 (S.D.N.Y. 2002), *rev'd*, 313 F.3d 49 (2d Cir. 2002).

47. See nn. 39–40.

48. See nn. 42–43.

49. *Furman*, 408 U.S. at 366 (Marshall, J., concurring).

50. *Id.* at 367–68.

51. See "The National Registry of Exonerations," Newkirk Center for Science and Society at University of California Irvine, University of Michigan Law School, and Michigan State University College of Law, accessed October 25, 2023, https://www.law.umich.edu/special/exoneration/Pages/about.aspx.

52. See Samuel R. Gross et al., "Rate of False Conviction of Defendants Who Are Sentenced to Death," *Proceedings of the National Academy of Sciences* 111, no. 20 (2014): 7230, https://www.ncbi.nlm.nih.gov/pmc/articles/PMC4034186/ (estimating an error rate of at least 4.1 percent).

53. *Furman*, 408 U.S. at 363 (Marshall, J., concurring).

54. See Death Penalty Information Center, *State Studies on Monetary Costs*, accessed October 25, 2023, https://deathpenaltyinfo.org/policy-issues/costs/summary-of-states-death-penalty.

55. Death Penalty Information Center, *Time on Death Row*, accessed October 25, 2023, https://deathpenaltyinfo.org/death-row/death-row-time-on-death-row.

56. Death Penalty Information Center, *Bureau of Justice Statistics Reports Number on Death Row Down, Average Time on Death Row Approaches 19 Years*, June 25, 2021, https://deathpenaltyinfo.org/news/bureau-of-justice-statistics-reports-number-on-death-row-down-average-time-on-death-row-approaches-19-years.

57. *Glossip*, 576 U.S. at 929 (Breyer, J., dissenting).

58. States authorized not only the electric chair but also the gas chamber, the firing squad, and hanging as possible modes of execution well into the modern era. See Bedau, *Death Penalty in America*, 12.

59. See Erik Eckholm, "In Death Penalty's Steady Decline, Some Experts See a Societal Shift," *New York Times*, December 19, 2013, https://www.nytimes.com/2013/12/19/us/in-death-penaltys-steady-decline-some-experts-see-a-societal-shift.html.

60. See Austin Sarat, *Lethal Injection and the False Promise of Humane Execution* (Stanford, CA: Stanford University Press, 2022).

61. Baze v. Rees, 553 U.S. 35, 113 (2008) (Ginsburg, J., dissenting).

62. *Id.* at 114.

63. *Glossip*, 576 U.S. at 949 (Sotomayor, J., dissenting).

64. *Id.*

65. See Louisiana ex rel. Francis v. Resweber, 329 U.S. 459 (1947).

66. Gregg v. Georgia, 428 U.S. 153, 179–81 (1976).

67. See, e.g., Lockett v. Ohio, 438 U.S. 586 (1978) (finding the Ohio scheme inadequate for the consideration of Lockett's mitigating evidence).

68. See, e.g., Godfrey v. Georgia, 446 U.S. 420 (1980) (finding Georgia's aggravating factor excessively broad).

69. See, e.g., Coker v. Georgia, 433 U.S. 584 (1977) (deeming the death penalty excessive for the offense of rape of an adult victim).

70. Gallup Poll, "Death Penalty," accessed October 25, 2023, https://news.gallup.com /poll/1606/death-penalty.aspx.

71. Death Penalty Information Center, *Facts about the Death Penalty*, last updated September 20, 2023, https://documents.deathpenaltyinfo.org/pdf/FactSheet.pdf.

72. Steiker and Steiker, *Courting Death*, 204–6.

73. *Id.* at 198–99.

74. See generally *Guidelines for the Appointment and Performance of Counsel in Death Penalty Cases* (American Bar Association, 1989).

75. See generally *Guidelines for the Appointment and Performance of Counsel in Death Penalty Cases* (American Bar Association, 2003).

76. See generally *Supplementary Guidelines for the Mitigation Function of Defense Teams in Death Penalty Cases* (American Bar Association, 2008).

77. Steiker and Steiker, *Courting Death*, 202–3.

78. *Id.*

79. *Id.*

80. See generally Carol S. Steiker and Jordan M. Steiker, "Little *Furmans* Everywhere: State Court Intervention and the Decline of the American Death Penalty," *Cornell Law Review* 107, no. 6 (2022): 1621–87 (describing state judicial regulation of the death penalty in the post-*Furman* era).

81. Steiker and Steiker, *Courting Death*, 203.

82. *Id.*

83. *Id.* at 205.

84. Corinna Lain also discusses the role of cost in the modern administration of the death penalty in her contribution to this volume.

85. Steiker and Steiker, *Courting Death*, 206.

86. See, e.g., Lackey v. Texas, 514 U.S. 1045 (1995) (Stevens, J., respecting denial of certiorari); Knight v. Florida, 528 U.S. 990, 993 (Breyer, J., dissenting from denial of certiorari).

87. *Glossip*, 576 U.S. at 908 (Breyer, J., dissenting).

88. *Id.* at 938.

89. Carol S. Steiker and Jordan M. Steiker, "The Court and Capital Punishment on Different Paths: Abolition in Waiting," *Washington and Lee Journal of Civil Rights and Social Justice* 29 (Winter 2023): 21–23.

90. *Id.*

91. *Id.*

92. *Baze*, 553 U.S. 35.

93. Steiker and Steiker, "Court and Capital Punishment," 22.

94. Bucklew v. Precythe, 139 S. Ct. 1112 (2018).

95. *Baze*, 553 U.S. 35; *Glossip*, 576 U.S. 863; *Bucklew*, 139 S. Ct. 1112.

The Foreignness of *Furman* / 129

96. *Bucklew*, 139 S. Ct. at 1125.

97. See Jason Evans, "The Innocent Welshman Wrongly Hanged for Killing His Wife and Child," WalesOnline, April 13, 2020, https://www.walesonline.co.uk/news/wales-news/timothy-evans-rillington-place-murder-18051253.

98. Herrera v. Collins, 506 U.S. 390 (1993).

99. Steiker and Steiker, "Court and Capital Punishment," 11.

100. See "National Registry of Exonerations."

101. *Aikens* brief at 6.

102. *Id.* at 28–29 (footnotes omitted).

103. *Id.* at 34.

104. *Id.* at 28n47 (describing Appendix E to the *Aikens* brief).

105. *Furman*, 408 U.S. at 278 (Brennan, J., concurring).

106. *Id.* at 295 (emphasis added).

107. *Id.* at 341 (Marshall, J., concurring); emphasis added.

108. Unlike Brennan, Marshall recognized that the widespread authorization of capital punishment at the time made it difficult to argue that the death penalty was unacceptable to contemporary American society. Hence, Marshall conjured a hypothetical fully informed citizenry that would reject punishment by death once in command of all the facts about the American death penalty.

109. *Coker*, 433 U.S. at 592n4 (1977) (emphasis added).

110. Enmund v. Florida, 458 U.S. 782, 788 (1982).

111. Atkins v. Virginia, 536 U.S. 304, 316n21 (2002).

112. Roper v. Simmons, 543 U.S. 551 (2005).

113. *Id.* at 578 (citing Brief for Human Rights Committee of the Bar of England and Wales et al. as amici curiae).

114. *Id.*

115. *Atkins*, 536 U.S. at 347 (Scalia, J., dissenting).

116. *Furman*, 408 U.S. at 250–51 (Douglas, J., concurring).

117. *Id.* at 251n15 (citation omitted).

118. *Id.* at 253.

119. *Id.* at 257; emphasis added.

120. McCleskey v. Kemp, 481 U.S. 279 (1987).

121. *Id.* at 287.

122. "Powell acknowledged in a memo to his law clerk that his 'understanding of statistical analysis—particularly what is called 'regression analysis' range[d] from limited to zero.'" Steiker and Steiker, *Courting Death*, 102 (footnote omitted).

123. The Court has repeated this move in other empirical contexts related to the death penalty. See, e.g., Lockhart v. McCree, 476 U.S. 162 (1986) (assuming arguendo that that the social science studies introduced in the courts below were adequate to establish that "death qualified" juries were more conviction prone but nonetheless rejecting the respondent's constitutional claim).

124. *Furman*, 408 U.S. at 353 (Marshall, J., concurring).

125. Robert Weisberg, "The Death Penalty Meets Social Science: Deterrence and Jury Behavior under New Scrutiny," *Annual Review of Law and Social Science* 1 (2005): 110.

126. *Gregg*, 428 U.S. 153.

127. Weisberg, "Death Penalty Meets Social Science," 110.

128. Death Penalty Information Center, *State by State*, accessed October 25, 2023, https://deathpenaltyinfo.org/state-and-federal-info/state-by-state. Several other states, including Delaware, Oregon, New York, New Mexico, and Vermont, partially abolished

the death penalty in the two decades prior to *Furman* or abolished only to have the death penalty reinstated. Michigan, which in the 1840s was the first state to abolish the death penalty (except for treason), constitutionalized its abolition in 1963. Death Penalty Information Center, *History of the Death Penalty*, accessed October 25, 2023, https://deathpenaltyinfo.org/facts-and-research/history-of-the-death-penalty.

129. Death Penalty Information Center, *History of the Death Penalty*.

130. *Id.*

131. Steiker and Steiker, "Little *Furmans* Everywhere," 1662–71.

132. *Id.* at 1627–32.

133. Death Penalty Information Center, *State by State*.

134. *Id.*

135. Death Penalty Information Center, *Facts about the Death Penalty*.

136. *Atkins*, 536 U.S. at 313n8.

137. Penry v. Lynaugh, 492 U.S. 302 (1989).

138. *Atkins*, 536 U.S. at 314–15.

139. *Id.*

140. Gilmore v. Utah, 429 U.S. 1012 (1976).

141. Jon Nordheimer, "Gilmore Is Executed after Stay Is Upset," *New York Times*, January 18, 1977, https://www.nytimes.com/1977/01/18/archives/gilmore-is-executed-after-stay-is-upset-lets-do-it-he-said-firing.html.

142. Katherine Bishop, "After a Night of Battles, A California Execution," *New York Times*, April 22, 1992, https://www.nytimes.com/1992/04/22/us/after-night-of-court-battles-a-california-execution.html.

143. *Atkins*, 536 U.S. 304.

144. Trevino v. Thaler, 569 U.S. 413 (2013).

145. *Bucklew*, 139 S. Ct. 1112.

146. *Id.* at 1133–34.

147. *Id.* at 1134.

148. *Id.* at 1146 (Sotomayor, J., dissenting).

149. Dunn v. Ray, 139 S. Ct. 661 (2019).

150. *Id.*

151. *Id.* at 662 (Kagan, J., dissenting).

152. In re Fed. Bureau of Prisons' Execution Protocol Cases, 980 F.3d 123, 125 (D.C. Cir. 2020).

153. Barr v. Lee, 140 S. Ct. 2590, 2591 (2020).

154. See Lee Kovarsky, "The Trump Executions," *Texas Law Review* 100 (2022): 622 (comprehensively discussing executions consummated in the last six months of the Trump administration).

155. See Stephen Vladeck, *The Shadow Docket: How the Supreme Court Uses Stealth Rulings to Amass Power and Undermine the Republic* (New York: Basic Books, 2023) (describing the Court's increased recourse to unsigned, unreasoned decisions issued without the benefit of full briefing or oral argument).

156. *Id.*

157. *Id.*

158. See Jordan M. Steiker, "The Long Road Up from Barbarism: Thurgood Marshall and the Death Penalty," *Texas Law Review* 71, no. 2 (1993): 1131 (discussing Justice Marshall's refusal to embrace *Gregg*'s upholding of the American death penalty).

159. Callins v. Collins, 510 U.S. 1141 (1994) (Blackmun, J., dissenting).

160. *Baze*, 553 U.S. at 71 (Stevens, J., concurring in the judgment).

The Foreignness of *Furman* / 131

161. *Glossip*, 576 U.S. at 908 (Breyer, J., joined by Ginsburg, J., dissenting).

162. *Furman*, 408 U.S. at 375 (Burger, C.J., dissenting).

163. *Id.* at 405 (Blackmun, J., dissenting).

164. *Glossip*, 576 U.S. at 889 (Scalia, J., concurring).

165. Linda Meyer also discusses the Supreme Court's move away from an "evolving standards of decency" framework and toward an originalist approach to the death penalty under the Eighth Amendment in her contribution to this volume.

166. *Bucklew*, 139 S. Ct. at 1122.

167. Rudolph v. Alabama, 375 U.S. 889 (1962).

168. Carol S. Steiker and Jordan M. Steiker, "The American Death Penalty and the (In)Visibility of Race," *University of Chicago Law Review* 82, no. 1 (2015): 255.

169. *McCleskey*, 481 U.S. 279.

170. *Id.* at 253–77.

171. *Id.*

172. *McCleskey*, 481 U.S. 279.

173. Franklin E. Zimring, *The Contradictions of American Capital Punishment* (New York: Oxford University Press, 2003).

174. Foster v. Chatman, 136 S. Ct. 1737 (2016).

175. Buck v. Davis, 137 S. Ct. 759 (2017).

176. State v. Gregory, 427 P.3d 621 (Wash. 2018).

177. See Steiker and Steiker, *Courting Death*, 285–89.

178. Trop v. Dulles, 356 U.S. 86, 101 (1958).

179. Steiker and Steiker, "Court and Capital Punishment," 7.

180. Steiker and Steiker, *Courting Death*, 282–85.

181. *Id.* at 271.

II

On the Road to Abolition?

II

On the Road to Abolition?

4

Catholicism and the Ongoing Struggle to End the Death Penalty, from *Furman v. Georgia* to the Present

Sara Mayeux

In 1960, John Cogley, one of the most prominent lay Catholic journalists in the United States, published a column expressing misgivings about capital punishment. Cogley acknowledged "the abstract argument for the State's right to take a life."[1] In this short column, he did not elaborate or cite theological sources, but versions of the argument to which he alluded had been standard Catholic teaching for centuries; St. Thomas Aquinas famously equated capital punishment with amputating a gangrenous limb, a necessary procedure to preserve the health of the body politic.[2] Under modern conditions, though, Cogley confessed that he "remain[ed] uneasy about the morality of capital punishment." He continued,

> Perhaps if it were true that society could be safe from the criminal only by killing, this argument would hold water. But aren't we reasonably capable these days of cutting such criminals off from normal life, as we do in the case of the violently insane? I am not convinced that the ultimate penalty is really necessary for the protection of society, and a cold-blooded killing that is not necessary, even if performed by a State executioner, strikes me as irrational. For that reason alone it is morally questionable.[3]

Cogley's reasoning, that the death penalty had become unnecessary and thus unjustified, prefigured the historic turn that the Catholic Church itself would take on the issue by the end of the twentieth century, both within the

136 / Sara Mayeux

United States and on the global stage. By the 1970s, growing numbers of U.S. bishops were speaking out against the death penalty in their states. For example, in 1973, Bishop Joseph Durick of Nashville wrote a pastoral letter dismissing as "weak" the traditional theological defenses for the death penalty.[4] In 1995, Pope John Paul II declared that capital punishment was justified only "in cases of absolute necessity"—and added that in the modern world, "such cases are very rare, if not practically non-existent."[5] Pope Francis has stated even more forthrightly an abolitionist position. Quoting Francis, the current version of the *Catechism* teaches that "the death penalty is inadmissible because it is an attack on the inviolability and dignity of the person" and calls "for its abolition worldwide."[6]

When *Furman v. Georgia* was decided in 1972, then, it might have seemed as though the U.S. Supreme Court and the Catholic Church were moving in roughly the same direction on the death penalty: away from rote acceptance of traditional justifications for the practice, both because modern state-building had undermined the case for its necessity and because of developing moral intuitions that the practice violated post–World War II conceptions of human dignity. In *Furman*, the Court held that the death penalty as then practiced in the United States amounted to "cruel and unusual punishment in violation of the Eighth and Fourteenth Amendments."[7] In the Supreme Court's parlance, constitutional doctrine must respond to "the evolving standards of decency that mark the progress of a maturing society"[8]—a concept that, although not a direct analog, resonated with the post–Vatican II spirit within Catholicism of aggiornamento and engagement with the modern world.[9] Two years after *Furman*, the U.S. Conference of Catholic Bishops (USCCB) went on record for the first time as opposing the death penalty.[10]

Instead, as it quickly turned out, the Church and the Court would not continue moving in tandem on the issue of capital punishment: already by 1976, their paths had diverged. That was because the Church would continue on its trajectory, becoming ever more categorical in its condemnation of the modern death penalty, while the Court, instead, would backtrack. In the 1976 decision of *Gregg v. Georgia*, a majority of the justices clarified that they had not intended in *Furman* to define capital punishment as categorically unconstitutional.[11] The problem pre-*Furman*, the Court now explained, was only that the states had been imposing the death penalty "capriciously and arbitrarily," at the unfettered discretion of juries. So long as the states reformed their sentencing laws to provide for a more structured process, tailored to "the particularized nature of the crime and the particularized characteristics of the individual defendant," then the death penalty could still be constitutionally imposed.[12] Post-*Gregg*, death penalty litigation at the Supreme Court would remain focused on procedural details rather than the basic morality of capital punishment, and there has never been a majority of the Court interested in holding the death penalty categorically unconstitutional.

At first glance, this pattern of short-lived convergence followed by sustained divergence between Church and Court may appear paradoxical. That is because by metrics other than death penalty jurisprudence, Catholicism only gained influence at the U.S. Supreme Court between the 1970s and the present. During these same decades, the Court transformed demographically due to a variety of factors, most importantly the diminished force of anti-Catholic prejudice in American public life. Historically, there was usually one Catholic justice at most. Since the 1980s, presidents have appointed numerous Catholics to the Supreme Court, and today, a supermajority of the justices either are practicing Catholics or were raised Catholic.[13] In addition, the majority of the Catholic justices on the Roberts Court (including, of course, Chief Justice John Roberts himself) are aligned with the Court's conservative wing. Although they do not overtly rely on Catholic authorities to explain their constitutional reasoning, there are several doctrinal areas where they have unmistakably shifted constitutional jurisprudence in ways that align with the Church's interests and positions, holding, for instance, that parochial schools are exempt from employment discrimination law.[14]

Most significantly, in 2022, the Roberts Court eliminated the constitutional right to abortion—a development that some pundits have attributed to the majority justices' conservative Catholicism. *Dobbs v. Jackson Women's Health Organization* was celebrated by many Catholics (though certainly not uniformly) as the culmination of decades of pro-life mobilization against *Roe v. Wade*, the 1973 decision that identified a right to abortion implicit in the Fourteenth Amendment and that *Dobbs* overruled.[15] Certainly, the *Dobbs* opinion—written by the devout Catholic justice Samuel Alito—was replete with echoes of pro-life-movement rhetoric. From the first few paragraphs of the opinion, Alito distinguishes abortion from other individual rights "because it destroys . . . 'fetal life' and what the [Mississippi state law] now before us describes as an 'unborn human being.'"[16] Although partly couched in deference to state legislators, Alito's respectful rhetoric here and throughout his *Dobbs* opinion implies his own sympathy with this characterization of fetal life. (As the longtime *New York Times* court-watcher Linda Greenhouse wrote, "the fetus is the indisputable star of the *Dobbs* opinion."[17]) Of course, that characterization is also the doctrinaire teaching of the Catholic Church, whose *Catechism* states, "Human life must be respected and protected absolutely from the moment of conception."[18] Noting these echoes, some media commentary has gone so far as to call Alito's *Dobbs* opinion "barely concealed theocracy."[19]

Yet Catholic teaching on the death penalty has made little dent in U.S. constitutional law. Indeed, it seems to have made little dent in the minds of at least some of the Catholic justices. In contrast to Alito's respectful summary of the pro-life argument against abortion, prominent Catholic justices have, at times, dismissed the campaign to abolish capital punishment as frivolous and disingenuous. In death penalty cases over the years, Justice Antonin Scalia deflated arguments against capital punishment as "sanctimonious,"[20] lampooned the Court's capital docket as a "Groundhog Day"–like experience, and laughed off constitutional arguments against the death penalty as obviously incorrect. Nevertheless, he lamented, "the capital convict will obtain endless legal assistance from the abolition lobby (and legal favoritism from abolitionist judges)."[21] Outside of his published opinions, Scalia also made public remarks in which he questioned the Church's modern position against capital punishment, voiced his own conclusion that the death penalty was not immoral, and made clear that he had no qualms about voting to affirm capital sentences.[22]

Clearly, then, there is a complex story to tell about the relationship between Catholicism and constitutionalism in the United States from the 1970s to the present. More generally, there is a complex story to tell about the interplay between religious beliefs, social movements, political mobilization, and constitutional law. Like abortion, the modern death penalty is offensive to Catholic doctrine and has been roundly condemned by recent popes. Unsurprisingly, then, there is a complex and international history of Catholic activism on both issues. In the United States, however, abortion has overwhelmingly dominated post–Vatican II Catholic legal and political mobilization. Catholic organizations, activists, and jurists have openly and indisputably played a central role in the fifty-year campaign to roll back the right to abortion recognized in *Roe*. In the death penalty context, the influence of Catholicism on American constitutional law appears murkier and more subtle. The Catholic Church's objections to the modern death penalty have translated into neither the scale of mass mobilization for constitutional change familiar from the history of the pro-life movement, nor the kind of morally charged rhetoric evident in conservative judicial opinions about abortion.

How, therefore, should we make sense of the relationship between Catholicism and U.S. constitutionalism in the post–Vatican II, post–Warren Court world? Looking solely at abortion, it might seem that Catholicism has had transformative influence on U.S. constitutional law in recent decades, but looking solely at the death penalty, it might seem that Catholicism has had little influence. This short symposium contribution, of course, cannot fully synthesize these seemingly disparate data points or fully resolve this legal-historical puzzle. Instead, this chapter aims to provide a brief summary and examination of some illustrative Catholic responses to the death penalty in the United States, both at the time of *Furman v. Georgia* and in

Catholicism and the Struggle to End the Death Penalty / 139

the fifty years since, and also to synthesize and recommend some recent scholarship by religious and political historians that may prove illuminating for legal scholars working on these issues. In noting the many contrasts with antiabortion activism in the same period, the chapter also makes a more general point about the need for scholarly nuance in characterizing the place of Catholicism in recent U.S. constitutional history. A single focus on abortion may mislead commentators into oversimplifying the relationship between the justices' religious identities and their views on constitutional law. Expanding the lens to include the death penalty can help illuminate the political pathways that connect some religious teachings to constitutional law and not others.

Catholicism and the Death Penalty at the Time of *Furman*

In 1972, when the Supreme Court decided *Furman v. Georgia*, some Catholic individuals and groups had begun questioning the death penalty, but the Catholic Church had not yet reached the official position that it would later take against capital punishment. It is not surprising, then, to learn that neither Catholic thought nor Catholic institutions played a major direct role in the *Furman* litigation. The litigation campaign that culminated in *Furman* was lawyerly and secular, spearheaded by legal-liberal stalwarts affiliated with the NAACP Legal Defense Fund and the ACLU.[23] Some Catholic individuals and groups participated as amici, whether in their personal or organizational capacities. For example, two Catholic entities (including a then-new and relatively radical group at least by Catholic standards, the National Coalition of American Nuns) were among the thirteen religious organizations that collectively filed an amicus brief in *Furman* urging the Supreme Court to invalidate the death penalty.[24]

However, *Furman* did reflect shifting religious views (including Catholic views) in various subtler ways. Even before civil liberties and civil rights groups had launched the specific litigation campaign that would culminate in *Furman*, many Americans had already become increasingly uncomfortable with the death penalty.[25] The number of executions carried out each year had been declining for decades, and several state legislatures had already abolished or sharply limited capital punishment under state law.[26] Those shifts comported with international trends; at the time of *Furman*, numerous countries had abolished or would soon abolish the death penalty, including most of Western Europe.[27] The modern and transnational trend toward the rejection of capital punishment had many long-term historical

140 / Sara Mayeux

causes, but among those causes must be counted the post–World War II concern with human dignity, which itself owed much to changing emphasis in Christian thought.[28]

Notably, in the United States, the mainline Protestant denominations—those that fell on the liberal side of the modernist-fundamentalist split—generally opposed the death penalty by the time of *Furman*.[29] Thus, they had moved away from the traditional acceptance of capital punishment within reformed Christianity, exemplified in Martin Luther's maxim, "Let no one imagine that the world can be governed without the shedding of blood."[30] The growing qualms of some number of Catholics reflected an analogous long-term shift within the Church of Rome, away from repetition of medieval and early modern apologies for capital punishment and toward independent moral reasoning about the death penalty in the new light of modern conditions. And *Furman*, in turn, while not produced solely by these shifts in religious sentiment, certainly comported with them and probably owed something to them, insofar as the Supreme Court justices are themselves part of their historical context and would have encountered a variety of arguments against capital punishment circulating in public discourse at the time, including religious ones.

Ironically, it was probably through this more convoluted and unquantifiable process of cultural miasma, rather than straightforwardly, that the Catholic tradition was a factor in the only *Furman* opinion actually written by a Catholic—the only Catholic justice at the time, William Brennan. The *Furman* Court was divided about the rationale for its holding, and so the case produced only a short per curiam opinion for the Court, followed by an excessively lengthy litany of separate concurrences and dissents. In his concurrence, Brennan strongly condemned capital punishment as a violation of the Eighth Amendment, using diction that had a Catholic ring to it and even might be read as anticipating the Church's later position. Brennan's concurrence observed that the death penalty may have been necessary to secure public safety in a world "without developed prison systems" but could not be justified on that basis in the world of the 1970s. Because the practice could no longer be defended as a practical necessity, Brennan instead framed the Eighth Amendment question as "whether a punishment comports with human dignity" and concluded that the death penalty did not.[31] Brennan had referred to dignity in speeches as early as the 1950s and later would describe the principle as his core constitutional value.[32] Famously, Brennan, along with Justice Thurgood Marshall, would subsequently reiterate his view that the death penalty was "cruel and unusual" by filing repetitive dissents in nearly two thousand capital cases in the years between *Furman* and his retirement.[33]

Notwithstanding these rhetorical echoes, scholars generally agree that Brennan's Catholic background had little direct influence on his jurispru-

Catholicism and the Struggle to End the Death Penalty / 141

dence. Indeed, one history of *Furman* asserts that Brennan's increasingly liberal jurisprudence over time "is often *mistakenly* attributed to his Catholicism" and suggests that his thinking on the death penalty owed more to other influences like his friendship with the liberal (and Jewish) DC Circuit judge David Bazelon.[34] Brennan's most recent biographers agree. They portray him as a cultural Catholic more than a devout believer and find no evidence that Brennan read or specifically read or referenced Catholic social teaching in developing his views. Instead of a specifically Catholic concept, they conclude that "his notion of human dignity aligns more closely with the liberal conception emphasizing autonomy and independence."[35]

That Brennan's jurisprudence blended midcentury legal liberalism with occasional flashes of Catholic moral vocabulary makes some sense, in light of his background. The oldest of eight children born in New Jersey to two Irish immigrants, he received in some respects a typical Irish Catholic formation.[36] However, in other ways, his background was less insular than was typical for Catholics of his generation. He attended parochial school only for a few years when he was very young, transferring to New Jersey public schools for the remainder of his education and then matriculating at the University of Pennsylvania and Harvard Law School. Although the family attended weekly Mass during his youth, Brennan remembered the experience as "an agony" and, according to his biographers, "retained a relatively unsophisticated understanding of Church doctrine."[37]

Brennan himself similarly denied that Catholicism directly informed his work as a judge. Of course, given the history of anti-Catholic suspicion in American political life, he could hardly have said otherwise. At his confirmation hearings, he gave the then-requisite assurances for Catholics in public office that he would keep his religious views separate from his oath to uphold the Constitution.[38] But it was indisputably true that, on issues from school prayer to contraception, Brennan did not vote according to the Church's preferences. And shortly after *Furman*, he joined the majority opinion in *Roe v. Wade* announcing a constitutional right to abortion, which opened a serious rift between Brennan and the Church.[39] By the 1970s, Brennan had already lapsed from regular churchgoing, but after *Roe* he became hesitant even to meet with priests he did not already know.[40] According to his biographers, he was "taken aback by antiabortion protestors who appeared outside subsequent Red Masses he attended, carrying signs that accused him of murdering babies."[41]

Still, Brennan's background meant that he would have been exposed to Catholic rituals, rhetoric, and ideas throughout his life, in contrast to his "brethren," who in that era mainly came from mainline Protestant traditions. His wife, Marjorie, remained a devout Catholic.[42] Brennan also valued his friendship with Father Ted Hesburgh of the University of Notre Dame, and "he identified strongly enough with the Church that criticisms by its leaders would sting, even if they never influenced how he actually voted."[43] Insofar as Brennan was influenced by Catholicism, the influence seems to have occurred at a high level of generality. Brennan took from his childhood formation not specific theology but a generic Gospel concern for the vulnerable.[44] Ironically, it was probably for that reason that Brennan could anticipate the Church's opposition to the death penalty. Had he memorized the doctrinaire teaching at the time of his childhood, it would likely have been something like St. Thomas Aquinas's justification for the necessity of capital punishment. Instead, Brennan applied to the death penalty, as he did to other topics, a more general framework of individual dignity and concern for the vulnerable.

In the decades post-*Furman*, one might also argue that the form of Brennan's increasingly absolutist opposition to the death penalty demonstrated a Catholic sensibility. He may not have reached his legal conclusion that capital punishment violated the Eighth Amendment through distinctively Catholic sources, but his refusal to compromise on the question by the end of his career resembled a Catholic-style absolute moral stance, at odds with the pragmatic liberalism that he himself, along with his former allies on the Warren Court, had once championed. Brennan had been more enamored of balancing tests and compromise positions during the tenure of Chief Justice Earl Warren, when he had some hope of corralling majorities by offering concessions.[45] As he found himself more often writing in dissent under Chief Justice Burger, the tone of his opinions became more extreme and strident.[46] Perhaps in these opinions one can hear some vestige of the latent voice of the Catholic moralist that he may have picked up on as a child in Mass, even if he himself was no longer much of a churchgoer.

The Post-*Furman* (and Post-*Gregg*) Catholic Witness against the Death Penalty

Although Catholicism played only a limited and indirect role in *Furman*, the opposite was not true: *Furman* had significant and direct influence on the Catholic Church, helping consolidate its emerging position on capital punishment. By the 1970s, most European countries with significant Catholic populations had already abolished the death penalty, so the United States became a major focus of Catholic concern about the issue. *Furman*, by putting states with the death penalty on the defensive and reopening debate in state legislatures about whether or how to reform their sentencing laws, also seems to have pushed Catholic clergy to refine their own views and positions on the question. In 1972, while the Supreme Court was still deliberating in

Furman, the bishops of Indiana became "the first group of Catholic bishops to issue a clear, public call for abolition of the death penalty." Their statement relied on the argument that each human life "is sacred . . . Any needless, purposeless taking of human life is an affront and threat to all of life."[47]

Once *Furman* was handed down, the decision provided further impetus for the U.S. bishops to reflect on the issue. According to Catholic death penalty scholar James Megivern, *Furman* forced "hard decisions" in particular for "some of the older and more conservative [bishops] who had long been defending the death penalty automatically," relying on the traditional theological arguments that were still "routinely taught in seminary manuals."[48] For younger bishops, the question was more complicated: just a few years earlier, Vatican II had urged Catholics to respond to "the signs of the times," and growing numbers of Catholic thinkers were no longer certain that those old theological arguments still obtained under modern conditions. Thus, the ingredients for Catholic opposition were already in place as a result of post–World War II humanitarianism generally and Vatican II specifically, but it was *Furman* and post-*Furman* legislative debates that spurred many U.S. bishops to put those ingredients together into a clear public statement of opposition to the death penalty.[49]

From the 1970s onward, it became routine for Catholic bishops to take public stands against the death penalty within their states.[50] The Jesuit priest Robert F. Drinan, S.J., who was then serving in Congress, also spoke out in 1973, cosponsoring a bill to abolish the federal death penalty.[51] But post-*Furman*, there was also growing pressure for the USCCB, the umbrella national organization representing the Church in the United States, to adopt a nationwide position. In the immediate aftermath of *Furman*, "Catholic conferences in several states had already asked for guidance on the question when the matter came up in their respective legislatures," and in 1974, the U.S. bishops began formally studying and deliberating about the question.[52]

The USCCB's first official statement against capital punishment, issued in 1974, reflected the divisions of opinion that remained within the Catholic Church. After much "squabbling and confusion," the conference declined to approve a more elaborate statement of opposition to the death penalty. Instead, the bishops approved by majority vote a resolution stating simply, "The United States Catholic Conference goes on record as opposed to capital punishment."[53] They gave no details about their rationale, about which there was not uniform consensus. And both the contentious deliberations and the vote tally demonstrated that "there was still a vocal minority" within the conference who remained committed to the traditional defense of the death penalty "rather than the Vatican II outlook."[54]

Furman was also among the line of dominos that pushed the global Church toward its modern position against the death penalty, because at the

144 / Sara Mayeux

same time as they issued their 1974 statement, the U.S. bishops also petitioned the Vatican to clarify its teaching on the matter.[55] Two years later, the reply came from the Pontifical Commission for Justice and Peace (a post–Vatican II institutional innovation that sought to develop and promote the Church's social teaching), constituting "the first time" that "the Vatican went on record against the death penalty."[56] The commission reaffirmed the state's traditional right to impose capital punishment and noted that capital punishment is not contrary to divine law, but added that neither is capital punishment required by divine law. In recent years, the statement continued, the Church had moved toward an emphasis on "the rights of the person" and a "medicinal" rather than retributive view of punishment. "Therefore," the statement concluded, "without reference to the American constitutional question, it can be concluded that capital punishment is outside the realm of practicable just punishments."[57] According to Megivern, the Vatican statement was essential in shifting the bishops' position and "probably swung the balance for many bishops who had hesitated over the question of the 'orthodoxy' of the change."[58]

Perhaps surprisingly, another 1970s Supreme Court decision, *Roe v. Wade*, also played an indirect role in pushing the Catholic Church toward a clear position against capital punishment. The Church had long opposed abortion as contrary to natural law, and from the beginning, both the Catholic hierarchy and many Catholics at the grass roots stood at the forefront of the pro-life mobilization against *Roe*. The Pontifical Commission cited that fact as a point in favor of mounting a similar witness against the death penalty. The Vatican statement noted, "The U.S. bishops have spoken out and acted firmly in defense of life against abortion and euthanasia. . . . There is an inner logic that would call Catholics, with their sense of the sacredness of life, to be *consistent* in this defense and extend it to the practice of capital punishment."[59]

By the end of 1976, the Supreme Court had decided *Gregg*, which greenlit the resumption of capital punishment in the United States; and thus, from 1976 onward, the Catholic Church's position diverged from the Supreme Court's on capital punishment. Even as constitutional law moved in the opposite direction, the Catholic position became only more forthright over time in its condemnation of the modern death penalty.[60] After *Gregg*, therefore, "the majority of the U.S. Supreme Court justices and the majority of the U.S. Catholic bishops were at loggerheads. The reinstatement of the death penalty enjoyed wide approval in the public opinion polls, but it collided squarely with the enhanced, Vatican II-inspired vision of human dignity."[61]

As states put the "machinery of death" back into motion, the Catholic hierarchy remained vocal against the practice. In 1977, Utah initiated the post-*Gregg* era of capital punishment when it killed convicted murderer

Gary Gilmore. It was the first execution carried out in the United States since 1968. Several state bishops' conferences had issued statements decrying *Gregg*, as did several individual bishops, although there remained a minority of bishops who continued to invoke the traditional defenses for the death penalty.[62] From 1979 onward, it became routine for Catholic bishops to object publicly to pending or scheduled executions within their states.[63]

In 1980, by which time executions had fully resumed under the *Gregg* regime, the USCCB issued a statement elaborating on their position against capital punishment and situating their views against the backdrop of ongoing legal developments. While acknowledging public fear of crime, the bishops observed that crime was, in part, "a manifestation of the great mysteries of evil and human freedom" and not susceptible to "simple or easy solutions." Although Catholic teaching had historically recognized "that the state may take appropriate measures to protect itself and its citizens from grave harm," the bishops doubted whether this rationale could justify capital punishment under late twentieth-century conditions. Under "the conditions of contemporary American society," neither rehabilitation, deterrence, nor retribution justified the death penalty, and the bishops called on "Christians and all Americans to support the abolition of capital punishment." Among other reasons, they explained that abolition would manifest "our belief in the unique worth and dignity of each person from the moment of conception, a creature made in the image and likeness of God."[64]

Behind the scenes, the bishops remained somewhat divided on the question in 1980, but since then, the number of pro-death-penalty dissenters has dwindled to only a handful. The vote on the 1980 statement endorsing abolition was 145 in favor, 31 opposed, and 41 abstaining.[65] By 2019, when the bishops voted in favor of updating the *Catechism* to include a forthright statement of the Church's abolitionist position, the vote was more lopsided: 194 in favor, 8 opposed, and 3 abstaining.[66]

In 2005, the U.S. bishops renewed their call for abolition, issuing a pastoral letter entitled *A Culture of Life and the Penalty of Death* and launching an initiative entitled the Catholic Campaign to End the Use of the Death Penalty.[67] The bishops' 2005 letter rehearsed many of the familiar secular arguments against the American death penalty, including its racially discriminatory implementation, but added a deeper layer of moral arguments. For Catholics, the bishops emphasized, the issue was not reducible to contingent statistics or details of procedure and implementation; it was fundamentally moral and theological. "The Catholic Campaign to End the Use of the Death Penalty is part of the Church's broad commitment to defend human life from conception to natural death whenever and wherever it is threatened," the bishops' statement explained. "While we do not equate the situation of persons convicted of terrible crimes with the moral claims of innocent unborn children . . . we are convinced that working together to end the use of the death penalty is an integral and important part of resisting a culture of death and building a true culture of life."[68]

Over time, the U.S. bishops' consolidating position against capital punishment was matched by the Vatican. Pope John Paul II's 1995 encyclical, *Evangelium vitae*, advocated for a "culture of life" and reiterated that the death penalty could be justified only "in cases of absolute necessity: in other words, when it would not be possible otherwise to defend society." It continued, "Today however, as a result of steady improvements in the organization of the penal system, such cases are very rare, if not practically non-existent."[69] At the time, according to Catholic death penalty scholar Christian Brugger, *Evangelium vitae* expressed "the strongest opposition to capital punishment in the ordinary magisterium in Christian history."[70] Megivern similarly observed that the 1995 encyclical was "singled out in the media as surprisingly newsworthy" because although Catholic individuals and groups had previously spoken out about the death penalty, this position could now clearly be understood as official Church teaching.[71]

Beginning with John Paul II, every recent pope has spoken out for the abolition of the death penalty, in addition to making appeals for clemency in individual cases. Speaking in St. Louis in 1999, John Paul II celebrated "the increasing recognition that the dignity of human life must never be taken away, even in the case of someone who has done great evil," and called again "for a consensus to end the death penalty, which is both cruel and unnecessary."[72] Pope Benedict XVI made similar remarks in 2011, expressing support for "the political and legislative initiatives being promoted in a growing number of countries to eliminate the death penalty."[73] Finally, Pope Francis has confirmed that under modern conditions, the death penalty is always unnecessary and therefore violates Catholic teaching, and the *Catechism of the Catholic Church* was updated in 2018 accordingly.[74]

The current version of the *Catechism* provides the following summary of Church teaching: "Legitimate public authority has the right and the duty to inflict punishment proportionate to the gravity of the offense," both to restore public order and to promote "the correction of the guilty party." In the past, the death penalty was considered "an acceptable, albeit extreme, means of safeguarding the common good" for certain grievous crimes. However, the *Catechism* continues, such conditions no longer hold:

> Today . . . there is an increasing awareness that the dignity of the person is not lost even after the commission of very serious crimes. In addition, a new understanding has emerged of the significance of penal sanctions imposed by the state. Lastly, more effective systems of detention have been developed, which ensure the due protection

of citizens but, at the same time, do not definitively deprive the guilty of the possibility of redemption.

Consequently, the Church teaches, in the light of the Gospel, that "the death penalty is inadmissible because it is an attack on the inviolability and dignity of the person", and she works with determination for its abolition worldwide.[75]

Pope Francis's 2020 encyclical *Fratelli tutti* reiterates this teaching, juxtaposing the death penalty alongside war as "false answers that do not resolve the problems they are meant to solve." The encyclical continues, "The firm rejection of the death penalty shows to what extent it is possible to recognize the inalienable dignity of every human being and to accept that he or she has a place in this universe. If I do not deny that dignity to the worst of criminals, I will not deny it to anyone."[76]

Catholic Grassroots Activism (or Lack Thereof?) against the Death Penalty

It would be an exaggeration to state that the Catholic position against the death penalty has had no effect on U.S. legal and constitutional culture. Both in the United States and around the world, many Catholics took the Church's teaching on capital punishment seriously throughout the post-*Furman* period. By 1994, according to one study of U.S. Catholics, "frequency of church attendance was consistently associated with *less support* for the death penalty," and this effect was especially pronounced among those who participated actively in parish life.[77] At the forefront of the global movement to abolish the death penalty have been lay Catholic organizations like the Community of Sant'Egidio, based in Rome.[78] In the United States as well, Catholics have remained a significant contingent within the movement to abolish the death penalty, small though that movement may be.[79] Sister Helen Prejean, a Catholic nun, has remained the public face of the movement since her work with death row inmates was adapted into the 1995 Hollywood film *Dead Man Walking*,[80] and popular movies and television shows occasionally include Catholic characters who voice absolute moral objections to capital punishment.[81] The Catholic Mobilizing Network to End the Use of the Death Penalty works in concert with the USCCB to engage in public outreach, advocacy, lobbying, and prayer.[82]

These efforts continue, although they have generally targeted state-level reform rather than constitutional change. In recent years, the Catholic Mobilizing Network has focused primarily on state-level campaigns to repeal or limit the use of the death penalty.[83] For example, in August 2022, the

Catholic Mobilizing Network hosted a webinar on capital punishment in Missouri, cosponsored by the archdioceses of St. Louis and Jefferson City.[84] Participants referenced a variety of ways in which Catholics remain involved in the campaign against capital punishment in the state, ranging from clergy who minister to men on death row to grassroots volunteers who participate in prayer vigils outside of the prison during scheduled executions and work on clemency campaigns. And Bishop Shawn McKnight, of Jefferson City, delivered remarks exemplary of the Church's current, absolute position against the death penalty: "I don't know how to say it more clearly: the death penalty is not pro-life. As Catholics we embrace a culture of life. There are no exceptions or exclusions."[85]

Yet, it must be observed that such efforts have never matched the volume and influence of the pro-life movement against legalized abortion, which one historian has called "the largest moral reform movement of the twentieth century,"[86] and which has now succeeded in convincing the Supreme Court to overrule *Roe v. Wade*, one of the most significant watershed decisions in twentieth-century constitutional law. That movement was initially Catholic-led, and, although increasingly ecumenical by the 1980s, has remained widely associated with the public face of American Catholicism.[87] If a movement's influence on the law is measured by the admittedly crude metric of whether the Supreme Court has adopted the movement's arguments, then it may seem that the pro-life movement has achieved significant (if not yet total) success in *Dobbs*. In contrast, by this metric, the movement to abolish the death penalty has achieved little, as capital punishment remains constitutional and the *Gregg* framework remains good law.

This discrepancy raises a variety of important questions about the relationship between religious doctrine, social movements, U.S. legal culture, and constitutional change. To some extent, there is a relatively straightforward explanation: large numbers of individual Catholics simply did not agree with the Church's position on the death penalty, or at least did not feel strongly enough about the issue to throw themselves into marches, rallies, letter-writing, and other time- and energy-consuming forms of grassroots activism. Of course, and notwithstanding the long history of caricatures of the lockstep, authoritarian Catholic Church, individuals who identify as Catholic nevertheless often express views at odds with Vatican doctrine. Even among observant Catholics, many have not translated the Church's position on capital punishment into their political views or voting behavior; in the United States, those who identify as Republicans or as politically conservative tend "toward greater support of the death penalty."[88] There is also an intra-denominational racial divide: a majority (59 percent) of white Catholics in the United States favor the death penalty, compared with 37 percent of Hispanic Catholics.[89]

Regarding the death penalty, there was also a generational divide, especially in the early years post-*Furman* and *Gregg*. Although the modern Catholic position could be explained as an application of the same principles to new facts (yielding the conclusion that the death penalty was no longer necessary for public safety), older Catholics often perceived the Church's updated position as novel and thus suspicious. Opposing the death penalty "was not what most [Catholics] had been raised on," especially pre–Vatican II, and some lay Catholics may have been simply confused or uncertain about the apparent shift in position.[90] For this reason, Cardinal Joseph Bernardin, the archbishop of Chicago, portrayed the death penalty as a special educational challenge for the clergy. Bernardin recalled, "If it really is the case that 75% to 80% of our people do not agree, well then, that means we really have a job ahead of us to explain to them why we take this position."[91] As James Megivern observed, by the 1980s, the reasoned Catholic case against the death penalty "had been more than adequately worked out on paper, but the task of communicating [the arguments] effectively to the Catholic laity and the broader public was proving to be more daunting than expected."[92]

Participants in the movement against capital punishment have also offered their own theories for the divergence between lay Catholics' relatively muted witness on this issue and the scale of passionate grassroots activism on abortion. Within the Catholic Church, one internal critique is that parish priests have failed to devote adequate attention to the issue. Sister Helen Prejean, for example, has asked, "In the pulpits of the churches, is the death penalty held up as an intrinsic evil like abortion?" Prejean posits that "for Catholics to come to the point of the recognition of the dignity of a murderer is a far harder journey than upholding the dignity of innocent life," and therefore, given the difficulty of the topic, local priests must devote more time and effort to helping parishioners learn about and reflect on the issue. "Just imagine if the church had a full-court press on this moral issue," she suggests, "running adult education programs in every Catholic parish to help people through this journey to see the inviolable dignity of all life, not just innocent life. Just imagine the change that would come of that."[93] Leaving aside Sister Helen's prescriptive recommendations to those within the Church, historians can distill an illuminating descriptive observation from her remarks. She implies that in the decades since *Roe* and *Furman*, local priests, along with lay volunteers who help organize parish programming, have devoted more time and attention to abortion than they have to the death penalty. But if so, then that just pushes the question back one step: Why is that?

To answer that question, it is necessary to zoom out beyond internal Catholic sources and consider external influences on American Catholics, including the broader religious and political context of the late twentieth century. Even as the bishops united in opposition to capital punishment, many Catholics at the grass roots jumped into the antiabortion cause with more gusto than they applied to advocacy against the death penalty. To understand their enthusiasm, it is important to recognize that politically active Catholics were shaped not just by the Church but also by American political culture, institutions, and discourse. Although Catholics did not uniformly agree with the Church's position against *Roe v. Wade* either, those who did agree would have found their antiabortion views reinforced not only by the Church but also by an expanding and increasingly powerful political coalition that encompassed evangelical Christians, the Republican Party (beginning in the 1980s), and elites within the conservative legal movement who criticized the reasoning of *Roe v. Wade* on originalist grounds. In contrast, the Catholic position against the death penalty remained outside of the political mainstream, particularly in the 1980s and '90s. That fact may have dissuaded some Catholics from adopting the position at all, but it likely discouraged some number of others from acting on it. As Megivern observed in his 1997 history of Catholics and the death penalty, the bishops became more opposed to capital punishment in the very same decades that Americans generally became more punitive. "The collision of these two contrary 'attitude adjustments' has resulted in making the bishops' reeducation programs for the Catholic people at large surprisingly ineffectual," Megivern lamented. "The popular American addiction to the death penalty is constantly reinforced in and by the media, which often drowns out the countercultural call for abolition."[94]

With the benefit of historical distance, new scholarship in religious and political history is beginning to look back on the 1980s and '90s and reconstruct in more detail how and why Catholics (and other religious believers) mobilized for legal and political change, yielding rich insights into the coalitions they formed and the trade-offs required. This scholarship, even if not focused on the death penalty as such, offers important insights for legal scholars interested in the dynamics of Catholic engagement (or lack thereof) on the issue of capital punishment. At least at the level of formal doctrine, the death penalty is an issue of great concern to the Catholic Church, and yet in the United States, it has failed to animate grassroots activism and legal mobilization on the scale of the pro-life movement.

Three insights from the emerging historiography on the late twentieth century stand out as most relevant for understanding the recent trajectory of the American death penalty. First, recent work in political history shows that the campaign against *Roe* depended for its political clout on dispelling the traditional perception that abortion was a sectarian "Catholic issue." Particularly in parts of the country where Catholics remained a small minority, such as most of the South, the pro-life movement gained power only once evangelical Protestants signed on to the cause. Abortion had long been viewed as a distinctively Catholic theological concern, of less interest to Protestants given the paucity of biblical references on the point. But as states began liberalizing their abortion laws in the late 1960s, evangelical Christians began to reconsider their views, and some went on record as opposed.[95] Into the early 1980s, the pro-life movement remained predominantly Catholic, but evangelicals were moving toward a strong pro-life position away from their earlier ambivalence.[96]

Second, the new ecumenical coalition on "family values" issues was never so frictionless as breathless media reports about the rise of the "religious right" sometimes implied. Neil Young's informative study *We Gather Together* provides granular detail about the conflicts that continued to arise between members of different denominations at the grass roots. In addition, Young documents that evangelicals did not simply adopt the Catholic theological line on abortion wholesale. Bringing Protestants into the fold required muting the Catholic emphasis on the "sanctity of life" across a range of issues including contraception and the death penalty. Evangelical Protestants remained likely to support the death penalty and to view abortion as a "singular horror" rather than symptomatic of a larger decline in societal respect for the dignity of life.[97] Jennifer Holland's work examines, in particular, how the pro-life movement benefited from cultivating in activists an emotional connection with the symbol of the fetus, as a uniquely innocent and vulnerable victim.[98] While not necessarily incompatible with opposition to the death penalty, this imagery did not lend itself readily to the kind of unconditional defense of human dignity required to expand activists' emotional concern to capital defendants.

Third, recent work on mass incarceration shows that evangelicals moved, if anything, farther apart from Catholics during this same period on issues of criminal punishment. As historian Aaron Blake observes in his recent work *God's Law and Order*, the post-1970s expansion of the carceral state coincided with the growing cultural and political prominence of evangelical Christianity, and evangelicals' religious views "meshed well with important aspects of America's penal culture."[99] Blake highlights a telling anecdote: In 1976, the ACLU Capital Punishment Project was seeking religious participation in the National Coalition against the Death Penalty, formed in response to *Gregg v. Georgia*. By then, numerous mainline Protestant groups had already taken public stances against capital punishment, and the Catholic bishops were moving toward such a stance. Yet the ACLU's overture to the National Association of Evangelicals proved unavailing. The NAE representative wrote back to the ACLU rehearsing at length some traditional biblical rationales for the death penalty, arguing "that the elimination of capital punishment devalued human life" and adding that a death sentence might benefit the condemned individual by hastening his conversion.[100]

More generally, evangelicals during this period were fusing traditional Christian accounts of temporal government with more specifically American conservative skepticism of the post–New Deal welfare state, and therefore developing an account of the purpose of temporal law in the modern world that revolved almost entirely around criminal punishment. On this view, the modern state had little capacity to promote good; progressive social programs had failed, and it remained the role of churches and families to instill morality. True freedom from sin would, of course, be achieved only in the world to come. However, as Blake explains, evangelicals did believe that the state retained "a divinely ordained role in restraining evil" by punishing wrongdoing.[101] In the 1950s and '60s, the evangelical magazine *Christianity Today* published several defenses of capital punishment and ultimately a special edition on the death penalty; meanwhile, the fundamentalist magazine *Sword of the Lord* published a lengthy article entitled "God Commands Death Penalty for Murder."[102]

There were, to be sure, Protestant theologians and ethicists who argued against capital punishment, particularly those within mainline and liberal traditions.[103] Just as the bishops increasingly rejected medieval and early modern Catholic arguments for capital punishment as inapplicable in the modern age, mainline Protestants in the twentieth century increasingly discarded both biblical proof-texting and Reformation-era rhetoric about the punitive role of the state, such as Luther's maxim about governing with bloodshed. But of course, in contrast to the Catholic Church, the debate necessarily remained just that; no entity had the authority to settle the question and establish an official Protestant position. Instead, the death penalty now became one of the many fault lines that divided liberal Protestants from conservative coreligionists, sometimes within denominations.[104] For some adherents of the Lutheran tradition, arguments to abolish the death penalty were not genuinely rooted in sound theological reasoning but instead were "merely part of the secular Enlightenment attack on the entire body of Christian theology," and Christians endorsed or participated in that attack at their peril.[105] Conservative Protestants assailed liberal elites for adopting what they regarded as soft, permissive stances on crime. Instead, they emphasized the traditional view "that where grace does *not* abound the law *must* abound," and social order required the temporal state to impose "restraints, police power, and punishment."[106] In the late twentieth century, as debates about "law and order" roiled both within Christian denominations and within American political culture more generally, Blake writes, "the death penalty proved to be particularly powerful glue for conservative Protestants."[107]

For our purposes, it is important to understand the breadth and depth of conservative Protestants' continuing support for the death penalty because it was leaders and activists within these same evangelical circles who were simultaneously forging alliances with pro-life Catholics to mobilize against *Roe v. Wade*. Abortion was maybe the only glue that could hold that otherwise theologically (and to some extent politically) disparate coalition together. That was especially true given that, as historian Daniel K. Williams has documented, the Catholic contingent in the pro-life movement spanned from conservatives like Phyllis Schlafly to leftists like Father Daniel Berrigan. Those from the latter group had previously protested the Vietnam War and racial discrimination, and some had protested capital punishment at the state level even before *Furman*.[108] Williams details divides within the pro-life movement about how to juggle these competing concerns, especially as growing numbers of politically conservative evangelicals signed on to the antiabortion cause. Before *Roe*, some activists had urged the Catholic pro-life movement to define itself as a coalition against all forms of violence, including war, nuclear weapons, and capital punishment.[109] Instead, after *Roe*, the increasingly ecumenical pro-life movement would also become increasingly coded as socially and politically conservative. Figures like Schlafly joined cause with evangelical leaders to portray abortion not as a form of needless violence akin to the death penalty but as a threat to "family values" akin to "gay rights, feminism, and 'secular humanism.'"[110]

Putting these insights together, then, we can see that it was overdetermined that grassroots mobilization against *Roe v. Wade* would limit the degree to which the Catholic Church's simultaneously developing position against the death penalty would get translated on the same scale into legal or political mobilization in the United States. To some extent, the simple fact that large numbers of lay Catholics joined the grassroots movement against *Roe* would have meant a shift in focus away from other issues of Catholic concern. Any individual or institution necessarily has finite time and resources. But beyond that basic observation, the specific political and religious context of the late twentieth-century United States channeled Catholic pro-life activism in a particular direction. For many Catholics, ending legalized abortion was the number-one priority, but Catholics alone remained a minority of the U.S. population. To achieve legal and political advances, the Catholic antiabortion campaign needed to maintain what was always a more fragile coalition with evangelical Protestants than it may now appear in retrospect.

All of these complex dynamics found pithy expression in a quotation that appeared in the *Washington Post* in 1983: the conservative Catholic organizer Phyllis Schlafly's reaction to Cardinal Joseph Bernardin's widely covered "seamless garment" speech. Before getting to the quote, some background is necessary. Bernardin, the archbishop of Chicago, gave a lecture at Fordham University in December 1983 in which he "challenged the church to build a 'constituency' that would battle capital punishment and human rights violations as vigorously as abortion."[111] Bernardin's remarks followed in the tradition of thinkers who have argued that Catholic teaching and the American political tradition can enrich one another rather than being at odds. He posited that the "Catholic moral vision," with its "consistent ethic of life," could offer a uniquely comprehensive response to multiple political controversies in the 1980s, from legalized abortion to the nuclear arms race. As Bernardin emphasized, no other major institution had connected these issues under one rubric "in the way the Catholic bishops have joined them."[112]

Bernardin's remarks came with several caveats. He framed the lecture as "an inquiry" rather than a manifesto, befitting the academic setting in which he delivered the lecture. He did not endorse the absolute position of some Christian pacifists that "life may never be taken." Rather, he started from the premise that "there should always be a *presumption* against taking human life," subject to certain "narrowly defined *exceptions*." And he emphasized that each of the issues he considered—nuclear war, abortion, capital punishment, and so on—presented "distinct problems," which he did not set out to analyze comprehensively in his relatively brief remarks.

But he made the global observation that, in moral theology, it seemed as though the list of exceptional circumstances that might justify taking life had been growing ever shorter over time, against the backdrop of modern technological development. In an elegant meditation, Bernardin clarified how age-old questions were now being addressed within a context that, on the one hand, made threats to human life greater than ever before, and, on the other hand, fostered "a sharper awareness of the fragility of human life." As Bernardin framed it, the "essential" modern question "is this: In an age when we *can* do almost anything, how do we decide what we *ought* to do? The even more demanding question is: In a time when we can do anything technologically, how do we decide morally what *we never should do*?"

Bernardin specifically discussed the bishops' recently articulated position against capital punishment. As Catholic thinkers and writers have long been wont to do, he first acknowledged "the classical position, found in the writing of Thomas Aquinas and other authors, that the state has the right to employ capital punishment." But he framed the modern question as whether the state, given the existence of alternative methods for protecting public safety, should exercise that right. He noted that the Church had increasingly taken positions "directed against the exercise of that right by the state." Under modern conditions, "more humane methods of defending the society exist and should be used."

Bernardin also posited that the antiabortion cause could not truly succeed unless it also encompassed related "life" issues. Just as the bishops hoped to cultivate a "broader attitude" of respect for life through their advocacy against abortion and nuclear war, so too with the death penalty: "We do not think its use cultivates an attitude of respect for life in society." Bernardin posited that "success on any one of the issues threatening life requires a concern for the broader attitude in society about respect for human life." As he insisted, "Consistency means we cannot have it both ways. We cannot urge a compassionate society and vigorous public policy to protect the rights of the unborn and then argue that compassion and significant public programs on behalf of the needy undermine the moral fiber of society or are beyond the proper scope of governmental responsibility."

Here was where Phyllis Schlafly entered: asked by the *Washington Post* about Bernardin's remarks, she criticized the speech as "divisive to the pro-life movement." Her full statement also alluded to the ongoing controversies over U.S. intervention in Central America. As the *Post* reported, "The genius of prolife movement, [Schlafly] said, has been to unite 'a tremendously wide variety of people who have other views' on other issues but come together on their opposition to abortion. 'Now to tell people they can't be prolife unless they attack Reagan on El Salvador . . . the net effect of that is to sabotage the prolife movement,' she said."[113] Just three years earlier, of course, four American Catholic churchwomen had been raped and murdered in El Salvador, and Oscar Romero, the archbishop of San Salvador, had been assassinated while celebrating Mass. These events—among others—remained heavy on the hearts of many Catholics and other Americans appalled by Reaganite adventurism in Central America.[114] Against that backdrop, Schlafly's remarks may have appeared insensitive, but they also crystallized how she defined the pro-life movement: not as part and parcel with the defense of all life, everywhere in the world, but more narrowly, as a movement against legalized abortion within the U.S. political context.

Perhaps, then, the line of Bernardin's "seamless garment" speech that is most illuminating for legal historians was this one: "A consistent ethic of life must be held by a constituency to be effective." In the United States of the 1980s and thereafter, it is not clear that the bishops ever had a unified constituency behind this ethic. At the grass roots, there were instead different subconstituencies within American Catholicism who held up some pieces of the "garment" and not others. Like everyone else, American Catholics' lives and choices were shaped not only by their personal beliefs but also by the political and religious dynamics of the larger society in which they were living. In the decades after *Roe*, Catholics made common cause with evangelical Protestants to battle against legalized abortion, which in various direct and indirect ways required the pro-life movement to focus on abortion rather than encompass other more distinctively Catholic life issues like the death penalty. Once in motion, these dynamics could also become self-reinforcing over time, as Catholics who became involved in grassroots pro-life efforts may have become thereby more solidified into thinking of themselves as having a conservative political identity and therefore increasingly unlikely to align with liberals (Catholic or otherwise) on issues related to crime and punishment.

Meanwhile, the Supreme Court began to look quite different from the *Furman* Court with its lone Catholic justice. Presidents Reagan, Bush, Obama, and Trump all appointed justices with Catholic elements in their biographies (whether family background, education, or current religious identity). Although, as Justice Brennan illustrates (and in our time, Justice Sonia Sotomayor), there is no necessary equivalence between Catholic background and conservative jurisprudence, it so happens that the Catholicization of the Supreme Court has been associated primarily with the rise of the conservative legal movement. Since the 1980s, the Supreme Court has always had a shifting contingent of conservative justices who publicly present themselves as active and observant Catholics, including the Reagan appointee and conservative legal icon Antonin Scalia, the Bush appointee Samuel Alito, and most recently the Trump appointee Amy Coney Barrett, a former law professor at Notre Dame.

The conservative Catholic justices (pace Barrett, about whom it may be too early to say) have generally appeared to share the typical tendencies of politically conservative lay Catholics in the United States: they have been far more vocal about abortion than about capital punishment, and in their opinions, their descriptions of the grassroots pro-life movement have always been respectful. In 1992, Justice Scalia memorably referenced the March for Life, a massive annual rally against *Roe v. Wade*, in his dissent in *Planned Parenthood v. Casey*, which (for a time) reaffirmed the holding of *Roe*. Scalia caricatured what he viewed as the majority's stubborn reaction to public outcry, offering a mocking paraphrase of their reasoning for preserving the abortion right: "We are offended by these marchers who descend upon us, every year on the anniversary of *Roe*, to protest our saying that the Constitution requires what our society has never thought the Constitution requires. These people . . . must be taught a lesson."[115] Yet these same justices, in their published opinions, have dismissed the campaign to abolish capital punishment as frivolous and disingenuous.

In sum, then, from the vantage point of 2022, Catholicism appears to have had a significant influence on U.S. constitutional law in the realm of abortion, but not much effect on U.S. constitutional law in the realm of criminal punishment. That discrepancy owes to some extent to many Catholics' priorities; many Catholics rated abortion as the more pressing crisis and either hoped that promoting a "culture of life" would also tend indirectly to undermine the death penalty or, like Scalia, simply disagreed with the Church's position on the death penalty. But decisions about priorities could be self-reinforcing; as the pro-life movement developed over time,

Catholic activists became increasingly wedded to tactical allies who may have agreed with their critique of *Roe* but little else. Evangelical Protestants—who famously moved into the antiabortion camp beginning in the 1970s—have never been persuaded by the Catholic position on the death penalty in large numbers; and although not a focus of this chapter, it is worth noting that secular legal conservatives too, whose commitment to originalism also made them valuable allies in the campaign to overturn *Roe v. Wade*, were for the same reason unlikely to turn against the death penalty. On the other hand, liberals and progressives (whether religious or otherwise) who might have agreed with the Church's anti-death-penalty position may have been hesitant to join cause with (or were simply disconnected from) Catholic pro-life activists who were increasingly coded as "conservative" in political discourse.

Conclusion

Scrolling through the website of the *New York Times* in July 2022, a reader might have encountered the following news:

> A Florida jury will decide if the young man who killed 17 people in 2018 will be sentenced to death. Follow for live updates on the trial of the Parkland school shooting gunman. . .[116]

> Abortion is now banned in at least eight states . . . More bans are expected in the coming weeks. . .[117]

Clicking further, the reader could watch live footage of opening statements in *Florida v. Cruz*, the legal aftermath of the 2018 massacre at Marjory Stoneman Douglas High School in Parkland, Florida. The defendant's culpability was not in dispute: several months earlier, Nikolas Cruz had pleaded guilty to seventeen counts of first-degree murder, among other charges. But because first-degree murder is a capital felony under Florida law, a sentencing jury had been empaneled to hear months of evidence about aggravating and mitigating factors and decide whether to recommend the death penalty. (Ultimately, the jury would reject the death penalty and consign Cruz to life without parole.) Or the reader could navigate to the abortion tracker, with its color-coded maps and state-by-state list of restrictions: "Alabama—Abortion is banned with no exceptions for rape or incest. Arkansas—Abortion is banned with no exceptions for rape or incest." And so on.

From the vantage point of 1972, few American legal observers would have predicted that such a juxtaposition of headlines would be possible fifty years later. It seemed then, certainly to legal liberals, that capital punishment

158 / Sara Mayeux

was headed for abolition, and abortion for expanding legal and constitutional protection. That year, the Supreme Court had invalidated several states' death penalty statutes as unconstitutional in *Furman*.[118] Meanwhile, advocates were increasingly arguing that abortion should be protected as a constitutional right, and in cases around the country, in both the state and lower federal courts, judges were beginning to agree. Soon, in *Roe v. Wade*, a 7–2 majority of the Supreme Court would accept and endorse a version of this argument.[119]

Yet from the vantage point of 2022, legal observers know that capital punishment survived *Furman*. Just four years later, in the follow-up case of *Gregg*, the Court clarified that it had not intended to define capital punishment as categorically unconstitutional. States could resume imposing the death penalty if they followed certain heightened procedural strictures, such as the separate penalty proceeding, with its requisite jury findings of aggravating factors, that began in July 2022 in *Florida v. Cruz*.[120] And we also know that earlier in 2022, in *Dobbs*, a very differently constituted Supreme Court overturned *Roe* as wrongly decided, returning abortion to the states to regulate—or ban—as their legislative majorities see fit.[121]

Not just a reminder that history is unpredictable, this juxtaposition of cases also raises questions of explanation that strike at the central problem of legal history: understanding why and how the law changes over time. For example, how much causal weight should be given to the personal beliefs of judges? *Furman* and *Roe* both addressed issues of life and death, issues that human societies have long debated not only as legal questions but also as moral and theological ones. Notably, the Supreme Court that decided *Furman* and *Roe* had only one Catholic member (and that member, William Brennan, was not especially observant), so the justices did not have any deep familiarity with the Catholic theological arguments against legalized abortion. In contrast, today's Supreme Court is predominantly Catholic. For some pundits, this fact alone goes far in explaining the outcome in *Dobbs*.[122]

But juxtaposing *Roe* with *Furman*, and *Dobbs* with the persistence of capital punishment, reveals a more complicated history of Catholicism and constitutionalism in the contemporary United States. Thus, one basic conclusion of this chapter is that, contra pundits, legal scholars should avoid simplistic commentary that describes Catholicism as having somehow captured or taken over constitutional law. It may be more accurate to observe that Catholicism as such, and on its own, is quite impotent to influence U.S. constitutional law—except on those issues, like abortion, where conservative Catholics have been able to make common legal and political cause with evangelical Christians and other religious conservatives. Constitutional law's recent rightward turn owes more to the political triumph of big-tent Reaganite conservatism than to the assimilation of Catholics to elite legal

Catholicism and the Struggle to End the Death Penalty / 159

culture, even if the Roberts Court certainly exemplifies both historical developments. Legal and historical scholarship about the relationship between religion, politics, and law will prove most illuminating when it encompasses not only the biographies and beliefs of individual justices but also the broader political, religious, and social contexts that shape which issues get prioritized and how they are framed in public discourse.

Contrasting the long-term fates of *Furman* and *Roe* thus underscores the need for caution in overattributing the Roberts Court's jurisprudence to the religious backgrounds of its members. It is overly simplistic to attribute the current direction of constitutional law to the fact that most of the justices identify as Catholic. But neither is the growing prominence of Catholics in American public life, particularly in elite circles within the conservative legal movement, irrelevant to the history of constitutional law. Rather, it was a complicated mix of religious identity, Church teachings, grassroots mobilization, and political context that produced *Dobbs*, and it was an equally complex mix of factors that have limited the influence of Church teaching (direct, indirect, or otherwise) on constitutional law when it comes to the death penalty.[123] Throughout, this chapter has sought to highlight recent scholarship in religious and political history that illuminates these dynamics and to emphasize how scholarship from these subfields can usefully be brought to bear on the study of constitutional law.

In concluding, though, I also want to venture into perhaps hazardous territory for a legal historian and consider some normative dimensions of the history presented here. One argument for the value of religious pluralism is that the public square is enriched by a diversity of moral arguments and theological traditions. It is therefore perhaps worth asking, in closing, what may have been lost in the years since *Furman* owing to the fact that, at least within the realm of popular constitutionalism, the Catholic position against capital punishment could be heard only at a relatively low volume. When the U.S. bishops reiterated their objections to the death penalty in 2015, they correctly observed that Catholicism as a moral tradition "offers a unique perspective on crime and punishment, one grounded in mercy and healing, not punishment for its own sake."[124] Whether or not that perspective is wholly unique in world history, it was certainly at odds with the dominant "punitive turn" in U.S. policymaking in the late twentieth century.[125]

In the years since *Furman* (and *Gregg*), the death penalty has declined in practice, but the Supreme Court has grown, if anything, only more resistant to making categorical moral judgments about whether capital punishment comports with human dignity.[126] If and when the death penalty peters out in the United States, it will likely be thanks to several decades of tireless, incremental campaigning to revise state-level laws and practices rather than to nationwide constitutional litigation. Few advocates dare to dream anymore about convincing the Supreme Court to declare capital punishment a per se violation of the Eighth Amendment—that is, for turning the old Brennan position, from all those dissents, into the majority statement of the law. That is especially true after the retirement of Justice Anthony Kennedy, another Catholic justice with a fondness for dignity rhetoric.

For conservative Catholics, the legacy of Cardinal Bernardin's "seamless garment" approach was negative, and its muted influence on popular constitutionalism was therefore presumably a desirable outcome. In the right-wing Catholic journal *First Things*, George Weigel has written critically about the years of Bernardin's influence—what he calls "the Bernardin machine"—as an era of "authoritarian Catholic liberalism," when the institutional voice of the clerical hierarchy seemed to march in support of the (then) seemingly permanent Democratic majority in Congress.[127] As Weigel acknowledged, "Cardinal Bernardin was a committed pro-lifer; charges that he developed the 'consistent ethic' approach in order to give cover to liberal (and pro-choice) Catholic legislators who were 'good on capital punishment and nuclear weapons' were false." But Weigel asserts that nevertheless, the circulation of the "consistent ethic" trope had the effect of "blunt[ing] criticism" of pro-choice Catholic politicians.[128]

Others have lamented the decline of Bernardin's "consistent ethic" and called for reviving the "seamless garment" approach to evaluating the morality of public policy. Cardinal Blase Cupich, the current archbishop of Chicago, argued in 2017 for "a fresh hearing" of Bernardin's 1983 speech, updated for "the signs of our times" in the Vatican II spirit. Following Bernardin's example of uniting several issues often treated as disparate in U.S. politics, Cupich celebrated both "a broad, vibrant, and increasingly young pro-life movement" and the decline in the death penalty "as prosecutors, juries, and Catholic and other Americans make the case that you cannot teach that killing is wrong by killing." But Cupich also emphasized Bernardin's more general contribution to public discourse: the recognition that the Catholic tradition "is uniquely able to assist our society in framing the moral calculi we, as a nation, are called to make, to define the terms and the values that should shape our public-policy discussions and decisions, to offer the moral and human vocabulary that is so often lacking in the technocratic paradigms dominant in our culture."[129]

Law is, of course, the technocratic paradigm par excellence in American policy debates, and many would say (and have said, from various directions) that it is indeed often lacking in "moral and human vocabulary." Perhaps, then, a useful vocabulary was lost with the relative muting of the Catholic voice on capital punishment. Today, Eighth Amendment jurisprudence and criminal justice policy discourse alike are extremely legalistic and technocratic discourses. In case-by-case litigation, in state-level lobbying, and in the pages of law reviews, the arguments that have succeeded in whittling away but never wholly eliminating the death penalty have been statistical and procedural: arguments about racial disparities, marginal deterrence, jury instructions, appellate delays, ineffective assistance of counsel. These are all important arguments so far as they go, and yet they are easy for the state to meet with statistical and procedural rejoinders: arguments about selection bias, omitted variables, standards of review, judicial efficiency, harmless error. These are the actuarial and proceduralist terms on which the post-*Furman* debate over capital punishment has been framed. On the American scene, what has so often been distinctive about the Catholic voice is the insistence on speaking in moral absolutes. This absolutism is what often infuriates and befuddles critics of the Catholic position on abortion, but for those who would wish to argue that the death penalty is simply wrong, it is a tendency that might have been a resource post-*Furman*.

NOTES

1. John Cogley, "Capital Punishment and Caryl Chessman," *Commonweal*, March 18, 1960, 671; James J. Megivern, *The Death Penalty: An Historical and Theological Survey* (New York: Paulist, 1997), 324–25. For background on Cogley, see Edward B. Fiske, "John Cogley Dies at 60; Expert on Catholicism," *New York Times*, March 30, 1976.

2. Megivern, *Death Penalty*, 115–17.

3. Cogley, "Capital Punishment and Caryl Chessman," 671.

4. Megivern, *Death Penalty*, 343; for other examples, see *id.* at 399–401, 408–9.

5. John Paul II, *Evangelium vitae*, encyclical letter, Vatican website, March 25, 1995, https://www.vatican.va/content/john-paul-ii/en/encyclicals/documents/hf_jp-ii_enc_25031995_evangelium-vitae.html; for a discussion, see Dorie Klein, "Human Dignity and the Death Penalty: Comparing Catholic Social Teaching and Eighth Amendment Jurisprudence," in *American Law from a Catholic Perspective: Through a Clearer Lens*, ed. Ronald J. Rychlak (Blue Ridge Summit, PA: Rowman and Littlefield, 2015), 150–51.

6. *Catechism of the Catholic Church*, 2nd ed. (Vatican City: Libreria Editrice Vaticana, 2019), 2266–67, https://www.usccb.org/sites/default/files/flipbooks/catechism/.

7. Furman v. Georgia, 408 U.S. 238, 239–40 (1972).

8. *Furman*, 408 U.S. at 269–70 (Brennan, J., concurring) (quoting Trop v. Dulles, 356 U.S. 99, 100–101 [1958]).

9. For a recent brief introduction to Vatican II, see John T. McGreevy, *Catholicism: A Global History from the French Revolution to Pope Francis* (New York: W. W. Norton, 2022), chap. 11.

10. E. Christian Brugger, "The Ancient, Medieval, and Early Modern Periods," in *Where Justice and Mercy Meet: Catholic Opposition to the Death Penalty*, ed. Vicki Schieber et al. (Collegeville, MN: Liturgical, 2013), 115–24, 131.

11. Gregg v. Georgia, 428 U.S. 153 (1976).

12. *Id.* at 206–7.

13. McGreevy, *Catholicism*, 418–19.

14. Our Lady of Guadalupe School v. Morrissey-Berru, 140 S. Ct. 2049 (2020); for a discussion of this and other recent cases expanding the rights of religious institutions and believers, see Erwin Chemerinsky and Howard Gillman, "Symposium: The Unfold-

162 / Sara Mayeux

ing Revolution in the Jurisprudence of the Religion Clauses," *SCOTUSblog*, August 6, 2020, https://www.scotusblog.com/2020/08/symposium-the-unfolding-revolution-in-the-jurisprudence-of-the-religion-clauses/.

15. See, e.g., "A Statement on the *Dobbs* Decision by the Catholic Bishops of New York State," New York State Catholic Conference, June 24, 2022, https://www.nyscatholic.org/a-statement-on-the-dobbs-decision-by-the-catholic-bishops-of-new-york-state/ (celebrating *Dobbs* as a "just decision" and thanking the "millions of heroic Americans who have worked tirelessly toward this outcome for nearly a half-century" through their participation in the pro-life movement).

16. Dobbs v. Jackson Women's Health Organization, 597 U.S. — (2022), slip op. at 5, https://www.supremecourt.gov/opinions/21pdf/19-1392_6j37.pdf.

17. Linda Greenhouse, "Religious Doctrine, Not the Constitution, Drove the Dobbs Decision," *New York Times*, July 22, 2022.

18. *Catechism of the Catholic Church*, 2270.

19. Laurence H. Tribe, "Deconstructing *Dobbs*," *New York Review of Books*, September 22, 2022. The subhead reads, "Whether or not one sees the Supreme Court's *Dobbs* decision as barely concealed theocracy, it fails to provide any coherent legal analysis of why the right to abortion is not protected by the Fourteenth Amendment." In the body of the article, Tribe ascribes *Dobbs* to "a five-justice bloc committed to a religiously inflected political agenda" and reads the opinion as demonstrating "the barely concealed belief of the majority . . . that they were doing the Lord's work by protecting unborn human life." See also Greenhouse, "Religious Doctrine"; Maureen Dowd, "Irish Eyes Aren't Smiling," *New York Times*, July 16, 2022, in which Dowd writes that "Ireland and the United States have traded places," with "Ireland less influenced by the dictates of the Catholic Church; America more influenced, reflecting the views of the five right-wing Catholics on the Supreme Court and Neil Gorsuch, an Episcopalian who was raised Catholic."

20. Kansas v. Marsh, 548 U.S. 163 (2006) (Scalia, J., concurring).

21. Glossip v. Gross, 576 U.S. 863 (2015) (Scalia, J., concurring).

22. "Scalia Calls Death Penalty Constitutional, Not Immoral," Pew Research Center, February 4, 2002, https://www.pewresearch.org/religion/2002/02/04/scalia-calls-death-penalty-constitutional-not-immoral/.

23. For a chronicle of the litigation campaign, see Evan J. Mandery, *A Wild Justice: The Death and Resurrection of Capital Punishment in America* (New York: W. W. Norton, 2013).

24. Megivern, *Death Penalty*, 339. In addition to the National Coalition of American Nuns, the other was the National Catholic Conference of Interracial Justice. As Megivern notes, their willingness to cosign an amicus brief with organizations representing other denominations "reflect[ed] the post-Vatican II ecumenical atmosphere." On NCAN, a then-relatively-new social-justice-oriented organization for feminist women religious, see "Document 11: National Coalition of American Nuns, 'Declaration of Independence for Women,' May 1972," in *How Did Catholic Women Participate in the Rebirth of American Feminism?*, by Mary Henold (Binghamton: State University of New York at Binghamton, 2005), https://documents.alexanderstreet.com/d/1000677520.

25. Corinna Barrett Lain, "*Furman* Fundamentals," *Washington Law Review* 82, no. 1 (2007): 1–74, 19–20.

26. *Id.* at 19–22.

27. *Id.* at 26–27.

Catholicism and the Struggle to End the Death Penalty / 163

28. See, e.g., Samuel Moyn, *Christian Human Rights* (Philadelphia: University of Pennsylvania Press, 2015).

29. Lain, "*Furman* Fundamentals," 32 (noting denominational statements from "the Methodist, Lutheran, Episcopal, and Presbyterian" churches).

30. Quoted in Megivern, *Death Penalty*, 142.

31. *Furman*, 408 U.S. at 270, 305 (Brennan, J., concurring).

32. Seth Stern and Stephen Wermiel, *Justice Brennan: Liberal Champion* (Boston: Houghton Mifflin Harcourt, 2010), 418.

33. Michael J. Graetz and Linda Greenhouse, *The Burger Court and the Rise of the Judicial Right* (New York: Simon and Schuster, 2016), 26. For an overview of the trajectory of Brennan's position throughout his career, see Stern and Wermiel, *Justice Brennan*, chap. 17.

34. Mandery, *Wild Justice*, 73–75 (quote at 73; emphasis added).

35. Stern and Wermiel, *Justice Brennan*, 419.

36. The information on Brennan's early life in this paragraph is drawn from *id.* at chap. 1.

37. *Id.* at 13.

38. *Id.* at 119. Stern and Wermiel note that such a promise "remained a prerequisite in this era for a Catholic hoping to gain widespread acceptance in American public life," as also evidenced in John F. Kennedy's presidential campaign.

39. Mandery, *Wild Justice*, 73–74.

40. He initially joined a Washington, DC, parish with his wife and daughter after joining the Court but was no longer attending regularly by 1963. Stern and Wermiel, *Justice Brennan*, 165, 210.

41. *Id.* at 376.

42. *Id.* at 19, 80.

43. *Id.* at 292–94.

44. *Id.* at 165–66 ("Brennan's jurisprudence mirrored the lessons he recalled from Sunday school as a child about 'taking care of the poor and the weak'").

45. *Id.* at 225.

46. *Id.* at 351–52.

47. Megivern, *Death Penalty*, 340.

48. *Id.* at 341.

49. See *id.* at 347.

50. For examples, see *id.* at 342–43, 385–86, 408–9, 442–43.

51. *Id.* at 344–45.

52. *Id.* at 346–49 (quote at 346).

53. *Id.* at 349; E. Christian Brugger, "The Church and Capital Punishment in the Modern Period," in Schieber et al., *Where Justice and Mercy Meet*, 131.

54. Megivern, *Death Penalty*, 349–50.

55. Brugger, "Church and Capital Punishment," 131–32.

56. *Id.* at 131 (citing Pontifical Commission for Justice and Peace, "The Church and the Death Penalty," *Origins*, December 9, 1976).

57. Brugger, "Church and Capital Punishment," 131–32.

58. Megivern, *Death Penalty*, 354.

59. Quoted in *id.* at 354.

60. For an overview of the Catholic position over time, see Klein, "Human Dignity."

61. Megivern, *Death Penalty*, 351–52.

62. *Id.* at 352, 356–57.

63. *Id.* at 360–69.

64. "Bishops' Statement on Capital Punishment, 1980," U.S. Conference on Catholic Bishops, 1980, https://www.usccb.org/resources/bishops-statement-capital-punishment-1980. For background on the bishops' deliberations and the content of the final statement, see Megivern, *Death Penalty*, 365–69.

65. Megivern, *Death Penalty*, 367.

66. Carol Zimmermann, "Bishops Vote to Revise U.S. Catechism's Capital Punishment Section," *National Catholic Reporter*, June 12, 2019, https://www.ncronline.org/news/bishops-vote-revise-us-catechisms-capital-punishment-section.

67. Michael Paulson, "U.S. Catholic Bishops Taking on Death Penalty," *New York Times*, March 22, 2005.

68. U.S. Conference of Catholic Bishops, *A Culture of Life and the Penalty of Death* (Washington, DC, 2005), https://www.usccb.org/issues-and-action/human-life-and-dignity/death-penalty-capital-punishment/upload/penaltyofdeath.pdf.

69. *Evangelium vitae*; for a discussion, see Klein, "Human Dignity," 150–51.

70. Brugger, "Church and Capital Punishment," 133.

71. Megivern, *Death Penalty*, 1.

72. John Paul II, homily at the TransWorld Dome, St. Louis, MO, July 27, 1999, quoted in Msgr. Stuart W. Swetland, "The Gospel of Life," in Schieber et al., *Where Justice and Mercy Meet*, 153.

73. Quoted in Swetland, "Gospel of Life," 155.

74. For news coverage, see, e.g., Merrit Kennedy, "Catholic Church Now Formally Opposes Death Penalty in All Cases," National Public Radio, August 2, 2018, https://www.npr.org/2018/08/02/634864608/catholic-church-now-formally-opposes-death-penalty-in-all-cases.

75. *Catechism of the Catholic Church*, 2266–67.

76. Francis, *Fratelli tutti*, encyclical letter, Vatican website, October 3, 2020, https://www.vatican.va/content/francesco/en/encyclicals/documents/papa-francesco_2020 1003_enciclica-fratelli-tutti.html.

77. Thoroddur Bjarnason and Michael R. Welch, "Father Knows Best: Parishes, Priests, and American Catholic Parishioners' Attitudes toward Capital Punishment," *Journal for the Scientific Study of Religion* 43, no. 1 (2004): 103–18, 107, 115 (emphasis in original).

78. See Mario Marazziti, *13 Ways of Looking at the Death Penalty* (New York: Seven Stories, 2015), 51–52.

79. On the current state of the movement, see Bill McCormick, S.J., "What Will It Take to End the Death Penalty?," *America*, January 13, 2021, https://www.americamagazine.org/politics-society/2021/01/13/abolition-death-penalty-federal-executions-culture-violence-trump-biden.

80. For a recent interview, see Kevin Clarke, "Sister Helen Prejean on Trump and Barr's Cruel Spree of Executions," *America*, January 11, 2021, https://www.americamagazine.org/politics-society/2021/01/11/trump-barr-federal-execution-death-penalty-helen-prejean-239560.

81. Such characters have furnished plot lines in, for instance, the HBO prison drama *Oz* and the Bush-era network political drama *The West Wing* (thanks to Austin Sarat for this reference).

82. The Catholic Mobilizing Network website, with an array of information about their activities, can be found at https://catholicsmobilizing.org.

Catholicism and the Struggle to End the Death Penalty / 165

83. Vicki Schieber, "Conclusion," in Schieber et al., *Where Justice and Mercy Meet*, 224.

84. "Webinar Recording: The Catholic Call to End Missouri's Death Penalty," Catholic Mobilizing Network, August 16, 2022, https://catholicsmobilizing.org/resource/webinar-recording-catholic-call-end-missouris-death-penalty.

85. *Id.*

86. Karissa Haugeberg, *Women against Abortion: Inside the Largest Moral Reform Movement of the Twentieth Century* (Urbana: University of Illinois Press, 2017).

87. On the early pro-life movement as led by liberal or human-rights-oriented Catholics, see Daniel K. Williams, *Defenders of the Unborn: The Pro-Life Movement before Roe v. Wade* (Oxford: Oxford University Press, 2016).

88. Bjarnason and Welch, "Father Knows Best," 107.

89. Elizabeth Bruenig, "The Catholic Church Opposes the Death Penalty. Why Don't White Catholics?," *New Republic*, March 6, 2015, https://newrepublic.com/article/121231/national-catholic-publications-announce-opposition-death-penalty.

90. Megivern, *Death Penalty*, 344.

91. Quoted in *id.* at 379.

92. *Id.* at 379–80.

93. Clarke, "Sister Helen Prejean."

94. Megivern, *Death Penalty*, 453.

95. Neil J. Young, *We Gather Together: The Religious Right and the Problem of Interfaith Politics* (Oxford: Oxford University Press, 2015), 99–102.

96. *Id.* at 119–20, 161.

97. *Id.* at 123, 127–28.

98. Jennifer Holland, *Tiny You: A Western History of the Anti-abortion Movement* (Berkeley: University of California Press, 2020).

99. Aaron Blake, *God's Law and Order: The Politics of Punishment in Evangelical America* (Cambridge, MA: Harvard University Press, 2020), 3.

100. *Id.* at 99–100. The ACLU lawyer (who was Jewish) wrote back that he found this position "appalling." The exchange was subsequently published in the liberal Protestant magazine *Christianity and Crisis. Id.* at 100–101.

101. *Id.* at 110–11.

102. *Id.* at 130.

103. *Id.* at 111–12.

104. E.g., Presbyterians, discussed in *id.* at 127–29.

105. Megivern, *Death Penalty*, 142.

106. Conservative Presbyterian position quoted in Blake, *God's Law and Order*, 129.

107. *Id.* at 130.

108. Williams, *Defenders of the Unborn*, 160–61.

109. *Id.* at 161–64; see also Haugeberg, *Women against Abortion*, 61–62 (discussing how pro-life activists who remained active in antiwar organizing felt strained from the other direction).

110. Williams, *Defenders of the Unborn*, 254–55.

111. Marjorie Hyer, "Bernardin Views Prolife Issues as 'Seamless Garment,'" *Washington Post*, December 10, 1983. For background on Bernardin's speech and its continuing relevance for intra-Catholic debates in the United States, see Michael J. O'Loughlin, "Can the 'Seamless Garment' Approach to Pro-life Issues Make a Comeback in the Catholic Church?," *America*, November 17, 2017, https://www.americamagazine.org/faith/2017/11/17/can-seamless-garment-approach-pro-life-issues-make-comeback-catholic-church.

166 / Sara Mayeux

112. All quotations in this and subsequent paragraphs are from the text of Bernardin's remarks, "A Consistent Ethic of Life: An American-Catholic Dialogue" (Gannon Lecture, Fordham University, December 6, 1983), https://www.hnp.org/publications/hnpfocus/BConsistentEthic1983.pdf (emphases in original).

113. Hyer, "Bernardin Views Prolife Issues."

114. See generally Theresa Keeley, *Reagan's Gun-Toting Nuns: The Catholic Conflict over Cold War Human Rights Policy in Central America* (Ithaca, NY: Cornell University Press, 2020).

115. Planned Parenthood v. Casey, 505 U.S. 833, 999 (1992) (Scalia, J., dissenting).

116. "Parkland School Gunman Faces Death Penalty in Rare Trial," *New York Times*, July 15, 2022, updated July 18, 2022, https://www.nytimes.com/2022/07/15/us/parkland-gunman-trial.html.

117. "Tracking the States Where Abortion Is Now Banned," *New York Times*, updated July 18, 2022, https://www.nytimes.com/interactive/2022/us/abortion-laws-roe-v-wade.html.

118. *Furman*, 408 U.S. 238; for a chronicle of the litigation campaign and legal liberal aspirations for abolition, see Mandery, *Wild Justice*.

119. Roe v. Wade, 410 U.S. 113 (1973); on abortion rights litigation in the years leading up to *Roe*, see Mary Ziegler, *Abortion and the Law in America: Roe v. Wade to the Present* (Cambridge: Cambridge University Press, 2020), chap. 1.

120. *Gregg*, 428 U.S. 153.

121. *Dobbs*, 597 U.S. —.

122. See, e.g., Dowd, "Irish Eyes Aren't Smiling"; Greenhouse, "Religious Doctrine"; Tribe, "Deconstructing *Dobbs*."

123. As social scientists have similarly noted, "the effects of formal and theological directives that emanate from the hierarchy of the Catholic Church . . . are conditioned by various geographical, political, and sociodemographic factors." Bjarnason and Welch, "Father Knows Best," 117.

124. U.S. Conference of Catholic Bishops, statement, July 16, 2015, https://www.usccb.org/issues-and-action/human-life-and-dignity/criminal-justice-restorative-justice/upload/joint-dp-message-dsd-pro-life-2015-07-16.pdf. See also Trudy D. Conway, "Rethinking the Death Penalty," in Schieber et al., *Where Justice and Mercy Meet*, 42 (describing the Catholic perspective on punishment as holistic and rehabilitative rather than retributive).

125. See generally, e.g., Michael S. Sherry, *The Punitive Turn in American Life: How the United States Learned to Fight Crime Like a War* (Chapel Hill: University of North Carolina Press, 2020); Julilly Kohler-Haussman, *Getting Tough: Welfare and Imprisonment in 1970s America* (Princeton, NJ: Princeton University Press, 2017); Jonathan Simon, *Governing through Crime: How the War on Crime Transformed American Democracy and Created a Culture of Fear* (New York: Oxford University Press, 2007).

126. Justices Kennedy and Breyer of course suggested such arguments, but they have now retired. Justice Sotomayor has raised serious questions but is usually writing in dissent.

127. George Weigel, "The End of the Bernardin Era," *First Things*, February 2011, https://www.firstthings.com/article/2011/02/the-end-of-the-bernardin-era.

128. *Id.*

129. Cardinal Blase J. Cupich, "Witnessing to a Consistent Ethic of Solidarity," *Commonweal*, May 19, 2017, https://www.commonwealmagazine.org/cardinal-blase-cupich-signs-times.

5

Abolition Then and Now

The Role of Furman's *Failure in*
Today's Abolition Success

CORINNA BARRETT LAIN

On the fiftieth anniversary of *Furman v. Georgia*,[1] one cannot help but see the similarities between the historical moment in which we find ourselves today and the historical moment in which the justices found themselves in 1972. Once again, the death penalty is dying—death sentences are down, executions are down, and states are slowly but surely abandoning the use of capital punishment. History, it would seem, is repeating itself.

But beneath these surface similarities lie important differences between the two eras in *why* these measures of death penalty support are low and what this means for the larger abolition story. Today's abolitionism is about bleeding the death penalty dry, making it more trouble than it is worth so that states will decide for themselves to let it go. Instead of aiming high, abolitionists are aiming low.

To be clear, this is not a comment on the quality of the abolitionist discourse. One might view aiming high as tapping into our better selves and lodging high-minded, fundamentally moral objections to the death penalty— arguments about why killing is wrong philosophically, ethically, or spiritually, as we see explored in other chapters in this book. By this view, aiming high is taking aim at the heart of the death penalty, while aiming low is just nibbling around the edges, focusing on practical realities instead. That is not the view of aiming high and aiming low that is the essence of my claim here.

My claim is more about *where* abolition is happening than what arguments are being made (although the two are not unrelated). In 1972, the aim of the abolition movement was ending the death penalty in one fell swoop by winning at the Supreme Court. Abolition was viewed as a top-down affair. Fifty years later, abolition is a movement from the bottom up, with states ending the death penalty on their own one jurisdiction at a time. Abolition today is not a story about the highest court in the land; it's a story about death by a thousand cuts.

In two ways, *Furman* itself played a part in this dramatic shift—not the only part, to be sure, but an important part nonetheless. First, *Furman*'s backlash taught abolitionists that the Supreme Court's "help" may do more harm than good. *Furman* was supposed to have ended the death penalty. Instead, the ruling helped revive it. In this way, *Furman* was not so different from other landmark rulings that instigated a backlash so strong that it set back the very cause that the Court was ostensibly supporting.[2] *Furman* showed that Supreme Court intervention could halt (or even reverse) change already in progress and that when this happened, the Court would be a fair-weather friend—there in good times but gone when needed the most. Hence the lesson to aim low.

Second, *Furman*—or rather, the Supreme Court's capitulation to *Furman*'s backlash in *Gregg v. Georgia*[3]—unwittingly provided the means to make this dramatic shift happen. *Gregg*'s attempt to tame the death penalty was a fool's errand. Like *Furman*, *Gregg* was a failure on its own terms. But the endeavor itself created a mass of complicated doctrine, and that gave rise to a cadre of specialized capital defenders to navigate it. Those defenders are the foot soldiers of today's abolition movement, killing the death penalty by saving one life at a time.

In the pages that follow, I tell a causal story, a descriptive (rather than normative) account of abolition then and now. At the heart of this story are the Supreme Court's decisions in *Furman* and *Gregg*, and in this sense, my account is unabashedly Supreme Court–centric. My aim is not to deify the Court, but rather to show that even the highest court of the land is subject to the law of unintended consequences. In the short run, those consequences were disastrous for the abolition movement, but in the long run, they may accomplish what the *Furman* ruling could not: abolition of the death penalty for good.

To make my point, I first turn to the similarities of abolition then and now. I then complicate the narrative by delving into the differences between the two historical moments. Finally, I connect the dots by showing the role that *Furman* played in getting us where we are today. The modern path to abolition is not without its downsides—surely it would have been better, as John Bessler argues in his chapter, had the Supreme Court in *Furman* stood its ground.[4] But there is an upside to doing abolition the hard way, from the bottom up: this time when the death penalty is abolished, it may actually stay that way.

The Road to *Furman*, Redux

Anyone familiar with the sociopolitical context in which *Furman* was decided knows that today's sociopolitical context is eerily similar in a number of ways. History, it would seem, is repeating itself. In this part, I make the point first by placing *Furman* in its larger historical context and then by examining the same indicia of death penalty support today.

The Dying Death Penalty in Furman

In the years leading up to *Furman*, it was widely believed that abolition of the death penalty was just a matter of time. *Time* magazine wrote about "The Dying Death Penalty" twice in 1967,[5] and other news magazines wrote about rising abolitionist sentiment as late as 1971.[6] Justice Potter Stewart, a pivotal part of *Furman's* five-justice majority, voted to invalidate the death penalty at least partly because, as he stated in conference, "If we hold it constitutional in 1972, it would only delay its abolition."[7] Justice Byron White, another pivotal vote in *Furman*, apparently shared this sentiment, writing in his concurring opinion that the death penalty had "for all practical purposes run its course"[8] and stating in conference that "we should not legalize the death penalty at this time in our history."[9]

Why the contemporary confidence in the death penalty's impending demise? The answer lies in a number of sociopolitical indications that the country was moving toward abolition on its own.

Start with executions. By the time the Supreme Court decided *Furman* in 1972, the United States had not seen an execution in five years. But even before executions had ground to a halt in late 1967, they had declined sharply in the two decades preceding *Furman*. In the 1940s, the average number of executions per year was 128.[10] By the 1950s, that average had dropped to 72,[11] and the numbers plummeted from there. In 1962, the country saw 47 executions, and in 1963, it saw just 21.[12] The year 1964 had 15 executions, 1965 had 7, 1966 had 1, and 1967 had 2.[13] From 1968 until the death penalty was reinstated in 1976 and states resumed executions in 1977, there were *none*.[14]

Granted, part of the reason that there were no executions in the five years before *Furman* was a litigation-based de facto moratorium in place while the Supreme Court waded through various constitutional challenges to the death penalty.[15] But as I have detailed elsewhere, executions also fell because a number of institutional actors were not interested in conducting them.[16] Contemporary commentators talked about growing opposition to the death penalty among governors, state attorneys general, and prison wardens, noting in particular an unusually high number of governor-issued commutations in the years leading up to *Furman*.[17]

170 / Corinna Barrett Lain

That said, another reason for the drop in executions was a drop in death sentences, which also strongly suggested the death penalty's impending demise. Death sentencing is a particularly important indicator of the death penalty's future because today's death sentences are tomorrow's executions. Without death sentences to feed the machinery of death, the cogs of the machine will eventually stop churning, leaving the death penalty to die on the vine (or just languish indefinitely in *Walking Dead* fashion).[18]

In the years before *Furman*, death sentences were in steep decline. In the 1940s, courts imposed an average of 142 death sentences per year.[19] By the 1960s, that number had dropped to 106 *despite* a significant rise in population and capital crimes.[20] By the 1960s, juries were returning death sentences only around 10 to 20 percent of the time they were asked to do so[21]— a remarkably low figure, especially given the fact that death-qualified "hanging juries" were not ruled unconstitutional until 1968.[22] As the National Crime Commission noted in its 1967 report, "all available data indicate that judges, juries, and governors are becoming increasingly reluctant to impose, or authorize the carrying out of a death sentence."[23]

These indicators, in turn, fed another: state legislative trends. Alaska and Hawaii abolished the death penalty as territories in 1957 (both became states in 1959), and Oregon followed suit in 1964, setting off a flurry of abolition activity in the states.[24] In 1965, two states (West Virginia and Iowa) abolished the death penalty completely, while another two (New York and Vermont) abolished it for all but extraordinary crimes such as murder by a prisoner already serving a life sentence.[25] New Mexico similarly chose limited abolition in 1969.[26] Before the late 1950s, no state had passed an abolition bill of any variety in thirty years.[27]

Granted, that still left forty states and the federal government with at least one death penalty statute on the books in 1972.[28] And granted, for every state that rescinded the death penalty or severely limited it in the lead-up to *Furman*, many more decided to keep it. In 1965, twenty states considered proposals to abolish capital punishment; the vast majority failed miserably.[29] But the fact that almost half the states were even considering abolition was itself significant. Before the 1960s, those proposals were not even on the table.[30]

Even the fact that forty states still had a death penalty statute in 1972 was deceptive as a measure of the death penalty's continued vitality. To be sure, death penalty statutes were on the books, but with one regional exception—the South—they were seldom invoked in practice.[31] Only in the South did the death penalty continue to thrive in the 1960s. At the time, the South accounted for nearly two-thirds of all executions in the country—double that of all other regions of the United States combined.[32] Yet even in the South, executions fell by 50 percent between 1940 and 1960.[33] In fact, the steep decline in executions nationwide was attributable in large part to the steep decline of executions in the South.[34]

Public opinion poll data also evidenced a turn away from the death penalty. In 1953, 68 percent of the public supported capital punishment.[35] By 1965, that figure was just 45 percent.[36] Those numbers came from Gallup polls, but a Harris poll in 1965 produced even more striking results, reporting death penalty support at just 38 percent and opposition at 47 percent.[37] Gallup's poll the next year similarly showed death penalty opponents outnumbering supporters, reporting in 1966 that 42 percent of the public supported capital punishment, while 47 percent opposed it.[38] In short, public support for the death penalty fell between 25 and 30 percent in just over a decade. Little wonder the Supreme Court referred to death penalty supporters as "a distinct and dwindling minority" in 1968.[39]

Granted, the Supreme Court decided *Furman* not in the mid-1960s, but in 1972, four years after Richard Nixon won the presidency on a law-and-order campaign in 1968. But even the public's sharp turn to the right on criminal justice matters had curiously little effect on support for capital punishment. Gallup reported death penalty support at 51 percent in 1969, 49 percent in 1971, and an even 50 percent in 1972, just before *Furman* was decided.[40] Harris polls reported death penalty support as consistently just under 50 percent during this time.[41]

Given the tenor of the times, these figures were truly remarkable. The public identified crime as the nation's top domestic problem in 1968,[42] yet could barely muster 50 percent support for the death penalty at the time. Tellingly, the 1972 Republican Party platform—still awash with crime-control rhetoric—was conspicuously silent about the death penalty, while the Democratic Party platform that year took a stand in favor of abolishing it.[43] The country may have been in a law-and-order moment, but it was still in the midst of an abolition *movement*.

Part of the reason that the abolition movement endured in such harsh conditions was the values driving it. Although people opposed the death penalty for a number of reasons, concerns about its discriminatory application were at the top of the list. Contemporary newspaper and magazine articles talked about racial and economic discrimination in the imposition of death.[44] The National Crime Commission's 1967 report talked about it.[45] And three of the five justices in *Furman*'s majority—Justices William Douglas, Thurgood Marshall, and Potter Stewart—talked about it in their concurring opinions.[46] The civil rights movement and the war on poverty had awakened the nation to the need to remedy long-standing racial and economic injustices, and that included injustice when the stakes were life and death. To many, the death penalty represented the ultimate expression of race and class discrimination. The civil rights movement and the war on poverty were

172 / Corinna Barrett Lain

propelling abolition sentiment, and the sheer strength of those movements was an ominous sign for the death penalty's future too.

All this is to say that in the years preceding *Furman*, there was good reason to think that the death penalty was an antiquated punishment whose end was in sight. Indeed, so confident were contemporary observers that the death penalty was coming to an end that the 1972 *Supreme Court Review* gave *Furman* little more than a figurative yawn, writing that with the ruling, "the inevitable came to pass."[47] None of this is to say that *Furman*'s result was predetermined or even predictable. For reasons I have discussed elsewhere, it was neither.[48] But when the justices decided *Furman* in 1972, the death penalty was dying. And it is dying again today.

The Dying Death Penalty Today

Today's death penalty discourse, like the discourse in the years before *Furman*, is marked by a sense of the death penalty's impending demise. *Time* magazine has once again written about "The Death of the Death Penalty" and "Why the Era of Capital Punishment Is Ending."[49] Numerous other newspapers and magazines have mused about the dying death penalty over the past decade as well.[50] One might even say that the question today is not whether the death penalty will end, but when and how.[51]

Here again, this sentiment makes sense in light of a number of sociopolitical indications that the death penalty is on its way out. Turning first to executions, 2021 saw just 11 nationwide, and for those interested in a pre-pandemic data point, 2019 saw just 22.[52] A year-end total of 22 executions nationally may not be stunning on its own, but that changes when considered against its larger historical context. Ten years earlier—in 2009—the United States saw 52 executions, more than double the 2019 figure.[53] And ten years before that—in 1999—the country saw 98 executions nationwide, more than four times the 2019 figure.[54] In the last two decades, executions have fallen 77 percent using 2019 as the relevant data point, and 88 percent using 2021 data. That's a larger decline in executions than what the nation experienced in the pre-*Furman* era (at least from the 1940s to the beginning of the 1960s, when a litigation-based moratorium started halting executions altogether).[55]

Death sentencing has likewise declined dramatically. In 2021, there were only 18 new death sentences in the entire country.[56] In 2019 (again, as a prepandemic data point), that number was 34.[57] Ten years earlier, in 2009, there were 118 new death sentences, and ten years before that—in 1999—that number was 279.[58] In the last two decades, death sentencing in the United States has fallen 88 percent using 2019 as the relevant data point, and

Abolition Then and Now / 173

93 percent using 2021 data. The pipeline of death sentences feeding the machinery of death has been reduced to a relative trickle.

These two data points—death sentences and executions—help explain state abolition trends, which likewise suggest that the death penalty is dying. Since 2007, eight states—New Jersey, New Mexico, Illinois, Connecticut, Maryland, New Hampshire, Colorado, and Virginia—have legislatively abolished the death penalty (with an honorable mention going to Nebraska, which legislatively abolished the death penalty in 2015 only to bring it back by popular referendum in 2016).[59] Moreover, in three states—New York, Washington, and Delaware—a court invalidated the state's death penalty statute and the state legislature failed to pass a new one, bringing the total number of states without the death penalty to twenty-three.[60] On top of that, the governors of three states—California, Oregon, and Pennsylvania—have declared an indefinite moratorium on executions, so although juries can still hand down death sentences in those states, the death sentences cannot be carried out.[61] Put all that together and the number of states with either no death penalty or no executions because of gubernatorial moratoria is twenty-six—more than half the nation for the first time in history.

That brings us to public opinion polls, which, as one might have guessed, also suggest that support for the death penalty is waning. In 2022, Gallup reported support for the death penalty at 55 percent, noting that it has ranged between 54 and 56 percent for the past five years.[62] For context, 54 percent is the lowest recorded support for the death penalty since *Furman* was decided in 1972.[63] The year 2022's reported 55 percent support—just one point above the post-*Furman* fifty-year low—marks a whopping 25-point decline from the all-time high of 80 percent support for the death penalty in 1994.[64]

Even the role of race in today's abolition movement is reminiscent of the earlier pre-*Furman* era. As before, those who oppose the death penalty today do so for a number of reasons, but race is high on the list. The murder of George Floyd at the hands of police in 2020 ignited a firestorm of criticism about the treatment of racial minorities by the police and criminal justice system more largely, leading to protests in all fifty states and countries around the world.[65] The 1960s had the civil rights movement. The 2020s have the Black Lives Matter movement. Like the civil rights movement before it, the Black Lives Matter movement has brought national attention to racial injustice in the criminal justice system, and that has brought renewed attention to racial injustice when the stakes are life and death. Indeed, the Black Lives Matter platform—"End the War on Black People"—explicitly calls for abolition of the death penalty, labeling it a "racist practice" that cannot be purged of its discriminatory taint.[66] Once again, a larger social movement is fueling abolition sentiment, adding momentum to a trend already underway.

174 / Corinna Barrett Lain

All this is to say that there are striking similarities between the historical moment in which we find ourselves today and the one in which the justices found themselves in 1972. Indeed, the similarities are so strong that they have sparked discussions about the Supreme Court's role in how the death penalty might end.[67] Could a *Furman*-type ruling work this time? Or would it once again spark a backlash that would reverse prevailing trends?

These questions are a testament to the fact that a dying death penalty is familiar. We've been here before. But beneath the surface similarities of the two eras lie important differences in the reasons *why* these measures of death penalty support are low and what this means for the larger abolition story.

Differences in Abolition Then and Now

History never really repeats itself. In any comparison, important differences remain. In this part, I explore the differences between abolition then and now, and how those differences have worked to flip the abolition script. *Furman*'s abolition story was about legislative failure, and a Supreme Court stepping in help. Today's abolition story is about the justices bending over backward to facilitate the death penalty, and state legislatures stepping in to abolish it on their own. Understanding the differences between abolition then and now is the key to understanding how today's upside-down state of affairs came to be.

Differences Underlying the Decline in Death Sentencing

In the pre-*Furman* era and today, the drop in death sentencing occurred mainly because juries were disinclined to return a death sentence, not because prosecutors were disinclined to ask for one (at least until recently).[68] But the reason *why* jurors were disinclined to return death sentences is vastly different between the two eras. A number of developments play an important part in this story—the discovery of innocent people on death row and the advent of life without parole as a sentencing option are prime examples—but my focus is the difference in the *process* by which jurors decide death, which, as we will see, has had cascading effects of its own.

In the pre-*Furman* era, jurors had unfettered discretion in capital sentencing. A typical instruction read: "Whether you recommend or withhold mercy is a matter solely within your discretion, calling for the exercise of your very best and most profound judgment."[69] The law provided no guidance; jurors were left to their own devices. Because capital sentencing was entirely unstructured, it is hard to know why jurors rarely returned death sentences in the pre-*Furman* era. The reason may have been resistance to the death penalty, or it may have been something else. That's the point—it was impossible to know.[70]

Gregg ostensibly solved this problem by validating death penalty statutes that purported to guide jurors' discretion in various ways.[71] Once *Gregg* blessed guided-discretion statutes, a new era in capital litigation was born, and it looked nothing like the pre-*Furman* era. In the pre-*Furman* era, capital trials were focused primarily on the guilt phase of trial; the sentencing phase was almost an afterthought, and the case for life was relatively rudimentary.[72] By contrast, today's capital trials are focused primarily on the sentencing phase of trial; the case for life is sophisticated and built on a mountain of mitigating evidence, all with the aim of guiding the jury's discretion away from death.[73] As Carol and Jordan Steiker note in their chapter in this book, guided-discretion statutes did not cure the arbitrariness of death sentencing; the core critique of *Furman* is still apt today.[74] But this shift in the capital litigation battlefield has had at least two consequences that are relevant to the discussion here.

First, it has vastly increased the cost of capital punishment. Mitigation costs money, and states have little choice but to spend it. Back in 1989, the American Bar Association promulgated guidelines for defense counsel in capital cases, stating that effective representation required (among other things) investigation into various aspects of the defendant's social history in order to build a case in mitigation.[75] But the guidelines were merely advisory, and in practice, they were viewed as more aspirational than operational—that is, until 2000, when the Supreme Court decided *Williams v. Taylor.*[76] Before 2000, the Court had never reversed a death sentence for ineffective assistance of counsel.[77] But that's exactly what it did in *Williams*, and the reason was the attorney's failure to conduct an investigation to support the case in mitigation.[78]

Williams was the first in a string of cases to reverse a death sentence based on defense counsel's failure to adequately investigate mitigating evidence, and it sent an important message: if states wanted to protect their death sentences, they needed to provide minimally competent counsel who would at least minimally investigate mitigating facts.[79] And so it came to be that when the American Bar Association revised its capital case guidelines in 2003 to call for at least two capital defenders, a fact investigator, and a mitigation specialist in every capital case, that became standard practice in a number of death penalty states.[80]

And that brings us to cost. As Carol and Jordan Steiker note in their chapter in this book (and as they have explored more deeply in other work), trying capital cases is stunningly expensive, and the cost to investigate, develop, and present a case in mitigation is a big part of the reason why.[81] A study in 2017 reviewed fifteen state studies of death penalty costs and found that on

176 / Corinna Barrett Lain

average, it costs around $700,000 more to try a capital murder case than a non-capital murder case.[82] At the federal level, another study found that the average cost of defending a capital murder case was over $620,000—around eight times the cost of defending a non-capital murder case.[83]

A second consequence of this shift in the capital litigation battlefield is what those hefty defense expenditures have produced: life sentences. Here again, the decline in death sentences is a story much bigger than the one I tell here, with a number of other developments also factoring into the equation. But the rise of mitigation as a chief capital defense strategy is a massive development having a massive effect. To see just how impactful this development is, consider my home state, Virginia.

Before *Furman* and after, Virginia was exceptional in its zeal for the death penalty. It was notoriously prolific in producing death sentences and notoriously efficient in carrying them out. No state executed faster once a death sentence was handed down.[84] And no state was more successful in converting death sentences to executions.[85] How, then, did Virginia go from all-in on the death penalty to abolition in 2021?

A host of factors played a role, but a critical piece of the puzzle was the ability of Virginia's capital defenders to essentially shut off the spigot of death sentences that were feeding the machinery of death. By the time Virginia abolished the death penalty, it had not seen a new death sentence in *ten years* and had only two people left on death row.[86] A critical part of the landscape that made abolition possible was the fact that as a practical matter, Virginia's death penalty was already dead.

Every state has its own story—its own death penalty statutes, capital defense systems, appellate review structures, and so on. Virginia's story may not be replicable in other states (although I have argued elsewhere that important parts of it are).[87] But replicable or not, Virginia offers a front-row seat to seeing just how impactful mitigation is in modern capital defense.

The story starts in 2002, when in the wake of *Williams* (which happened to be a Virginia case), the Virginia General Assembly created regional capital defender offices as a way to save money on capital defense.[88] If Virginia was serious about its death penalty—and it very much was—then it needed to make sure that its death sentences would stick, and to do that, it needed to shore up its capital defense. The Virginia State Crime Commission studied the issue and wrote a report recommending the creation of six regional capital defender offices to handle the sheer volume of capital cases.[89] The General Assembly went with four.[90] It equipped each office with two capital defenders, one mitigation specialist, one fact investigator, and an administrative assistant—the bare minimum.[91]

The offices started taking cases in 2004, and the difference was dramatic. Importantly, the rate of capital murder indictments being filed for eligible first-degree murders did not change much during this time—the rate was 79 percent before 2004 and 73 percent in 2015, when my colleague John Douglass ran the numbers.[92] Capital murder indictments were still coming down the pike. What changed was the number of cases going to trial and what happened when they did.

The numbers tell the tale. Altogether, the regional capital defender offices handled over 250 capital cases.[93] Of those, only *ten* went to trial with death as a possible outcome.[94] The rest were negotiated for a sentence short of death or went to trial with death off the table.

As to the ten cases that the regional capital defenders took to trial with death as a possible outcome, only four resulted in a death sentence. Before 2004, when the regional capital defenders started taking cases, the death sentencing rate of cases that went to trial in Virginia was 84 percent.[95] Prosecutors were asking for death, and over 80 percent of the time, they were getting it. After 2004, the death sentencing rate in Virginia fell to 47 percent,[96] and it was lower than that for the cases that the regional capital defenders (as opposed to retained or court-appointed defenders) handled—four of ten is just 40 percent.

Even the four death sentences attributed to the regional capital defenders is a bit of an overstatement. One of those four death sentences was reversed on appeal based on the improper exclusion of mitigating evidence.[97] On remand, the prosecutor announced that he would not seek death,[98] so four death sentences became three—and three became two when the governor commuted another of those death sentences after it was discovered that prosecutors used (to quote the governor) "false information, plain and simple" to convince the jury to return a sentence of death.[99] That left just *two* death sentences of the more than 250 cases that the capital defenders handled, and in one of those two, the regional capital defenders were only partly involved in the case.[100]

To be sure, this astounding figure was not entirely due to mitigation; the regional capital defenders litigated these cases to the hilt in a number of ways.[101] But as capital defenders themselves attested, mitigation was the key to winning at trial, which meant mitigation played a key role in keeping cases from going to trial in the first place. Here is what one regional capital defender had to say:

> The prosecutor shows the jury our client's worst day of his life. We try to show the jury all the other days. We're not trying to excuse the conduct. We're trying to explain it—to help the jury understand why a defendant did what they did, and to use that understanding to make the case for life. . . .
>
> If you want to know where the capital defender offices had the most impact, where our involvement made the biggest difference in

178 / Corinna Barrett Lain

terms of ending the death penalty in Virginia, it was here. The biggest thing we did was stop death sentences, and we did that mostly by stopping those cases from going to trial. Trial is bad for capital defendants. Around half the time, the jury comes back with death. So, job one was keeping those cases from going to trial, at least if the case was going to come down to sentencing. . . .

It is hard to overstate how important it was that prosecutors were losing some of the cases that they took to trial. It made them look bad when they asked for death and didn't get it, despite all their time and effort. They started getting worried that they could lose, and that created an opening for us to deal the case. It's hard to say, but it's also possible that they were affected by the same mitigating evidence that we were preparing to submit to the jury. . . . It's easy to ask for death if you think the defendant is pure evil. It's a little harder if you come to conclude that the person never had a chance from the start.[102]

Gregg's guided-discretion scheme may have revived the death penalty, but it also provided a key weapon for killing the death penalty by saving lives one capital case at a time.

Differences Underlying the Decline in Executions

In some ways, the reason for the low number of executions then and now is quite similar. In both the pre-*Furman* and modern eras, postconviction litigation has kept death sentences from being carried out—back then because of the unofficial moratorium it created, and in the modern era, because of the sheer time it takes for a capital case to wind its way through the postconviction review process and the growing reversal rate as it does.[103] Thus, both then and now, one might accurately attribute low execution numbers to the fact of capital litigation itself.

But even when that is not the case—even when courts have given states the green light to execute—a new problem has kept states from doing so: the inability to get lethal injection drugs. In the pre-*Furman* era, this was not a problem because lethal injection did not exist. States did not start adopting lethal injection as an execution method until 1977, and even then, there were no problems acquiring lethal injection drugs until 2009, when a shortage of the raw ingredients needed to produce sodium thiopental (the all-important first drug in the traditional three-drug protocol) first slowed and then halted production of the drug.[104]

But while an upstream supply-side shortage was holding up production, another development would prove to be even more consequential. The sole domestic producer of sodium thiopental was a company called Hospira, and in 2010, an FDA inspection of Hospira's aging plant in North Carolina revealed numerous deficiencies that would need to be addressed.[105] Hospira decided that the better move was to relocate its operation to a production plant in Italy, and that is when the real trouble for executing states began.

Italy, like other European nations, is staunchly opposed to the death penalty, and refused to license Hospira's plant without a guarantee that the drugs made there would not be used in executions.[106] Hospira decided that the easiest way to comply with this demand was to stop producing sodium thiopental altogether, stating in a January 2011 press release that "we cannot take the risk that we will be held liable by the Italian authorities if the product is diverted for use in capital punishment."[107] With that, the sole domestic supplier of the all-important first drug in the three-drug lethal injection protocol exited the market.

States scrambled to get sodium thiopental anywhere they could, borrowing from each other and buying bulk quantities of the drug from sketchy sources abroad (consider, for example, Dream Pharma, a pharmaceutical distributor that turned out to be nothing more than two desks and a file cabinet in the back of a London driving school).[108] States also turned to substitute drugs—pentobarbital at first, then others—in a desperate attempt to get their execution chambers up and running again.[109]

The fallout of Hospira's exit revealed a weakness in the lethal injection enterprise, and that had cascading effects of its own. The European Union, which had been trying for decades to get the United States to see the error of its executing ways, discovered that the best way to stop the American death penalty was to stop equipping states with execution drugs. In 2011, the EU adopted strict export controls on drugs associated with lethal injection, requiring authorities to halt the export of any drug that they had "reasonable grounds" to believe would be used in executions.[110] That prevented states from buying drugs for lethal injection from any of Europe's Big Pharma suppliers, while FDA import controls prevented states from buying drugs from gray-market suppliers in other countries.[111] States had no choice but to turn to the domestic market for the supply of lethal injection drugs.

This created its own headaches for executing states as abolitionists seized on the opportunity to put the squeeze on domestic drug suppliers. A prime example is the U.K.-based organization Reprieve, which launched SLIP—the Stop Lethal Injection Project—in a concerted campaign to get major pharmaceutical companies to take steps of their own to keep their products from being used in executions.[112] Turns out, those companies were not willing partners in the execution enterprise in the first place; states were just capitalizing on lax drug distribution systems to make purchases for purposes that the companies did not condone. As the Danish pharmaceutical company Lundbeck stated upon learning that its drugs were being used for executions, "We invent and develop medicine with the aim of alleviating people's burden. This is the direct opposite of that . . . It's against everything we stand for."[113]

By all (abolitionist) accounts, SLIP has been a smashing success. One by one, major pharmaceutical companies have adopted strict distribution systems and end-user agreements to keep their products out of executioners' hands. The most recent is Pfizer, an American pharmaceutical giant whose slogan is "Life is our life's work."[114] *That's* potentially awkward. In 2016, Pfizer adopted measures to control the downstream distribution of its drugs, becoming the last domestic drug manufacturer to do so.[115] "With Pfizer's announcement, all FDA-approved manufacturers of any potential execution drug have now blocked their sale for this purpose," Reprieve stated in response to the announcement.[116] The supply side of the market for lethal injection drugs had just become even smaller.

In response, states have turned to grossly underregulated compounding pharmacies, which are now the primary supplier of lethal injection drugs because no one else is left. Compounding pharmacies create customized versions of FDA-approved drugs for those who cannot take medicines in their commercially manufactured form.[117] They are typically small local businesses, often selling gifts and curio items on the side, and they are uniquely situated to provide a single dose of a drug made to order—just what states need for a given execution at a given time.

As the last supplier standing, compounding pharmacies have likewise been targeted by abolitionist activists, who have written letters, made calls, posted on social media, and picketed stores that have sold drugs for lethal injection.[118] This is the "guerilla war against the death penalty" (also known as the exercise of free speech) that is apparently driving Justice Samuel Alito nuts,[119] and the reason is that it works. Consider, for example, Greenpark Compounding Pharmacy and Gifts, the Houston compounding pharmacy that supplied Texas with lethal injection drugs—that is, until it was outed for its sales and withdrew as a supplier.[120] Indeed, the sheer effectiveness of these tactics is the reason that states have passed a slew of secrecy laws to protect the identity of their lethal injection drug suppliers.[121]

Today, every possible supply line of Big Pharma drugs has been more or less cut off, and even compounding pharmacies have grown increasingly wary of lending a helping hand. "I can no more flap my arms and fly across the state than I can carry out an execution," one attorney general stated in 2012[122]—and what was true then is even more true today. States cannot get the drugs they need for lethal injection, and the ripple effects of that predicament are creating delays at every turn—delays to find a willing supplier, delays to fight a myriad of lawsuits, and delays to quell public outrage because when botched executions occur, putting executions on hold is the only publicly acceptable thing to do.

Now states are exhausted and thinking about new ways to execute—old ones too. Nitrogen gas, firing squads, and the electric chair are all on the table, and as South Carolina's recent experience has shown, any attempt to move to a new execution method will likely have destabilizing effects of its own.[123] The abolition movement today is about wearing states down—making the death penalty more trouble than it is worth. And it is working.

Flipping the Abolition Script

Understanding what is happening in the trenches helps us understand why eight states—including Virginia, the former capital of the Confederacy—have legislatively abolished the death penalty in the last fifteen years.[124] Death sentences are increasingly hard to come by, and executions are practically impossible for all but the most committed states. Meanwhile, costs continue to mount.

Herein lies today's abolitionism. States are not abandoning capital punishment because they have awakened to the moral depravity of the government killing its own citizens with people filing into a room to watch. They are abandoning capital punishment because keeping it no longer makes sense. The death penalty is breathtakingly expensive, and we do not get much bang for buck. As David McCord writes, capital punishment is what those in the consumer protection field would call a "lemon."[125]

States themselves have made clear that the cost of capital punishment, and what they were getting in return, was an important part of their decision to abolish the death penalty. Illinois reported that it had spent some $100 million on the death penalty in the ten years prior to its abolition in 2011 and had executed no one during that time.[126] New York estimated that it spent $170 million on the death penalty in the modern era, and New Jersey estimated that it spent $253 million—and neither of those states had a single execution to show for it.[127] New Mexico, Connecticut, Colorado, and Maryland all had a similar story to tell; high costs and a host of problems made retaining the death penalty untenable.[128] So they decided to let it go.

Because the cost calculus is not only what states pay to maintain their capital punishment systems, but also what they get in return, calculations of the cost of the death penalty today are frequently expressed in terms of cost per execution.[129] In California, which maintains the largest death row in the country and has spent $5 billion on the death penalty in the modern era but executed just thirteen people during that time, calculating cost this way produces an astronomical figure—$384 million per execution.[130] In Florida, which has a much smaller death row and a much larger number of executions, the cost comes to a more modest $24 million per execution.[131] Either way, the price tag is take-your-breath-away high.

Granted, for diehard death penalty states like Texas and Oklahoma, these costs are unlikely to make a difference. Money is no object for those who believe that killing killers is the right thing to do. But for many states today, what the death penalty costs, and what states get in return, *does* matter. Money is its own morality. For these states, the only fiscally responsible thing to do is to end the death penalty, and spend the public fisc on more worthy endeavors.

This brings us to how the modern era has flipped the script. In *Furman*, the case for Supreme Court intervention rested largely on legislative failure. A handful of states had abolished the death penalty, but many more had not, and in the South, where the death penalty's application was most problematic, there was reason to believe that states never would. As the talented Anthony Amsterdam explained at oral argument,

> The penalty remains on the statute books only to be—and because it is—rarely and unusually inflicted. . . . There is nothing in the political process by which public opinion manifests itself in legislated laws that protects the isolated individual from being cruelly treated by the state. . . . Legislatures neither must nor do take account of such individuals.[132]

The death penalty was tolerated only because of its sporadic use, Amsterdam argued, "sterilizing the ordinary political processes that keep . . . legislation reflective of the public conscience."[133] When it came to the death penalty, the democratic process was like a turtle on its back—it was stuck and needed the Supreme Court's help to get righted again.

We know this claim was persuasive in *Furman* because a number of the justices talked about it. Justice White wrote that the "past and present legislative judgment with respect to the death penalty loses much of its force when viewed in light of the recurring practice of delegating sentencing authority to the jury," and juries were refusing to return a sentence of death.[134] Justice Marshall wrote that the death penalty's sporadic and discriminatory use "undercuts the argument that since the legislature is the voice of the people, its retention of capital punishment must represent the will of the people."[135] And even Justice Lewis Powell, who dissented in the case, lamented in conference that "our legislative guardians have abdicated their responsibilities, hoping that this Court would take the problem off of their backs."[136] In *Furman*, the justices stepped in because they were convinced that by and large, state legislatures would not.

Today's abolition story is exactly the opposite. Today's story features the justices bending over backwards to facilitate the death penalty's operation in every way. When it comes to lethal injection, for example, anything goes.

Short of states "superadding" pain to their execution methods—going out of their way to torture inmates (which nobody does anymore, and even if they did, who would admit it?)—a majority of the Supreme Court has concluded that the Eighth Amendment has nothing to say about how inmates are executed.[137] And when lower courts have put a pause on executions to merely consider an inmate's lethal injection challenge, the Court has used the shadow docket to lift the stay, without argument or explanation, sometimes even in the dead of night.[138] We can fault the justices in *Furman* for being tepid and uncommitted, but a majority of today's justices are aggressively pro-death—despite their Catholic precommitments to the contrary, as Sara Mayeux discusses in her chapter.[139] So much for being pro-life.

Yet even a decidedly bloodthirsty Supreme Court can do nothing to stop the death penalty's seemingly inexorable demise (much to the justices' chagrin) because abolition today is coming from the bottom up rather than the top down. What Anthony Amsterdam said about legislatures not being responsive to those without power or political clout may still be true, but today's abolition movement is founded on something that state legislatures *are* responsive to—exorbitant costs with miniscule returns. Abolition today is happening at the state level, and it is happening not because of the justices but despite them. One by one, the sister states are doing what the Supreme Court would not. As Aretha Franklin would say, sisters are doin' it for themselves.[140]

To show just how flipped the script is at this point in time, I pause for a moment to consider Carol and Jordan Steiker's article "Abolition in Our Time."[141] "Abolition in Our Time" is a particularly apt point of reference on the fiftieth anniversary of *Furman*, because although it was published in 2003, it imagines what the death penalty landscape might look like fifty years after *Furman*. "It is 2022," the opening line reads.[142] *How fun.*

In the article, the Steikers creatively offer one possibility of the future in the form of a hypothetical Supreme Court case considering the constitutionality of the death penalty at the federal level and in three states—Texas, Virginia, and Florida.[143] In 2003, it was simply unfathomable that Virginia would not even have the death penalty in 2022. Virginia was a reliable death penalty stronghold.

In their hypothetical case, the Steikers consider a number of arguments that might form the basis of a constitutional challenge to the death penalty in 2022. Ultimately, they focus on the claim that the death penalty is inconsistent with the nation's "prevailing standards of decency."[144] If only the Steikers had known just how strong that argument would be in 2022—and ironically, just how unlikely the Supreme Court would be to accept it!

In the Steikers' hypothetical world, thirty-three states still have the death penalty, and executions have fallen to just over fifty per year.[145] The majority and dissent spar over whether the drop in executions shows that society has turned against the death penalty, with the dissent pointing to a number of alternative explanations for the low execution rate.[146] A shortage of lethal injection drugs is not on the list. In 2003, when the Steikers' article was published, it was simply unfathomable that states would be given the green light to execute but lack the supplies to get it done.

Most interesting is the epilogue to the article, where the Steikers talk to their readers directly. "The route to nation-wide abolition in the United States is almost certainly through constitutional litigation in the courts rather than through state-by-state legislative abolition," they write, noting "the much greater resistance to abolition through the political branches of government."[147] At the time, they were undoubtedly right. What a difference twenty years makes.

To be clear, my point here is not about Carol and Jordan Steiker's ability to predict the future. After all, I too left my crystal ball at home. (For the record, even now I think they were right about nationwide abolition coming from courts rather than state legislatures, as some states will likely never let the death penalty go.) My point here is to show how utterly unimaginable this moment in time is—and was even twenty years ago. All that remains now is to show the role that *Furman* played in getting us here.

How *Furman*'s Failure Contributed to Today's Abolition Movement Success

Thus far, the story I have told has separated today's abolition movement from the one that came before it. But the abolition movements of yesterday and today are not as separate as I have suggested. In this part, I connect the two movements, exploring the *Furman*'s contributions to today's abolition success.

Furman's *Lesson*

Furman's first contribution to today's abolition movement is a lesson: aim low. *Furman* was a failure on its own terms. The justices thought they were ending the death penalty, but instead their ruling played a key role in reinvigorating it. Indeed, *Furman* set in motion one of the most dramatic legislative backlashes that the nation had ever seen.[148]

This is not to say that *Furman* was solely responsible for the backlash that followed. After all, the country had already turned sharply conservative on criminal justice issues by the late 1960s, and the nation's renewed support for capital punishment may also have reflected rising crime rates between 1972 and 1976.[149] But as I have discussed elsewhere, crime rates had risen before *Furman* as well, with little to no effect on death penalty support, and the crime rate actually dropped in 1976, while support for the death penalty skyrocketed.[150] Moreover, crime had begun to occupy the public consciousness as early as 1966, when public opinion polls named it as the second most important domestic problem and President Johnson issued a special message to Congress on the issue.[151] Yet as already noted, the year 1966 marked the lowest level of death penalty support in recorded history, and even in the years immediately preceding *Furman*, when the country was awash in crime-control rhetoric, support for the death penalty was barely 50 percent.[152]

All this is to say that other factors may have played a part in the backlash to *Furman*—history is always a complex smattering of a number of contingencies—but the clearest cause of the backlash was the *Furman* decision itself. "In a curious way, [*Furman*] has had the opposite effect of what many who favor abolishing the death penalty had hoped," *The New York Times* wrote in 1973, the year after the case was decided.[153] Similarly, *The Nation* observed in 1973 that *Furman*'s chief effect was a "retrogression" of death penalty support.[154] As contemporary commentators saw it, the problem was not that the justices in *Furman* had misread the tide of public opinion; the problem was that they had unwittingly turned it. Instead of settling the death penalty debate, *Furman* galvanized those who were losing it, mobilizing death penalty supporters and tapping into nearly two decades of bitterness and hostility that had been building in Southern states since the Supreme Court's decision in *Brown*.

The rest, as they say, is history. In the wake of *Furman*, thirty-five states passed new death penalty statutes, public support for the death penalty rebounded, and death sentences surged, hitting the highest year-end figure ever recorded (at least at that time).[155] When the Supreme Court revisited the death penalty's constitutionality four years later in *Gregg*, the death penalty was substantially stronger, and the Court's commitment to *Furman*'s values substantially weaker. The Court was gone when abolitionists needed it the most—hence the lesson to aim low (as if today's abolitionists have a choice!).

Furman's *Cascading Effects*

Furman's second contribution to the modern abolition movement lies in its cascading effects. *Furman*'s backlash gave rise to *Gregg*, and *Gregg* too was a failure on its own terms. In *Gregg*, the Supreme Court tried to tame the death penalty by regulating it, and guided-discretion statutes were the way to make that happen. But guided-discretion statutes raised more questions than they answered, and those questions became a slew of challenges that came to the Supreme Court for resolution. By one unofficial count, the Court

186 / Corinna Barrett Lain

issued over eighty opinions in capital cases between 1976 and 1995—roughly four per year in the first two decades of the modern death penalty era.[156]

By way of sheer numbers, it at least *looked* like the Supreme Court was making good on its promise to take special care when the penalty was death.[157] But as studies showed (and as Carol and Jordan Steiker have written about elsewhere), the Court's regulatory project was largely a façade—over 90 percent of those sentenced to death before *Gregg* were just as death eligible afterward.[158] The only difference in the cases was the complexity.

Yet that complexity had cascading effects of its own. Complexity required lawyers—lawyers to litigate the myriad of questions that the Supreme Court's regulatory project raised, and lawyers to try the increasingly complex capital cases. Both gave rise to a specialized capital defense bar that over time became skilled in harnessing the law's complexity and making it work for them. From investigation to mitigation to voir dire to pre- and post-trial motions and collateral review—even lethal injection litigation, as Carol and Jordan Steiker note in their chapter in this book[159]—these newfangled capital defense lawyers left no stone unturned and no legal argument overlooked. They mounted a vigorous defense, negotiated the case when they could, fought tooth and nail at sentencing, and sought reversal of death sentences and off-ramps to executions everywhere they could. They became the foot soldiers of today's abolition movement, killing the death penalty by saving one life at a time.

None of this is to suggest that capital defense today is a panacea. States with the most executions still don't have statewide specialized capital defender offices, and although some court-appointed capital defense attorneys are superb, some are downright terrible—so terrible, in fact, that even a Supreme Court disinclined to overturn death sentences has seen fit to reverse on grounds of ineffective assistance of counsel in case after capital case.[160]

Still, the larger point remains: *Furman* may have been a failure on its own terms, but it inadvertently set in motion the developments that would prove critical to today's abolition success. *Furman* led to *Gregg*, and *Gregg* ratified guided-discretion statutes, legitimating the death penalty and ushering in an era of renewed commitment to state killing. That was a tragedy, to be sure, but the story didn't end there. The next chapter saw the very lawyers who were forged from that tragedy beating the state at its own game. Guided-discretion statutes gave rise to complexity, and complexity gave rise to specialized capital defense attorneys, who figured out how to make guided discretion work for them. The preeminence of mitigation as a modern capital defense strategy has changed the landscape of capital litigation and shrunk the footprint of the death penalty. And that's not just a Virginia story. In 2022, for example, mitigation was the key to saving what many saw as an unsavable defendant's life in the Parkland school shooting case, a mass

shooting in Florida that took the lives of seventeen people, including fourteen students.[161] *Furman* turned abolition from a top-down affair to a movement from the bottom up and set in motion the means to make it successful.
That's not all bad for a failure on its own terms.

Conclusion

The modern path to abolition is not without its downsides. Gone is the day
when one Supreme Court ruling can save over six hundred lives.[162] Today,
states continue to kill in our name, and gross injustices remain. But abolition is once again on the horizon, and this time it is coming from the states
themselves. The upside to states ending the death penalty because it is their
best move, and not because the Supreme Court said so, is that this time when
the death penalty dies, it may well stay dead for good.

NOTES

Many thanks to Jim Gibson, Danielle Stokes, and my fellow symposium participants
for their comments on an earlier draft, and to Joanie Fasulo for her excellent research
assistance in preparing this chapter for publication.

1. Furman v. Georgia, 408 U.S. 238 (1972).

2. Prominent examples include Engel v. Vitale, 370 U.S. 421 (1962) (invalidating state-
sponsored prayer in public schools); Roe v. Wade, 410 U.S. 113 (1973) (recognizing the
right to abortion); Brown v. Board of Education, 347 U.S. 483 (1954) (invalidating de jure
segregation in public schools).

3. Gregg v. Georgia, 428 U.S. 153 (1976).

4. Bessler, this volume.

5. "The Dying Death Penalty," *Time*, February 17, 1967, 50; "Killing the Death Penalty," *Time*, July 7, 1967, 47 ("By inches, the death penalty is dying in the U.S.").

6. "Death Sentence for Manson Clan, But," *U.S. News and World Report*, April 12, 1971,
26 ("Sentiment to abolish the death penalty altogether appears to be growing throughout the United States"); "Signs of an End to 'Death Row,'" *U.S. News and World Report*,
May 31, 1971, 37 ("Now a nationwide drive to do away with the death penalty is gaining
momentum"); "No Work for the Hangman," *The Nation*, January 27, 1969, 101–2 (noting growing opposition to the death penalty despite public concern over crime in the
streets).

7. Del Dickson, *The Supreme Court in Conference, 1940–1985: The Private Discussions behind Nearly 300 Supreme Court Decisions* (Oxford: Oxford University Press,
2001), 617 (reporting Justice Stewart's comments in conference).

8. *Furman*, 408 U.S. at 313 (White, J., concurring).

9. Dickson, *Supreme Court in Conference*, 618 (reporting Justice Stewart's comments
in conference).

10. Walter C. Reckless, "The Use of the Death Penalty: A Factual Statement," in *Capital Punishment*, ed. James A. McCafferty (Chicago: Aldine-Atherton, 1974), 51 (charting
executions from 1930 through 1970).

11. *Id.*

12. *Id.*

188 / Corinna Barrett Lain

13. *Id.*

14. *Id.*

15. Corinna Barrett Lain, "*Furman* Fundamentals," *Washington Law Review* 82 (2007): 20.

16. *Id.* at 20–22.

17. *Id.* at 22, nn. 105–6.

18. According to *Urban Dictionary*, "the title of the series [*The Walking Dead*] does not (only) refer to the actual zombies. The title mostly refers to the group of survivors, as they are walking around but are as good as dead." "The Walking Dead," *Urban Dictionary*, accessed October 21, 2022, https://www.urbandictionary.com/define.php?term=The%20Walking%20Dead.

19. Stuart Banner, *The Death Penalty: An American History* (Cambridge, MA: Harvard University Press, 2002), 244.

20. Lain, "*Furman* Fundamentals," 18.

21. *Id.*

22. Witherspoon v. Illinois, 391 U.S. 510 (1968).

23. President's Commission on Law Enforcement and the Administration of Justice, *The Challenge of Crime in a Free Society* (1967), 143, https://www.ojp.gov/ncjrs/virtual-library/abstracts/challenge-crime-free-society.

24. Lain, "*Furman* Fundamentals," 19.

25. *Id.*

26. *Id.*

27. *Id.*

28. *Id.* at 21.

29. *Id.* at 19.

30. *Id.*

31. *Id.* at 21.

32. *Id.* at 25.

33. *Id.* at 26.

34. *Id.*

35. *Id.* at 28.

36. *Id.*

37. *Id.*

38. *Id.*

39. *Witherspoon*, 391 U.S. at 520.

40. Lain, "*Furman* Fundamentals," 31.

41. *Id.*

42. *Id.* at 37.

43. *Id.* at 33. For the Republican Party platform of 1972, see the American Presidency Project, at https://www.presidency.ucsb.edu/documents/republican-party-platform-1972.

44. Lain, "*Furman* Fundamentals," 25.

45. President's Commission on Law Enforcement, *Challenge of Crime*, 143 ("The death sentence is disproportionately imposed and carried out on the poor, the Negro, and the members of unpopular groups").

46. *Furman*, 408 U.S. at 249–50 (Douglas, J., concurring) ("The death sentence is disproportionately imposed and carried out on the poor, the Negro, and the members of unpopular groups") (internal citation omitted); *id.* at 365–66 (Marshall, J., concurring) ("It also is evident that the burden of capital punishment falls upon the poor, the

ignorant, and the underprivileged members of society. It is the poor, and the members of minority groups who are least able to voice their complaints against capital punishment."); *id.* at 310 (Stewart, J., concurring) ("If any basis can be discerned for the selection of these few to be sentenced to die, it is the constitutionally impermissible basis of race").

47. Philip Kurland, "1971 Term: The Year of the Stewart-White Court," *Supreme Court Review* 1972, no. 181 (1972): 297.

48. Lain, "*Furman* Fundamentals," 36.

49. David Von Drehle, "The Death of the Death Penalty: Why the Era of Capital Punishment Is Ending," *Time*, June 8, 2015, https://time.com/deathpenalty/.

50. Scott Bland, "Is the Death Penalty Dying?," *National Journal*, September 30, 2022, https://www.nationaljournal.com/s/62088/; Bill Clutter, "Death Penalty's Dying Days," *Illinois Times*, November 21, 2012, https://www.illinoistimes.com/springfield/death-penaltys-dying-days/Content?oid=11448945e; Rebecca Kesby, "Is the Death Penalty Dying Out in the US?," BBC News, June 8, 2015, https://www.bbc.com/news/world-us-canada-33006105; Chelsea Follett, "Despite Federal Return, Capital Punishment Is Dying Out," Cato Institute, July 29, 2019, https://www.cato.org/blog/despite-federal-return-capital-punishment-dying-out; Stephen Reeves, "The Death Penalty Is Dying a Slow Death; It's Time We Pulled the Plug," *Baptist News Global*, January 27, 2021, https://baptistnews.com/article/the-death-penalty-is-dying-a-slow-death-its-time-we-pull-the-plug/#.Yy2kvHbMI2w.

51. Carol S. Steiker and Jordan M. Steiker, "Entrenchment and/or Destabilization? Reflections on (Another) Two Decades of Constitutional Regulation of Capital Punishment," *Law and Inequality* 30 (2012): 213; Jordan Steiker, "The American Death Penalty from a Consequentialist Perspective," *Texas Tech Law Review* 47 (1995): 214; Matt Watkins, "How Will the Death Penalty End?," Center for Court Innovation, March 2021, https://www.courtinnovation.org/publications/let-the-lord-sort.

52. Death Penalty Information Center [hereinafter DPIC], *Facts about the Death Penalty*, accessed October 21, 2022, https://documents.deathpenaltyinfo.org/pdf/FactSheet.pdf.

53. *Id.*

54. *Id.*

55. Lain, "*Furman* Fundamentals," 20. The decline from the 1940s (128 executions on average) to 1962 (47 executions) is 63 percent.

56. "Death Sentences in the United States Since 1977," DPIC, accessed October 21, 2022, https://deathpenaltyinfo.org/facts-and-research/sentencing-data/death-sentences-in-the-united-states-from-1977-by-state-and-by-year.

57. *Id.*

58. *Id.*

59. "State by State: States with and without the Death Penalty—2021," DPIC, accessed October 21, 2022, https://deathpenaltyinfo.org/state-and-federal-info/state-by-state. For Nebraska's story, see "State and Federal Info: Nebraska," DPIC, accessed October 21, 2022, https://deathpenaltyinfo.org/state-and-federal-info/state-by-state/nebraska.

60. DPIC, "State by State." For an excellent discussion of the role of state courts in today's abolition movement, see generally Carol S. Steiker and Jordan M. Steiker, "Little *Furmans* Everywhere: State Court Intervention and the Decline of the American Death Penalty," *Cornell Law Review* 107, no. 6 (2022).

61. DPIC, "State by State." In December 2022, Oregon's governor commuted all death sentences in the state to life without parole. Hillary Borrud, "Gov. Kate Brown Com-

mutes Sentences of All 17 People on Oregon's Death Row," *Oregonian*, December 13, 2022.

62. Megan Brenan, "Steady 55% of Americans Support Death Penalty for Murderers," *Gallup*, November 14, 2022, https://news.gallup.com/poll/404975/steady-americans-support-death-penalty-murderers.aspx.

63. *Id.*

64. *Id.*

65. Audra D. S. Burch et al., "How Black Lives Matter Reached Every Corner of America," *New York Times*, June 13, 2020, https://www.nytimes.com/interactive/2020/06/13/us/george-floyd-protests-cities-photos.html.

66. Movement for Black Lives Platform, "End the War on Black People," accessed October 21, 2022, https://m4bl.org/end-the-war-on-black-people/. For an excellent discussion, see Michael Cholbi and Alex Madva, "Black Lives Matter and the Call for Death Penalty Abolition," *Ethics* 128 (2018): 517.

67. J. Steiker, "American Death Penalty," 214; Watkins, "How Will the Death Penalty End?"

68. C. Steiker and Steiker, "Entrenchment," 240 (noting that jurors' reluctance to return a death sentence, along with other developments, "has radically altered the calculus of prosecutors, who have sought death sentences much more frequently over the past years, sending the absolute number of death sentences to modern-era lows").

69. Robert Weisberg, "Deregulating Death," *Supreme Court Review* 1983 (1983): 363 (quoting pre-*Furman* jury instructions).

70. Although the focus of capital trials in the pre-*Furman* era was undoubtedly the guilt phase of trial, it is almost certainly the case that the low 10–20 percent death sentencing rate was not because juries were refusing to convict. If accused capital murderers were being acquitted 80–90 percent of the time, surely that would have been a topic of conversation in the contemporary discourse. It is possible that residual doubt was playing a role in the low death sentencing rate in the pre-*Furman* era, but this brings me back to the point: it is just impossible to know precisely why juries were refusing to impose death in any given case.

71. *Gregg*, 428 U.S. at 206–7 ("No longer can a jury wantonly and freakishly impose the death sentence. . . . It is always circumscribed by the legislative guidelines").

72. C. Steiker and Steiker, "Entrenchment," 231–32.

73. *Id.* at 232.

74. C. Steiker and Steiker, this volume.

75. "1989 Guidelines for the Appointment and Performance of Counsel in Death Penalty Cases," American Bar Association, accessed October 21, 2022, https://www.americanbar.org/groups/committees/death_penalty_representation/resources/aba_guidelines/1989-guidelines/.

76. Williams v. Taylor, 529 U.S. 362 (2000).

77. Brandon L. Garrett, "The Decline of the Virginia (and American) Death Penalty," *Georgetown Law Journal* 105 (2017): 676.

78. Corinna Barrett Lain and Douglas A. Ramseur, "Disrupting Death: How Specialized Capital Defenders Ground Virginia's Machinery of Death to a Halt," *University of Richmond Law Review* 56 (2021): 243. The attorney failed to request social services records, failed to get mental health experts, failed to return the call of a potential character witness, and failed to present the testimony of prison officials, who by the time of trial had awarded Williams two commendations for his exemplary behavior.

79. Wiggins v. Smith, 539 U.S. 510 (2003) (reversing for ineffective assistance of counsel based on counsel's failure to adequately investigate mitigating evidence); Rompilla v. Beard, 545 U.S. 374 (2005) (same); Porter v. McCollum, 558 U.S. 30 (2009) (same); Sears v. Upton, 561 U.S. 945 (2010) (same); Andrus v. Texas, 140 S. Ct. 1875 (2020) (same).

80. "2003 Guidelines for the Appointment and Performance of Counsel in Death Penalty Cases," American Bar Association, accessed October 21, 2022, https://www.americanbar.org/groups/committees/death_penalty_representation/resources/aba_guidelines/ (providing guidelines and links to states that have adopted them).

81. C. Steiker and Steiker, this volume; Carol S. Steiker and Jordan M. Steiker, "Costs and Capital Punishment: A New Consideration Transforms an Old Debate," *University of Chicago Legal Forum* (2010): 139.

82. DPIC, "State Studies on Monetary Costs," accessed October 21, 2022, https://deathpenaltyinfo.org/policy-issues/costs/summary-of-states-death-penalty.

83. *Id.*

84. For an extended discussion of the point, see Lain and Ramseur, "Disrupting Death," 203–29.

85. For an extended discussion of the point, see *id.*

86. *Id.* at 187.

87. *Id.* at 303–6.

88. *Id.* at 245–46. I'd like to say that the exoneration of Earl Washington in 2000 also had an effect, but I'm skeptical. Although Washington's exoneration drew national attention, and poor capital defense was part of the reason he was falsely convicted in the first place, the Virginia General Assembly's miserly approach to capital defense suggests that it was more concerned with making death sentences stick than with preventing the occasional wrongful conviction. After all, DNA testing first excluded Washington back in 1993, which is how he was able to secure a commutation to a life sentence, but in 1993, Virginia was nowhere near creating dedicated offices for capital defense. For a deeper discussion, I recommend Margaret Edds's excellent book *An Expendable Man: The Near-Execution of Earl Washington, Jr.* (New York: New York University Press, 2003).

89. Lain and Ramseur, "Disrupting Death," 245.

90. *Id.*

91. *Id.* at 246.

92. John G. Douglass, "Death as a Bargaining Chip: Plea Bargaining and the Future of Virginia's Death Penalty," *University of Richmond Law Review* 49 (2015): 885; Lain and Ramseur, "Disrupting Death," 295. (Quoting Doug Ramseur, former capital defender, as saying, "There is this impression out there that capital indictments were slowing down, and the death penalty was fading away. That was not what was happening, at least not until the very end. It was not that capital indictments were slowing down; it was that we were pleading them more. That's why Virginia did not have any death sentences. We were pleading almost all of those cases for something less.")

93. Lain and Ramseur, "Disrupting Death," 250.

94. *Id.*

95. *Id.* at 249 (discussing figures from the 2013 ABA Virginia Death Penalty Assessment Report).

96. *Id.* (discussing figures from the 2013 ABA Virginia Death Penalty Assessment Report and a 2015 study by Brandon Garrett).

97. *Id.* at 250.

98. *Id.*

99. *Id.* at 251.

100. *Id.* at 250, 280–89 (discussing partial involvement in Ricky Gray case).

101. For an extended discussion, see *id.* at 253–99.

102. *Id.* at 260, 296–97 (quoting Doug Ramseur).

103. James S. Liebman et al., "Capital Attrition: Error Rates in Capital Cases, 1973–1995," *Texas Law Review* 78 (2000): 1839 (reporting an average reversal rate for capital cases of 68 percent).

104. Emma Marris, "Death-Row Drug Dilemma," *Nature News*, January 27, 2011, https://www.nature.com/articles/news.2011.53. ("For some time, all the sodium thiopental in the United States has come from a drug company called Hospira, based in Lake Forest, Illinois. In the summer of 2009, Hospira had to suspend the production of the drug. The company that made the active ingredient—which Hospira would not name, but US Food and Drug Administration (FDA) records identify as Abbott Laboratories—stopped making it.")

105. This is a story more fully detailed and documented in James Gibson and Corinna Barrett Lain, "Death Penalty Drugs and the International Moral Marketplace," *Georgetown Law Journal* 103 (2015): 1223.

106. *Id.* at 1240.

107. *Id.* at 1241 (quoting Hospira, Inc., "Hospira Statement Regarding Pentothal [Sodium Thiopental] Market Exit," January 21, 2011).

108. A picture speaks a thousand words. For the visual, see "London Firm Supplied Drugs Used for US Lethal Injections," *The Guardian*, January 6, 2011, https://www.theguardian.com/world/2011/jan/06/london-firm-drugs-us-lethal-injections.

109. Gibson and Lain, "Death Penalty Drugs," 1227–30.

110. Comm'n Implementing Reg. 1252/2011 of Dec. 20, 2011, amending Council Regulation (EC) No. 1236/2005 Concerning Trade in Certain Goods Which Could Be Used for Capital Punishment, Torture, or Other Cruel, Inhuman or Degrading Treatment or Punishment, 2011 O.J. (L 338) 31.

111. Gibson and Lain, "Death Penalty Drugs," 1225–26. For a frightening look at who these gray-market suppliers are, see Chris McDaniel, "This Is the Man in India Who Is Selling States Illegally Imported Execution Drugs," *BuzzFeed News*, October 20, 2015, https://www.buzzfeednews.com/article/chrismcdaniel/this-is-the-man-in-india-who-is-selling-states-illegally-imp.

112. Mary D. Fan, "The Supply-Side Attack on Lethal Injection and the Rise of Execution Secrecy," *Boston University Law Review* 95 (2015): 439 (discussing SLIP); "Helping Pharmaceutical Companies Stop Their Medicines Being Used to Kill," Reprieve, February 9, 2017, https://reprieve.org/us/2017/02/09/helping-pharmaceutical-companies-stop-medicines-used-kill/.

113. Rob Stein, "Ohio Executes Inmate Using New, Single-Drug Method for Death Penalty," *Washington Post*, March 11, 2011 (quoting Lundbeck spokesperson).

114. "Pfizer," Slogan List, accessed October 21, 2022, https://www.sloganlist.com/plug/search.asp?key=Pfizer.

115. Erik Eckholm, "Pfizer Blocks the Use of Its Drugs in Executions," *New York Times*, May 13, 2016, https://www.nytimes.com/2016/05/14/us/pfizer-execution-drugs-lethal-injection.html?searchResultPosition=1.

116. *Id.*

117. To quote the FDA, drug compounding is a process that "combines, mixes, or alters ingredients of a drug to create a medication tailored to the needs of an individual patient." "Human Drug Compounding," Food and Drug Administration, accessed

October 21, 2022, https://www.fda.gov/drugs/guidance-compliance-regulatory-infor
mation/human-drug-compounding. Compounding pharmacies are like regular pharmacies—they are in the business of filling prescriptions—they just do it in a tailor-made
way. 21 U.S.C. § 353a (2012) (requiring a valid prescription by a licensed practitioner for
dispensing of compounded drugs).

118. Keri Blakinger, "'Struggling with It Ever Since': Former Texas Lethal Injection Drug
Supplier Speaks Out," *Houston Chronicle*, May 3, 2019, https://www.houstonchronicle
.com/news/houston-texas/houston/article/Struggling-with-it-ever-since-Former-Texas
-13818277.php (describing these activities as "always non-violent but always unnerving").

119. Sam Baker, "Alito: Critics Waging 'Guerilla War against the Death Penalty,'"
Atlantic, April 29, 2015, https://www.theatlantic.com/politics/archive/2015/04/alito
-critics-waging-guerilla-war-against-the-death-penalty/440232/ (discussing Justice
Alito's comment during oral arguments that abolitionists were waging "a guerilla war
against the death penalty").

120. Blakinger, "Struggling with It Ever Since."

121. Gibson and Lain, "Death Penalty Drugs," 1235. For an extended discussion, see
Michael Rooney, "Lethal Secrecy: State Secrecy Statutes Keep Execution Information
from the Public," *News Media and the Law*, Spring 2014, https://www.rcfp.org/wp-con
tent/uploads/2019/01/Spring_2014.pdf.

122. Kimberly Leonard, "Lethal Injection Drug Access Could Put Executions on
Hold," Center for Public Integrity, July 11, 2012, https://publicintegrity.org/health/lethal
-injection-drug-access-could-put-executions-on-hold/.

123. Daniel Victor, "South Carolina Judge Rules against Use of Firing Squad and Electric Chair," *New York Times*, September 7, 2022, https://www.nytimes.com/2022/09/07/us
/south-carolina-unconstitutional-executions.html.

124. DPIC, "State by State."

125. David McCord, "If Capital Punishment Were Subject to Consumer Protection
Laws," *Judicature* 89 (2006): 35.

126. Corinna Barrett Lain, "Following Finality: Why Capital Punishment Is Collaps-
ing under Its Own Weight," in *Final Judgments: The Death Penalty in American Law and
Culture*, ed. Austin Sarat (Cambridge: Cambridge University Press, 2017), 42.

127. *Id.*

128. *Id.*; David Ariosto, "Connecticut Becomes 17th State to Abolish Death Pen-
alty," CNN, April 25, 2012, http://www.cnn.com/2012/04/25/justice/connecticut-death
-penalty-law-repealed (discussing Connecticut's rationale for ending the death penalty);
Ian Simpson, "Maryland Becomes Latest U.S. State to Abolish Death Penalty," Reuters,
May 2, 2013, https://www.reuters.com/article/us-usa-maryland-deathpenalty-idUS
BRE9410TQ20130502 (same); Scot Kersgaard, "Colorado's Death Penalty: Spending
Millions to Execute Almost No One," *Colorado Independent*, February 7, 2013, https://
www.coloradoindependent.com/2013/02/07/colorados-death-penalty-spending-mil
lions-to-execute-almost-no-one/; DPIC, "State Studies on Monetary Costs" (discussing
a meta-analysis of cost studies conducted around the country showing that the death
penalty costs states with capital punishment an average of $23.2 million more per year
than those with alternative sentencing).

129. C. Steiker and Steiker, "Costs and Capital Punishment," 148.

130. This was one of the arguments in favor of California's failed Proposition 62,
which would have replaced the death penalty with a maximum sentence of life without
parole. California Proposition 62, Death Penalty Initiative Statute, 2016, https://vigar
chive.sos.ca.gov/2016/general/en/propositions/62/arguments-rebuttals.htm.

131. DPIC, "State Studies on Monetary Costs."

132. Corinna Barrett Lain, "Upside-Down Judicial Review," *Georgetown Law Journal* 101 (2012): 131 (quoting Anthony Amsterdam at oral argument in *Furman*).

133. *Id.*

134. *Furman*, 408 U.S. at 314 (White, J., concurring).

135. *Id.* at 361n145 (Marshall, J., concurring).

136. Dickson, *Supreme Court in Conference*, 617–18; *Furman*, 408 U.S. at 465 (Powell, J., dissenting) ("Many may regret, as I do, the failure of some legislative bodies to address the capital punishment issue with greater frankness or effectiveness").

137. Bucklew v. Precythe, 139 S. Ct. 1112 (2019). ("As originally understood, the Eighth Amendment tolerated methods of execution, like hanging, that involved a significant risk of pain, while forbidding as cruel only those methods that intensified the death sentence by 'superadding' terror, pain, or disgrace. To establish that a State's chosen method cruelly 'superadds' pain to the death sentence, a prisoner must show a feasible and readily implemented alternative method that would significantly reduce a substantial risk of severe pain and that the State has refused to adopt without a legitimate penological reason.")

138. Barr v. Lee, 140 S. Ct. 2590 (2020) (vacating lower court stay, reversing DC District Court injunction); Rosen v. Montgomery, 141 S. Ct. 1232 (2020) (mem) (vacating DC Circuit stay); United States v. Montgomery, 141 S. Ct. 1233 (2020) (mem) (vacating Eighth Circuit stay); Barr v. Hall, 141 S. Ct. 869 (2020) (mem) (vacating DC District Court stay without waiting for DC Circuit review); United States v. Higgs, 141 S. Ct. 645 (2020) (mem) (granting certiorari while case was still pending in court of appeals and vacating lower court stay without an opinion); Barr v. Purkey, 140 S. Ct. 2594 (2020) (vacating DC District Court injunction); "Supreme Court's 'Shadow Docket' Shapes Death Penalty Litigation," American Bar Association, January 25, 2021, https://www.americanbar.org /groups/committees/death_penalty_representation/project_press/2020/year-end-2020 /the-influence-of-the-shadow-docket-on-death-penalty-litigation/. ("Often via unsigned or summary orders issued late at night, the Court repeatedly cleared the way for the execution in question to go forward. These stays and injunctions would have temporarily halted the scheduled executions to allow lower courts to conduct a thorough review of ongoing factual and legal disputes.")

139. Mayeux, this volume.

140. For those unfamiliar with the reference, sadly, see Aretha Franklin, "Sisters Are Doin' It for Themselves," YouTube, accessed October 21, 2022, https://www.youtube .com/watch?v=g9tziRkNql8.

141. Carol S. Steiker and Jordan M. Steiker, "Abolition in Our Time," *Ohio State Journal of Criminal Law* 1 (2003): 323.

142. *Id.*

143. *Id.* at 324.

144. *Id.* at 331.

145. *Id.* at 332.

146. *Id.* at 332, 338.

147. *Id.* at 340.

148. Lain, "*Furman* Fundamentals," 46.

149. *Id.* at 49–50.

150. *Id.* at 50.

151. *Id.*

152. See nn. 41–43 and accompanying text.

153. James Q. Wilson, "The Death Penalty: Is It Useful? Is It Just? Or Is It Only Cruel?," *New York Times*, October 28, 1973, 273.

154. "Death Row Returns," *The Nation*, October 15, 1973, 356.

155. Lain, "*Furman* Fundamentals," 47–49.

156. *Id.* at 33.

157. *Gregg*, 428 U.S. at 187 ("When a defendant's life is at stake, the Court has been particularly sensitive to insure that every safeguard is observed"); Woodson v. North Carolina, 428 U.S. 280, 305 (1976). ("The penalty of death is qualitatively different from a sentence of imprisonment, however long. Death, in its finality, differs more from life imprisonment than a 100-year prison term differs from one of only a year or two. Because of that qualitative difference, there is a corresponding difference in the need for reliability in the determination that death is the appropriate punishment in a specific case.")

158. David C. Baldus, George Woodworth, and Charles Pulaski, *Equal Justice and the Death Penalty: A Legal and Empirical Analysis* (Boston: Northeastern University Press, 1990), 102; Charles L. Black Jr., *Capital Punishment: The Inevitability of Caprice and Mistake* (New York: W.W. Norton, 1982). For an excellent, in-depth discussion of the Supreme Court's regulatory project in the death penalty arena, I recommend Carol and Jordan Steiker's book *Courting Death: The Supreme Court and Capital Punishment* (Cambridge, MA: Belknap Press of Harvard University Press, 2016), and Carol and Jordan Steiker's article "Sober Second Thoughts: Reflections on Two Decades of Constitutional Regulation of Capital Punishment," *Harvard Law Review* 109 (1995): 355.

159. Steiker and Steiker, this volume.

160. *Wiggins*, 539 U.S. 510 (reversing for ineffective assistance of counsel); *Rompilla*, 545 U.S. 374 (same); *Porter*, 558 U.S. 30 (same); *Sears*, 561 U.S. 945 (same); *Andrus*, 140 S. Ct. 1875 (same).

161. Lori Rozsa, "Judge Formally Sentences Parkland School Shooter to Life in Prison," *Washington Post*, November 2, 2022 (reporting that the gunman who killed seventeen people, including fourteen students, at Marjory Stoneman Douglas High School in 2018 was sentenced to thirty-four consecutive life sentences without the possibility of parole, much to the astonishment and outrage of victims and members of the community).

162. Lain, "*Furman* Fundamentals," 5 (noting that in 1972, when *Furman* was decided, there were 631 men and 2 women on death row).

6

When the Killing Law Stops Killing

Thoughts about Furman

JAMES R. MARTEL

Introduction

In the height of the French revolutionary terror, Georges Danton famously said that the Committee for Public Safety had to "be terrible so as the spare the people the need to be so."[1] Despite the fact that this seems to apply to a most extreme situation, the bloody apogee of the French revolution, my claim is that in fact what Danton says here applies more generally to the practice of law—only not quite in the same way that Danton intended. My argument in what follows is not that the law has to be terrible to save the people from having to be but rather that within the law, certain locations and practices have to be terrible so that the law more generally can appear to be benign and neutral. This argument helps explain how a phenomenon like *Furman v. Georgia*, a 1972 U.S. Supreme Court decision that, at least for a time, stopped the application of the death penalty in the United States, is possible. As I explain further, as per the thinking of Walter Benjamin in his "Critique of Violence," the law *must* kill. It must kill because of its anxiety over its own status and origins. It kills not to create justice but rather to continually establish its own existence and authority. But what Benjamin doesn't discuss in this essay is the fact that the law doesn't always or only kill. There are vast areas of the law that have nothing to do with killing, with police violence, prison guard abuse, and so on, and there are furthermore large areas of law that address the remediation or prevention of violence (albeit, generally speaking, more in the population rather than in the law itself).

More to the point, with *Furman*, we see that the United States, arguably the belly of the beast when it comes to the power of the rule of law, the "global policeman" and the one constant superpower of the last century, actually formally suspended the practice of legal killing. How, I ask, was that outcome possible when the law cannot exist without killing and the law is, in this case, perhaps most especially, represented on a global scale by its greatest hegemon and enforcer? Whereas many of the other essays in this volume ask the question "How is it possible that the United States still has the death penalty," in this essay I look at this question from the other side: How is it possible that the United States got rid of the death penalty, even for a short amount of time?[2]

My argument proceeds in three parts. First, I lay out (briefly) Benjamin's understanding of the law—at least in its mythic instantiation, which is akin to what I call archism—and why it is inherently violent. Second, I adapt Karl Marx's argument about rights in "On the Jewish Question" to show that, just as with rights, when the state or the law in this case formally retreats from a certain position, this can serve to cement that practice all the more in civil society (with, for example, lynch mobs but also with "extrajudicial" cop killings, principally of Black and Brown people). Finally, by doing a close reading of *Furman* (principally the opinion of Justice William Brennan but looking at Justice Thurgood Marshall and other members of the Court as well), I further explain how, even as the death penalty was being suspended, *Furman* reflected what could be called archist logics, resulting in the decision itself being very short lived. Finally, for a conclusion I connect an analysis of abolition to Benjamin's understanding of the general strike, offering what getting rid of the death penalty once and for all could look like.

Archism, Mythic Violence, and the Law

To begin this discussion, let me first go over some points from Benjamin's "Critique of Violence" to better establish his claim that the law is inherently violent. In that essay, one of Benjamin's main contributions to legal theory is his notion of "mythic violence." As he explains it, mythic violence constitutes—or perhaps more accurately speaks for—the entirety of what passes for the practice of law (it covers other concepts such as the state and other institutional and political, social, and economic forms of authority too, a question that I return to shortly). Mythic violence is so named because it is not based on anything real or ontological. Benjamin contrasts this power to what he calls "divine violence," which is the power of a real deity, one that is actual in the face of invented and false forms of projection.

Because mythic violence has no real basis, it is permanently anxious about its status in the world and thus must turn to violence (the German

198 / James R. Martel

term *Gewalt* that Benjamin employs means not only literal violence but also any forms of power or force) in order to continually assert not only its right to existence but even the fact of its existence in the first place. Benjamin writes,

> If violence, violence crowned by fate, is the origin of law, then it may be readily supposed that where the highest violence, that over life and death, occurs in the legal system, the origins of law jut manifestly and fearsomely into existence. [The purpose of capital punishment] is not to punish the infringement of law but to establish new law.[3]

Here, Benjamin tells us that the law "juts manifestly and fearsomely into existence," through violence, and in particular through the highest form of violence, murder. In this depiction, the law, as it were, pulls itself into reality by its own act of self-assertion, an assertion that can only be realized through the sign of blood.

Mythic violence is essentially a form of projection. It projects onto blank, false externalities that do not actually exist in order to return to earth in the form of undeniable laws and forms of authority. It therefore readily transfers itself from a theological to a secular practice (albeit one that is no less theological in structure and origin). Mythic violence could be said to be an extensive set of false prophecies that serve particular and very local ends in the name of some universal that is itself merely evoked as a form of justification of those ends (not serving as the end itself). It is, in effect, a form of bad immanentism, wherein it pretends to engage with an externality that only serves to justify its all-too-human desires (the desires of political and economic rulers, which are then foisted onto the rest of the population).

Benjamin tells us that divine violence serves not so much to rival mythic violence but rather merely as a way to undermine and destroy mythic forms of projection that are nominally done in its name. Because divine violence is undertaken by an actual deity instead of a false one, it does not share the same sense of insecurity, nor does it feel the same need to ceaselessly prove its existence that we find with mythic violence.

One way to understand the difference between mythic and divine violence is to look at Machiavelli's telling of the story of Numa, the second king of Rome. Finding the Romans lawless, Machiavelli tells us that Numa thought that if he gave the Romans a set of laws directly from his own hands, they would not follow them.[4] Numa therefore lied and said that a nymph had given him a set of divine laws and that anyone who disobeyed these laws would be struck down by the gods. The ruse worked, and the Romans accepted the law as such.[5]

This could be said to be one origin story for mythic violence; here, a false externality becomes the screen by which Numa projects his own will onto the people of Rome. Machiavelli appears to approve of this (although he also is exposing the trick in the guise of praising it). He thinks of Numa as a good king, but what if Numa wasn't so good? Mythic violence serves as a constant temptation for would-be rulers to project whatever they want outwardly to be received as an inviolable edict.

But now imagine if the nymph that Numa lied about (in the original telling by Livy, it is a goddess) suddenly appeared. Imagine if she took whatever tablets the law was inscribed on and smashed them to pieces, leaving the scene without saying a word. Here, the nominally blank screen that mythic violence projects itself onto (be it God, nature, reason, or what have you) suddenly speaks back, using its voice and power to deny that projection without attempting to create any new truths in its stead. This would be an act of divine violence.

In thinking more generally about these two forms of power, Benjamin tells us,

> If mythical violence is lawmaking, divine violence is law destroying; if the former sets boundaries, the latter boundlessly destroys them; if mythical violence brings at once guilt and retribution, divine power only expiates.[6]

As a "law destroying" power, then, divine violence serves to allow human beings a space that is constrained by neither false nor true gods. Human agency and freedom become possible only through the disruptions that divine violence ceaselessly causes for mythic violence.

In my own work I prefer to speak of "archism" rather than mythic violence. The term *archism* is derived from the ancient Greek verb *arkein*, which means both "to begin" and "to rule." Archism is roughly the same concept as mythic violence except where mythic violence may explain the why, archism is more concerned with the what. That is to say, archism describes the modalities of power in our time, while mythic violence may be an explanation for the source of those modalities.

The term *archism* is far more unfamiliar than its opposite, *anarchism*. This is because archism does not wish (if I can risk anthropomorphizing it) to have a name. It seeks rather to be effectively melted into the background, presupposed as the nature and basis of all political, social, economic, and legal authority. To give it a name is already to begin to challenge the self-granted supremacy of archist power.

Perhaps the best way to describe archism is as a metaphysics of hierarchy. Archism seeks to render the entire world (certainly all that falls within its attention) under regularized and taxonomized forms of identity that are then put in their place and ordered. The imagined spot from which archism projects its power (once again God or nature or reason, etc.) is itself exempt from this taxonomization so that there is always an imagined center or node of power (even though that center can never actually be identified or articulated, being as it is entirely mythic).

Although I think the two terms can be used somewhat interchangeably, I think that *mythic violence* describes the basis for the hierarchical power systems in the world, while *archism* describes the effect of that power. Furthermore, while Benjamin sees mythic violence as a ubiquitous form of power since the fall of Adam (and Eve, although she is not Benjamin's focus), archism speaks to a much more recent phenomenon: the contemporary world, which is a result of Western imperialism, slavery, and genocide. Archism covers a wide variety of political and economic forms of power ranging from liberalism to fascism. Perhaps above all, it is deeply associated with capitalism.

Perhaps most critically for the purposes of my discussion here, archism is a purely parasitical power. With no reality of its own, it must draw upon the subjects who live in its shadow. Although he does not use the language of archism, Benjamin succinctly sums this up when he states,

> Mythic violence is bloody power over mere life for its own sake; divine violence is pure power over all life for the sake of the living.[7]

Here, we see the political and legal upshot of this idea. Mythic violence or archism reduces us to mere life. It rules for its own sake. Divine violence allows for a life that is untrammeled by such rule. Where Benjamin speaks of "the living," I think of anarchism. In contrasting anarchism to archism, I do not think of these as a binary. I think that archism is one particular (perhaps one of the worst) forms of political and economic organization, while anarchism is an infinite variety of other forms. When we introduce the term *archism* as a contrast to *anarchism*, the latter term itself expands from being simply a strand of European leftist thought in the tradition of Bakunin, Kropotkin, and Goldman to something much bigger, life itself (i.e., "the living") when it is not dominated by archism. As Maia Ramnath argues in *Decolonizing Anarchism*, when the term *anarchism* is considered with a small *a* (as opposed to what she calls "Circle-A Brand," the European variety), it can be applied to multiple contexts that assert collective and horizontal forms of organization in opposition to the forms that archism always presents (my word, not hers).[8]

In thinking about the contrast between archism and anarchism, the passage from Benjamin quoted earlier shows us that by juxtaposing "mere life" to "the living," he is reminding us that even when we are reduced to being the former, we are also always the latter. This means that no matter how dire the situation, no matter how subjected people are to archist forces and projections, they are always also living an anarchist life. Insofar as archism predates on that life, it cannot utterly reduce the living to itself (which is to say to nothing). It requires some aspect of the living to have a bit of autonomy from itself not only so that it can disguise the degree to which it feeds off the living but also so that it allows for the very vitality of life to continue to feed archism itself.

Archism always maintains that its human subjects are somehow deficient. Thus, workers, it maintains, cannot possibly handle their own issues without managers, and political subjects cannot figure out politics on their own. Without the police, we would all be at one another's throat in a matter of minutes. In each case the parasitical element (the archons) not only claim better knowledge and so forth but even take credit for whatever creativity and invention and even peaceability the human life that it parasitizes produces.

This already helps explain one of the paradoxes that I brought up earlier in this chapter. When people say that they are involved in law but in a way that is nonviolent or even counterviolent, I think Benjamin's answer to this is to say that their nonviolence (not in a literal sense; Benjamin himself saw moments when physical violence was justified) comes from their status as the living, what I am calling anarchism, rather than from archism itself. To put this in a nutshell, everything good that comes from law or the state or even capitalism does not come from it directly but comes from the life that these things predate on. The law, the state, and the corporation all have a benign face that they show to the world (until they don't; liberalism readily turns into fascism when the capitalist core of things is threatened). These creative, nonviolent acts bolster that image, but they do not come from archism itself.

In this way, the law and other archist institutions "need" the living in a double sense. They need the living to transfer their own realness unto the law itself, to steal from them their own tangibility, and in the process derealize the living, turning them into mere life (so that the law becomes more real, more vivid than the communities that it preys on). But it also needs the living in a second sense, to provide the decency and the peacefulness, the benign face that the law claims as its own. This is why you can have lawyers who work against domestic violence or police officers coming to neighborhood barbecues. It is not the law or its components as such that do these things; it is the human beings who are subjugated to the law (including those who work for and as part of the law) and who allow the law the plausibility of its own claims to being benign and just.[9]

You can see a bit of Benjamin's understanding of the parasitical nature of archism when he talks early on in the "Critique" about the nature of the police. He tells us that, whereas the law may imagine itself to be entirely benign and in search of justice, in its actual application, which is to say when it manifests itself in the world through the police, it shows its truer face. He writes,

> The assertion that the ends of police violence are always identical or even connected to those of general law is entirely untrue. Rather, the "law" of the police really marks the point at which the state, whether from impotence or because of the immanent connections within any legal system, can no longer guarantee through the legal system the empirical ends that it desires at any price to attain. Therefore, the police intervene "for security reasons" in countless cases where no clear legal situation exists, when they are not merely, without the slightest relation to legal ends, accompanying the citizen as a brutal encumbrance through a life regulated by ordinances, or simply supervising him. Unlike law, which acknowledges in the "decision" determined by place and time a metaphysical category that gives it a claim to critical evaluation, a consideration of the police institution encounters nothing essential at all. Its power is formless, like its nowhere-tangible, all-pervasive, ghostly presence in the life of civilized states.[10]

In other words, the law is not to be found in textbooks or in legal imaginations in the minds of judges and legal administrators. Rather, the law only really materializes in direct applications, perhaps most especially in the case of the police. The law here is, he tells us, a "brutal encumbrance" that is entirely about itself, about the power and authority of those authorized to kill versus the rest of us who are explicitly denied this right.

Robert Cover says something very similar when he discusses how the seemingly innocuous act of a judge pronouncing a sentence is deeply linked to an entire apparatus of legalized violence. Speaking, for example, of the fact that when they are sentenced, the newly convicted appear to accept this sentence and walk rather than being dragged off to prison, he writes,

> I think it is unquestionably the case in the United States that most prisoners walk into prison because they know they will be dragged or beaten into prison if they do not walk. They do not organize force against being dragged because they know that if they wage this kind of battle they will lose—very possibly lose their lives.[11]

For Cover, as for Benjamin, the surface calm of the judicial procedure disguises its true nature but also through that disguise permits an entire array of deep violence to continue to function, to turn a simple human word (like *guilty*) into an apparatus of law.

To put all of this in a nutshell, when the police kill a Black or Brown person, they are in fact truly representing the law because this is what the law requires in order to exist at all. When they engage in nonviolent behavior, they are expressing their own status as the living (but in a way that the law also draws up into itself to help disguise its own murderousness).

Benjamin's language is paradoxical in the passage quoted earlier in that he sees the police as a "ghostly presence in the life of civilized states" even as it is the main material application of legal power. This language is telling because it indicates a reversal of sorts where the "truth" of the law—its violence—seems more ephemeral, even metaphysical, than the more abstract concept of law as such. This reversal speaks to the larger concept of archism that I have been describing. Here again, the law (but other forms of archism as well) takes up the tangibility of the world that it dominates, transferring the reality and tangibility of that world to itself, rendering the actual world less real, less tangible, in the process.

By way of concluding this initial argument, it may seem as if Benjamin is opposed to law altogether, but I do not think that is the case. He is opposed to mythic law, certainly, and divine law for him is a purely negative feature (he even tells us that a commandment as seemingly obvious as "thou shalt not kill" cannot be interpreted to mean one thing only and must be "wrestled with").[12]

But this leaves still the possibility of what could be called "human law" or perhaps more accurately a law for "the living," that category that I associate with anarchism. If we think of this other nonmythic form of law, we can see that law's function, which is to tie together a disparate and complex community with certain boundaries, can be exercised, in some sense *is* exercised, even under conditions of archism, although of course the extent of such law is totally eclipsed and overwritten by archism's own claim to be the only kind of law that exists or could ever be.

I will leave a larger consideration of the law of the living to another time except to say that, without the existential anxiety of mythic forms of law, this other form of law is not required to kill; its existence is granted by the community itself, and so it has a tangibility to it that does not need to be siphoned off from somewhere else.

Perhaps the most extended vision of what that law might look like in the "Critique" comes from Benjamin's description of the general strike, a subject that I return to at the end of this essay. The general strike is for Benjamin an instance of nonviolence. It is an act neither of mythological projection nor of divine intervention but is rather entirely a product of human actors, action by "the living." The general strike is for Benjamin "anarchistic" because it represents a rejection of mythic violence in its entirety.[13] Rather than negotiating with capitalism or the state as do liberal forms of strikes, the general strike is a refusal to engage with capitalism at all. It is a form of counter

204 / James R. Martel

law in this sense, a denial of the authority that mythic violence—and archism—gives to itself. This is a power that mythic violence can never take away from the living; insofar as divine violence is for Benjamin ceaselessly canceling out and rejecting mythic violence, disallowing it to coalesce as a real and actual truth, human actors can always step into the breach made by such cancellations and act as and for themselves in promoting other forms of law and life.

I am not here making a utopian argument about how anarchist forms of law will always be nonviolent. As I said previously, I think that anarchism is as varied as human life itself, and some versions of it will undoubtably be violent to some extent, but without the *need* to be violent, these forms of law will tend to be much less hostile, less predatory, less racist and misogynistic—that is to say, less in keeping with the systemic violence of archism, which is only ever terrible. Perhaps more to the point, for Benjamin, nonviolence is always possible even if human beings do not always engage in it. If we recall that under conditions of mythic violence, even as we are reduced to "mere life" (and this is a category that has within it further subcategories insofar as the mereness of this life is experienced far more directly by Black and Brown subjects of archism than white ones, by the poor rather than by the rich, by women and trans and queer people rather than cisgendered straight men, and so on), we are also always the living; we can see that human communities are already practicing these kinds of laws—albeit in ways that generally go unrecognized—even as the archist forms of law continue to predate on and steal from us.

Getting Out of the Business of Murder

Having laid out this initial discussion, let me now turn to the *Furman* decision to try to explain better how it might have come to pass. How, to repeat my original question, could the U.S. Supreme Court, the veritable center of law in a nation that is itself emblematic of the law (through its neoimperial and now neoliberal global power) throughout the planet, have made the decision to break with the death penalty? It is true that *Furman* was eventually reversed and the United States has been back to legalized murder ever since, but it is equally true that even before *Furman* (and this is something that Justice Brennan makes much of in his legal decision) the death penalty was being applied less and less frequently and, after a period of reaction, has become even more infrequent since its return as a condoned practice in whichever states have not banned it.

The first point I'd like to stress about this is that the fact that a legal or state apparatus formally declares its disassociation from a certain practice does not mean that this practice is ended but rather that it can be presupposed into civil society itself. This is in fact the argument that Marx makes about liberal rights in "On the Jewish Question." There, Marx tells us that when the state formally abolishes a certain practice, they do so only in order to presuppose it into the social order itself, rendering that category essentially depoliticized and therefore all the harder to address or eliminate.

Thus, for example, Marx states (quoting Gustave de Beaumont in this case), "There is not in the United States, either a state religion or a religion declared to be that of the majority. . . . The state remains aloof from all religion." And yet, "no one in the United States believes that a man without a religion can be an honest man."[14]

In other words, by formally renouncing a state religion, the United States allowed religion to be preserved in the spaces that were not available to political solutions, relegating religion to the "private realm," which, as Marx astutely points out, is the realm of actual life, akin to what Benjamin refers to when he speaks of "the living."

In making these claims, Marx makes a distinction between what he calls "political emancipation" and "human emancipation."[15] The latter category is indeed very much like the category of the living—that is to say, the material and real practices of human life. If human beings are to be free from religion (a goal that Marx supports), the solution is not to banish it from the public realm (the mythical level of false, liberal rights and formal equality) but rather to address it within that realm and undermine it once and for all.

Marx goes on to say of this that

> the limits of political emancipation appear at once in the fact that the state can liberate itself from a constraint without man himself being really liberated; that a state may be a free state without man himself being a free man.[16]

Here, as with Benjamin, you can see that the state worries more about freeing itself than freeing its subjects. To formally rid itself of religion or whatever else is at question, the state can bolster its self-image as benign and just even as the necessary hierarchies that it is based on are allowed to flourish elsewhere. Setting up an analogy between the mythical nature of the state and the mythical nature of religion (for Marx), he says,

> Just as Christ is the intermediary to whom man attributes all his own divinity and all his religious bonds, so the state is the intermediary to which man confides all his non divinity and all his human freedom.[17]

Here, the state is set up as a mythical realm that is, as with Benjamin's claims, more real than the actual world that it rules over. As citizens of the state, we go about our daily lives, Marx argues, in a state of abject subjection (i.e., mere life), but our eyes go to a realm in which everyone is considered free and equal. Marx goes on to describe how this works, not for religion only but for many other rights and institutions as well, perhaps the most important of which is property. By formally emancipating itself from property considerations (by, for example, eliminating the requirement that one have a certain amount of property in order to be allowed to vote), the state similarly ensures not only that property is depoliticized but also that class itself becomes a nonpolitical (or even antipolitical) category insofar as the state makes no formal recognition of class distinctions and thereby allows capitalism to go along on its untrammeled way.[18]

In turning to Marx in this way, we can see how this might apply to law too, albeit with some critical distinctions. In the *Furman* decision, the courts formally separated (or emancipated) themselves from state murder, but in doing so they did not eliminate murder as a political category.[19] This tracks with what Benjamin says as well about how the law imagines itself versus how the law actually operates. It makes sense that the higher echelon of the judiciary in the form of the Supreme Court would rid itself of the taint of murder only to ensure that state killings continue in the form of police violence, vigilantism, and so on (but also, as Linda Ross Meyer points out, punishments that are just short of death such as life without parole, which is a kind of living death).

This is one of the places where it is useful to speak of archism instead of just states because it becomes easier to see how state violence can effectively still be carried out by nonstate actors like lynch mobs or also, as already mentioned, by the police themselves who continue to kill with impunity despite the states' formal abandonment of this practice. The fact that the lynch mob is "unauthorized" and the police is "authorized" (although in a complicated way) makes no difference in this case; all that matters is that the (archist) law in all of its hydra-headed forms continues to kill in a way that is highly visible.

From this perspective, *Furman* becomes something other than it initially seems. Rather than a decision to end the death penalty once and for all, it could be said that *Furman* distracts from the way that legal murder operates. Here again we can see that in the gap that Benjamin describes between how the law thinks of itself (benign, just, etc.) and the reality of the law (brutal, violent), *Furman* enabled the law, at least for a time, to think that it was coming closer to its own self-idealization, even as this was never actually the case.

This reminds me of the passage I started this chapter with where Danton says that the Committee for Public Safety has to be "terrible" (i.e., to kill) so that the people do not have to be. Yet in this case, the statement implies something different, maybe even the opposite of what Danton has in mind in his own historical context. In this case the Court is saying that they (i.e., the equivalent of the Committee of Public Safety in terms of its centrality and authority) are no longer going to be terrible so that the people (at least people who promote an archist agenda) now have to be terrible instead. The law, in purifying itself formally of violence, has now ensured that legal violence will be continued by nonstate actors and even by its own agents, although in ways that are not condoned by the law itself. This helps cover over a seeming glaring contradiction that Benjamin has noted at least insofar as the law's own self-regard is concerned.

The point here is that the killing that establishes the reality of the law, its parasitical archist function, does not have to reside in any one site, not even the law or the state itself, as long as it happens *somewhere* (and by somewhere I mean somewhere that is still identifiable as an arbiter of archism and its attendant institutions of white supremacy, patriarchy, capitalism, etc.). Getting out of the "murder business" once again allows the state and the law both more plausibility in their claim that they are neutral and just, not violent and mythical.

Here too, the central issue is the nature of archist parasitism and its need to feed off the vitality and diversity of the living. In the case of law, that parasitism is hidden by the law's own conceit that it is about justice, but as we have already seen, Benjamin tells us that the truth of the law lies not in its own mythic self-imagination but rather at the point of contact between the law and the living, and on that level (i.e., the level of the police) it is a brutal if ghostly encumbrance.

This answer then goes part of the way to explaining how a given legal system can abandon the death penalty when Benjamin insists that the law (at least in its mode as mythic law) is only ever violent. We can understand how in Denmark or some other country celebrated for its decency and humanism, the law can appear to be utterly benign (although no country on earth is innocent of police violence and racism) because the United States is holding up the existence and the power of the law by itself. The U.S. legal system spills blood (not literally anymore, but I don't think that Benjamin is as tied to the literalness of that image as Jacques Derrida, for one, assumes him to be) to establish law not only on its own territory but all over the world, especially those parts of the world that are tightly connected to it.[20] But this begs the question, What does it mean when the U.S. state and legal system itself stops killing?

As a hegemon for the world, the United States has some unique qualities that especially qualify it for the role of "being terrible so that others do not have to." The United States has the highest rate of imprisonment as well as the highest absolute number of prisoners.[21] Among wealthy countries, the

208 / James R. Martel

United States dwarves every other state in terms of police killings.[22] And, of course, the United States is quite distinct among developed nations for its continued practice of the death penalty itself. Hegemony is not the only explanation for why the United States is unique in its ongoing pursuit of capital punishment.

Carol Steiker, one of the authors in this volume, argues that the fact that the United States is a far more populist state than other more parliamentary-style democracies in Europe is also a major factor in explaining U.S. exceptionalism on the death penalty.[23] This tracks with a larger point about archism, that it adheres not only in states but in large segments of the population, who benefit from and support archism (in this case via white supremacy) so that the two explanations, one empirical and one theoretical, are mutually supportive.

Furman Revisited

In any case, the uniquely resilient nature of capital punishment in the United States, paired with the fact that for one brief moment state killing was suspended via *Furman*, remains the central puzzle of this essay. In light of this, a deeper level of analysis of *Furman* is important since Benjamin's "Critique" would lead us to expect that the U.S. state could never really give up on the death penalty precisely because it is at the heart of what Derrida calls "the arkheion," the place from which judgment occurs, the site where the "truth" of law must be centered.[24] That truth of the law, Benjamin tells us, lies in killing, and if the law passes that duty down to civil society, it loses to an extent some control over how that killing is practiced or even whether it is practiced at all. Doesn't this devolution of power over killing threaten the law at its most fundamental level?

As I explain further (and as the many essays in this volume attest), *Furman* is not in itself a moment of abolition. The justices did not come out and say that the death penalty was unconstitutional according to the Eighth Amendment but rather stated that as it was currently practiced it amounted to cruel and unusual punishment, opening the door for *Gregg*, a few years later, to specify how state killing could and had to be undertaken henceforth.

But even a partial and temporary suspension is significant. My answer to the question of how *Furman* was possible at all is in two parts, first to understand how the *Furman* decision is itself saturated with an archist logic. The second and final part focuses on how I believe that so long as the United States remains the global hegemon and a center of archist belief structures, we should not expect an utter condemnation of the death penalty that is much more robust than *Furman*.

Let me start by looking at the *Furman* decision to show how, while it did constitute a break with the most critical feature of archism—its power to kill—it nonetheless remained very much ensconced in an archist logic. In the *Furman* decision, there was not one majority opinion with several concurrences and dissents but rather a series of concurring opinions and then dissents. This itself may speak to the centrality of *Furman* for the law's own self-regard and the lack of a clear-cut and absolute ruling that multiple people could sign on to. An ambivalence that I see going throughout these opinions is reflected even in the nature of how those opinions are rendered.

In what follows, I focus mainly on Justice William Brennan's opinion because it is, in my view, the heart of the argument for why the death penalty must be ended (at least for now). Let me say at the outset that Brennan, like all archons, is both a part of a larger (anarchist) community, one of the "living," and a perpetrator and source of archist logics. In that duality, we can see the source of a visible tension between Brennan's own nonviolent (and, as Sara Mayeux points out in her essay, Catholic) views and his role as a member of the Supreme Court and hence someone who is especially concerned with the status and authority of the law. Here, we see in a single person a microcosm of the larger struggle Benjamin describes between the law's desire to be just and the requirement that the law be violent in order to exist at all. Each member of the Court struggles with this tension in one way or the other, and I would just reiterate here my claim that what comes out of these opinions that is antiviolent is not due to the law itself (at least not in its archist variety) but rather reflects the ensconcement of these justices (to a greater or lesser degree) in larger conversations that come from the living rather than from archism itself, which is only ever violent.

In his opinion, Brennan laid out four criteria for why the death penalty amounted to cruel and unusual punishment and was thus, in his view, a violation of the Eighth Amendment. The four criteria are based on his reading of the Fourteenth and Eighth Amendments as well as a variety of legal cases that help him reach his conclusions. Brennan tells us that to avoid being classified as cruel and unusual, a punishment must not be (1) unusually severe and degrading, (2) arbitrary, (3) against community judgments, or (4) "excessive in view of the purpose for which it is inflicted."[25]

Summarizing these principles, toward the end of his opinion, Brennan states,

> In sum, the punishment of death is inconsistent with all four principles: Death is an unusually severe and degrading punishment; there is a strong probability that it is inflicted arbitrarily; its rejection by contemporary society is virtually total; and there is no reason to

believe that it serves any penal purpose more effectively than the less severe punishment of imprisonment. The function of these principles is to enable a court to determine whether a punishment comports with human dignity. Death, quite simply, does not.[26]

Let me treat each of these criteria in turn to show how collectively they reflect an archist form of thinking even as they allow for a moratorium on the death penalty as an official state act. Beginning with the question of whether the death penalty is uniquely severe and degrading, Brennan notes famously that "the unusual severity of death is manifested most clearly in its finality and enormity. Death, in these respects, is in a class by itself."[27] He goes on to say that in being put to death (in a way that connects to Hannah Arendt's own concept of the same phrase), the prisoner loses "the right to have rights"—that is to say, they become unavailable for any other form of law.[28]

In stating that "death is truly an awesome punishment," Brennan is recognizing its centrality to law. Death, as he shows, is a way for the law to enact a form of finality on a prisoner; it trumps any attempt at resistance or usurpation. Even though for Brennan these are all negative features as pertains to the death penalty, it does not stop him from understanding that what the death penalty ultimately does is to assert the absolute power of the law over that of any given person or group of persons. It offers that the law has a power that makes it unquestionably higher, better, and in a very literal sense more real than the life that serves beneath it, precisely because it can take that life away while it itself remains ongoing and intact.[29]

Even if the law ceases to perform this function, it seems clear to me that Brennan is indicating that the law always *could* return to killing to reestablish its absolute authority. This reminds me of Carl Schmitt's argument that liberalism is at the end of the day no different from authoritarianism in that under conditions of liberalism the state forebears to enact its absolute power to suspend the constitution, in keeping with Schmitt's famous adage that "sovereign is he who decides upon the exception."[30] Whether the state actually engages that power or not, it always remains within its purview to do so. Such a power remains the potential and right of the law, and so in effect the truth of the state is not its show of benign self-control but rather the possibility that it could at any moment cease that restraint and assert its true power. This may help explain too why *Furman* is so incomplete, not the abolition of death but its abeyance for a time.

Precisely by recognizing the ways that the law might choose *not* to kill, Brennan is in effect reminding us that it could always change its mind (it is up to the law itself to allow or forebear to engage with capital punishment, albeit in way that is connected to the principle of community judgment, which I come to shortly). To put this in a nutshell, Brennan's argument that capital punishment is in fact too severe and degrading does not contradict his understanding that it is a primary legal power. That status is enshrined even in a decision to suspend the penalty (for the time being).

The second principle, that a punishment is cruel and unusual when it is arbitrarily enforced, only reinforces this first point. Brennan speaks of a punishment ideally being "regularly and fairly applied."[31] Here, Brennan argues that because the death penalty has become so rare, the fact that it is inflicted at all becomes effectively arbitrary. But this argument begs the question of whether the solution to this "arbitrary" violence would be to allow a much greater number of executions. If every rape and murder were met with the death penalty, then this criterion would disappear, and so the argument against the arbitrary nature of the death penalty does not preclude that outcome but only articulates (and this may speak in part to why the *Furman* decision was ultimately temporary) one condition under which it could be prevented.

Perhaps more to the point, from a Benjaminian perspective, the death penalty is always arbitrary in that the subject of execution is not killed for what they have done per se but rather for the sake of the law itself. Some criteria for who must pay that ultimate price are always required, and yet those criteria are not really about the subjects of the law as such; rather, they serve as an excuse for state killings in the first place. This may help explain why the actual application of the death penalty is so piecemeal and effectively random. The true reason for execution is never, of course, mentioned, and so the reasons for execution are inherently arbitrary and cannot ever not be so.

We see some evidence for this not in *Furman* itself but in the *Gregg* decision that effectively superseded *Furman* (albeit based on *Furman*'s own principles). As Corinna Lain pointed out to me, in early deliberations about *Gregg* Justice Lewis Powell sought to openly adopt vengeance as a basis for capital punishment. Lain records the following conversation: "Justice Powell told his clerk that he wanted the opinion to say, 'Society has a need for revenge.' When the clerk told him 'You can't put that in an opinion,' Powell replied 'It's honest,' to which the clerk responded, 'It's wrong.'"[32] Lain also records that "Powell had the last word, telling his clerk, 'You're just more Christian than I am.'"[33]

In the end, the final form this took in *Gregg* was as follows:

In part, capital punishment is an expression of society's moral outrage at particularly offensive conduct. This function may be unappealing to many, but it is essential in an ordered society that asks its citizens to rely on legal processes rather than self-help to vindicate their wrongs. The instinct for retribution is part of the nature of man, and channeling that instinct in the administration of criminal justice serves an important purpose in promoting the stability of a society governed by law.[34]

Here, Powell comes close to acknowledging what the law is always doing when it engages in capital punishment (in the *Furman* decision four years earlier, it is Justice Marshall who most openly considers and then repudiates the idea that legal state executions are a form of retribution). What he does not say (and I wouldn't expect any Supreme Court justice to say this) is that the revenge Powell is citing may not be for the sake of the family of the murder victim in question but rather revenge by the law itself for its own nonexistence, a revenge that it takes out on the living (but which tracks nicely with the claim that it is on behalf of human victims).

In light of this, to claim that the death penalty is arbitrary serves to acknowledge its false justifications as well as its true purpose. Being arbitrary, the death penalty does not serve to prevent crime (as so many studies have shown) but rather serves to show that the state has the power to kill as it sees fit and to remind all of its subjects that they are potentially (but also potentially not) subject to that ultimate act of violence. The very idea that the law may kill at random enhances its power precisely because it makes the state more dangerous and unpredictable, according not only with killing itself but also, via the whole apparatus of the capital punishment bar (a creation of *Gregg* and thus in some way of *Furman* too), with what John Bessler calls "state-sanctioned death threats."[35] Here too, Brennan is renouncing rather than condoning this condition, but he is recognizing the way such arbitrary killing sends a particular—and necessary—message about the law.

The third principle lies with the community and its evolving judgments of what constitutes cruel and unusual punishment. In this case, Brennan states that arguments over the death penalty have existed since its inception. He tells us that these arguments were not ultimately debates over the efficacity or nature of the death penalty but rather over its moral qualities. Brennan cites the increasing rarity of the penalty as a sign that the U.S. population has come to reject the use of capital punishment. He says that "rejection could hardly be more complete without being absolute. At the very least, I must conclude that contemporary society views this punishment with substantial doubt."[36]

Here, Brennan acknowledges that social mores can change over time. This suggests that the law is in fact cognizant of having to reflect community standards and having to adapt accordingly (part of its attempt to show that it is not for itself but for everyone else). What is interesting and perhaps unique about capital punishment is that, in this case, the community standard in question involves something very fundamental to the law itself. One way to reconcile this is to say that if community standards can change in one direction, they can change in another as well. Perhaps the U.S. population will become more bloodthirsty in the future (arguably that is happening right now, even though, as Corinna Lain points out, the percentage of the population that supports the death penalty is about what it was when *Furman* was decided).

Or perhaps they won't. Either way, one can see that having once approved of the death penalty (Brennan notes repeatedly that it was relatively uncontroversial for much of the history of the U.S. republic), the people's opinion on this matter becomes somewhat secondary to the law's own decision (it is one of several principles, after all). If there was popular consent for capital punishment back in the day, then state-sanctioned killing can always refer itself to this earlier authorization (an argument the originalists on the Court today could surely point to, as Linda Ross Meyer makes clear in her own contribution to this volume).

Given that the people's opinion is currently turning against the death penalty, it could be argued that perhaps the fact that the law has killed for over two centuries suffices to give it a sense of authority that can sustain it in the future without having to kill any further (especially if that formal nonkilling is bolstered by other agents of archism like vigilantes, "Karens," the police, prison guards, etc.). As I argue further, however, this argument may hold for a time, but I do not think that ultimately it can succeed in taming the law's need to kill. Here again, we may get a sense for why *Furman* was in the end only a temporary measure. Even if community standards have been "evolving" (a teleological term that I would reject out of hand), they can never come to the point where the law itself does not need execution for its own purposes.

The final principle that Brennan considers is that the death penalty may be too excessive for the purposes that it purports to serve. He cites Justice Marshall's own concurring opinion that the death penalty does not prevent crime from occurring (and here, once again, the increasing rarity of the death penalty is part of that equation).

More to the point, Brennan argues that the enormity of inflicting death on a convicted prisoner makes it inherently excessive to the crime committed (even the crime of murder). He writes that, given the principle of proportionality itself, "our laws distribute punishments according to the gravity of crimes and punish more severely the crimes society regards as more serious. That purpose cannot justify any particular punishment as the upper limit of severity."[37] Brennan's claim is that, accordingly, the law requires a lighter sentence than death because, compared to any prison sentence, even

214 / James R. Martel

life without parole, death is utterly beyond that range of punishment; it is so beyond other forms of punishment that it defies any sense of proportionality by definition.

In my own view, I would say that Brennan's discussion here reflects a frustration of the law as much as it does a moral point. In seeking to establish its own existence via the death penalty, I would say that the law cannot kill enough to once and for all establish its own reality. Certainly, as already noted, the law cannot kill everyone, lest it remove its own host and the basis for its parasitical existence. But even within the limited range of who it can kill, death serves as a limit rather than a facilitation of its own desire to exist. As Michel Foucault tells us, with death, the law discovers the end rather than the beginning of its power, and this motivation may be seen (at least implicitly) in Brennan's recognition of death's unique status as a form of punishment.[38] Thus, even as death is the ultimate punishment that the law can mete out, it is perhaps not ultimate enough in that it fails to make the law permanent, needing no more violence to establish its own right to exist (and rule).

In his film *Salò, 120 Days of Sodom*, the director and writer Pier Paolo Pasolini offers us a scene of pure archist power.[39] In the film, toward the end of World War II in Italy, four political, legal, and religious leaders (archons one and all) set up in a villa where they establish a reign of absolute terror (the context is the short-lived republic of Salò, a last-gasp effort to create a fascist state in northern Italy as the Allies advanced from the south). Kidnapping a group of young people, they commence to torture and otherwise abuse them in ways that become increasingly horrible (and indeed unwatchable). But the upshot of the movie is not that these four archons are rewarded with their power but rather that they show the limits of power in the end. They lament in fact that they cannot kill their victims multiple times, and in the end, when they resort to pure violence (mutilation and murder), their faces are contorted with rage at their inability to do even more to their victims.[40]

Clearly, Brennan is not motivated by similar concerns, but there is, even in his comments, a recognition that the law is not in fact all powerful, that it must recognize, at least formally, its own limitations, its dependence— even if it does not want to admit it—on the community that it reigns over (an ambivalence that is also present to some degree in his comments on community standards). Whether death is a check on or a bolster to the law's authority, it retains a unique status, and Brennan recognizes this even as he claims that the death penalty per se must cease.

Moving beyond a focus on the four principles that he cites, we can see that more generally, Brennan's opinion suggests a suspension and not the abolition of the death penalty not only in terms of temporality but also in terms of its most basic approach. Near the end of his concurrence, Brennan states that "there is, then, no substantial reason to believe that the punishment of death, as currently administered, is necessary for the protection of society."[41] Here, we can see that his judgment does not entirely preclude the return of the death penalty. All it would require would be a change in the way it is "currently administered"; if a way to kill that was truly painless (and somehow also overcame the mental anguish that accompanies being put to death), if societal mores changed once again, if strict criteria could be established that allowed for a regular and orderly form of sentencing, if the process by which death was determined was streamlined and made regular, if it could be shown that the death penalty was in fact a proportional response to crime, then perhaps the death penalty could be restored. And furthermore, it is quite logical to conclude that the *Gregg* decision, just four years later, was precisely that response.[42]

With *Gregg*, the claim that the problem with the death penalty lies in its nature as a form of punishment (i.e., the fact that it is cruel and unusual) allows some wiggle room for the law to "decide" that the death penalty can be reinstated after all. Holding the death penalty up to *Furman*'s set criteria (even if at times those criteria claim to base themselves in part on the larger society and its own mores), *Gregg* was almost the logical conclusion of *Furman*. Had *Furman* embraced true abolitionism, it would have rendered the law, I would argue, too far removed from the true purpose of the death penalty, which serves, as I've said several times already, the law itself rather than the community as a whole.

One can argue that the federal government might pass a law (as has happened in many states) that prevents capital punishment, and this would stand outside of the law itself, which would never abrogate its own power to decide whether to kill or not kill. This is one more of those places where the usefulness of a concept like archism comes into play. The state, just like the law, is a product of archism, and, as such, it is subject to the same anxieties, the same relationship to mythic violence. When the law kills, it does so not just for its own sake but for the sake of all archist power, the state very much included. Indeed, this may be the unique purpose of the law per se. Just as the United States stands as the law for much of the world and accordingly kills so that other legal systems "don't have to" (although of course there are plenty of legal systems that kill with impunity), so too does the law kill for the sake of its fellow archists, allowing them to keep their hands clean of the violence that establishes and preserves all of their parasitical authority.

At the end, I would just reiterate that the ongoing conflict in the text between Brennan's distaste for capital punishment and his recognition (and perhaps appreciation) for the awesome power of the law, a power that he is entirely caught up with and within, reflects his own dual status as both a

216 / James R. Martel

member of the living and someone who is at the heart of the legal apparatus. Given the outsized status of the United States, including in terms of its legal system, throughout the world and given the centrality of the Supreme Court in U.S. jurisdiction, Brennan sits at the very pinnacle of the law. One might expect someone in that position to be the most "in the know" and perhaps the most aware of what the law really is and what its true motivations are, but as Benjamin shows us, in fact the opposite may be true. It is the police officer who kills Black and Brown people with impunity who knows what the law is. The justice who sits on the U.S. Supreme Court is much more invested in what the law *wants* to be and, in that way, more in conflict with the violence—especially capital violence—of the law even as he or she is also very much part of its apparatus.

Other Readings in *Furman*

Looking at the other concurrent opinions and the dissents in *Furman*, we can see similar thought processes to what has already been discussed. Of the other concurring judgments, I would say that those of Justices William Douglas, Potter Stewart, and Byron White can be classified as weaker defenses of the decision to suspend the death penalty. The other concurring opinion, that of Justice Marshall, can be read as a more robust defense of reasons to suspend the death penalty. Marshall also structures his argument around more or less the same principles as does Brennan. He speaks of the "traditional humanity of modern Anglo-American law" and suggests that the death penalty is out of sync with this tradition even if it has in fact long been a practice of both the United States and the United Kingdom (although by then, the United Kingdom had abolished the death penalty).

As previously noted, one area that Marshall expands on from Brennan's opinion brings up the question of retribution. He argues that just because someone is being punished due to the fact that they have broken the law does not imply that the law is thus a form of retribution. He writes, "It is undoubtedly correct that there is a demand for vengeance on the part of many persons in a community against one who is convicted of a particularly offensive act. But the Eighth amendment is our insulation from our baser selves."[43] In other words, Justice Marshall is here offering the law as a corrective to the human desire for vengeance, suggesting that the law itself is not a form of retribution (nor should it be). It is interesting to note that, as previously mentioned, Justice Powell will reverse this point a mere four years later in *Gregg*, once again demonstrating a tension, in this case not only within a particular justice but between justices of the Court.

Unlike Powell, Marshall's statement about retribution in *Furman* seeks to absolve the law from its own violence and thereby bolster the way that law imagines itself as nonviolent or at least not essentially violent (he writes that the law might "tolerate" punishment so long as it serves better purposes).[44] It may well be that as the sole Black member of the Court, Marshall is more aware than his fellow justices of the dangers of law's violence, and so his desire to make the law just is stronger (stronger, certainly, than Powell's will be in *Gregg*).

Marshall's unique perspective may also be seen in his discussion of how capital punishment may serve eugenic purposes. Although he doesn't mention race explicitly here, Marshall may once again be indicating the fact that the law disproportionately puts to death Black and Brown people. He says that the law has not formally accepted eugenics as a criterion to justify punishment (or even as a criterion at all) and that in the absence of such a claim, eugenics cannot be considered as a legitimate factor in allowing for capital punishment.[45]

For all of this, Marshall shares with Brennan a hesitancy to come out and condemn capital punishment full stop. For example, if the state did adopt an explicitly eugenicist model for punishment, Marshall's arguments would seem to allow for this development (although that is clearly something that he would vehemently oppose). In some ways, Marshall's hesitancy may be more a matter of the way Supreme Court justices express themselves than any indication of Marshall's own views. The pose of law is always that it does not legislate but works with existing statutes. Yet one gets the sense that Marshall's arguments, even more than Brennan's, implicitly condemn all of the ways that the death penalty is wrong and unacceptable even if they do not quite come out and say that (but the difference between saying and not saying this has huge consequences, as *Gregg* will go on to show).

Paradoxically, we see the same tension about the law's desired and actual nature even in those justices who dissent from the majority opinion. Justice Harry Blackmun, for one, announces his own personal opposition to the death penalty (he is not the only justice to do so). In his dissent, Blackmun says that he finds the death penalty to be anathema, offering that "I yield to no one in the depth of my distaste, antipathy, and indeed abhorrence, for the death penalty."[46] Yet, Blackmun refuses to go along with the majority in the Court because he notes that the founders plainly accepted the death penalty in their own time (i.e., when they passed the Eighth Amendment), and so it is up to the legislature and not the courts to end the practice.

In the scholarly literature on the subject, there has been much criticism of the *Furman* decision for being too lukewarm in its condemnation of the death penalty more generally. S. Tao, for example, argues that "on constitutional doctrine, the Court settled very little in *Furman*."[47] Tao further argues that insofar as Justices Brennan and Marshall in particular argued against the arbitrary nature of the application of the death penalty, the solution that states seeking to reimpose the death penalty turned to was to limit judicial discretion in such cases, potentially making capital punishment more rather than less common.[48] As many of the authors in this volume argue, *Furman* led more or less directly to *Gregg*, and a whole industry was created to manage (but also to limit) capital punishment. None of the justices on the Court opted for full abolition (although Marshall comes the closest to that position), and as a result we get what could be called a "zombie life" for the death penalty. After a resurgence thanks to *Gregg* and a backlash that *Furman* itself produced, the death penalty is even rarer now than when *Furman* was decided. It is rare but not gone, and even those who are not actually killed get instead a kind of living death, subjected over and over again to the threat of death, which, as John Bessler aptly chronicles in his essay, amounts to a form of torture (a sentiment that echoes Robert Cover's own views on the violence of the law).

Conclusion: Can the Law Ever Not Kill?

While Tao and other authors may be correct in their criticisms, in my view it makes sense that *Furman* would be ambivalent. After all, even without bringing Benjamin's analysis of mythic violence into the picture, the law tends to want to keep for itself the ultimate prerogative over matters of life and death. To renounce the death penalty forever might then have been a bridge too far for a court that sat at the heart of a global hegemon, as well as reflecting the bloodthirstiness of a large number of its citizens who benefit (or at least think that they benefit) from that position with, as Carol Steiker notes, a concomitant system that allows for a high degree of populism. This leads once again to the question of whether the law, and in particular the U.S. law, could ever fully break with legal killing once and for all. Could any of the archist features of the United States—the state, the courts, and so on—decide not just to suspend but to abolish the death penalty?

I wouldn't go so far as to say that this would be impossible, and I certainly hope that the death penalty *is* abolished, along with a broader form of police and prison abolition. Yet, I think that we are unlikely to see the death penalty completely rejected in the United States unless and until its global position is sufficiently reduced so that it no longer holds pride of place in determining what "the law" intends on a global, universal basis. It is always dangerous to make predictions, but if I were to venture one, it would be that the death penalty will continue on in its zombie existence, killing increasingly rarely, maybe effectively stopping to kill altogether, but never quite abolishing the power that gives the law its vital life in the first place.

There is some precedent for thinking that the end of the U.S. empire might also spell the end of its reliance on the death penalty. The British suspended the death penalty in 1965 and abolished it in 1969, a period that corresponds more or less to the end of their global empire.[49] But this comparison may be a bit misleading because, even in decline, the British were not giving up on the law as such but mainly transferring that responsibility to the United States, a country that was highly compatible with Britain's own devotion to global liberalism and capitalism. Without another kindred hegemon to step into the ranks as it loses its own grip on global domination (I doubt the United States would like to hand this kind of authority over to China, for instance), the United States may well hold on to the power to legally kill for longer than the British did in their own decline as an empire. For a nation that purports not only to stand for but also in some sense to embody the rule of law, the United States, as was the case with the British empire before it, must show its power to kill both internationally (through episodic invasions, supported coups, and the like) and domestically (via the death penalty, police killings, and so forth).

In the West, the United States remains an outlier in terms of its continued use of capital punishment. Besides Britain, other European countries similarly abandoned the death penalty over the course of the twentieth century, and in 1985 a protocol was adopted by the European Convention on Human Rights abolishing the death penalty in peacetime for all member states.[50] Russia enacted a moratorium on the death penalty in 1996 when it joined that convention.[51] Today, the only country in Europe with an active death penalty practice is Belarus.[52]

In other parts of the developed world, Japan holds on to the death penalty, as does India.[53] As a rising hegemon in its own right, China is an enthusiastic proponent of the death penalty, although the actual number of executions that it commits is difficult to ascertain due to a great deal of state secrecy on this issue.[54]

The tenacity of the death penalty in the United States may show the difference between the way rights function as Marx describes them in "On the Jewish Question" and the way that the law seeks to wash its hands of formal violence. Individual liberal rights, as already noted, are entirely ephemeral things. It is up to the state to give them or not to give them as it sees fit. But the right to kill is one that is existential for the law and the state, for archism in general, and so this "right" has a different quality. Precisely because the power to kill is one key mechanism whereby the reality of the subject population is stolen and transferred to the archeon itself, this is not a right that the law will give up readily (except in partial ways with an eye toward being overruled, which is arguably the case with *Furman*).

Furman helps illuminate the paradoxical nature of Benjamin's discussion of the discrepancy between how the law sees itself and how it is actually applied (via the police). Here, the law sees itself as an ever-progressing institution that over time becomes increasingly rational and humane even as the fact of the death penalty remains an inconvenient truth against this self-regard. In some ways this discrepancy is papered over by the idea of progress itself wherein the courts and the community as a whole are both progressing toward a greater and fuller humanism. One of the key points that I am trying to make in this chapter is that we should not invest too much energy in the false hope that this progress will be achieved. We may get closer to the end of legal killing, but for reasons that I have already explained, I do not think that we will get full abolition anytime soon. In the meantime, the central question then becomes, How does the law appear to be progressing even as it holds on to, at least in some form or other, the right to kill? How can the law be a killer even as it is the self-described paragon of liberal humanism?

One of the values of turning to Benjamin is that he helps inure us against reading the law according to its own teleological narrative. When we think in teleological terms, we imagine that it is only a matter of time before the death penalty is abolished in the United States. We say to ourselves, how anachronistic is it that the most powerful, most democratic nation on earth (we may say this latter part less after January 6, 2021) still permits capital punishment? But from a Benjaminian viewpoint, it is not anachronistic at all. This discrepancy is rather what permits a sense of time progressing more generally over the whole world where, once again, the U.S. legal system is "terrible so that others do not need to be." The practice of capital punishment in the United States is not an isolated incident but tied in with archist narratives of space and time so that the law is revealed to be more of an international and interrelated system than we generally acknowledge it to be.

The role that the United States plays in maintaining a global regime of rule of law reminds me of an argument that Jodi Dean makes in *Crowds and Party* where the mere existence of the Soviet Union, regardless of how dysfunctional it was, allowed there to be a sense of the possibility (the horizon) of communism across the world. When the USSR fell, it took that possibility with it, at least for a time.[55] The United States in a sense performs the same function for the global liberal system that the USSR did for global communism. It will not be able to play that role forever, and when it does cease these functions, the nature of law may change. Yet the requirement for law to kill *somewhere* and at *some time* will not change without a major alteration of the bases of our political and economic life. Only the death of archism itself (and archism can definitely die—in a sense it is already dead but living a kind of undead violent existence nonetheless) can lead once and for all to the end, not just of capital punishment, which I hope I have demonstrated is just the tip of the killing iceberg in archist society, but of the entire killing machine that unites the state, the law, the police, the prison carceral, the "Karens" of all genders, the lynch mobs, the vigilantes, all of that massive apparatus of archist murder.

Furman did save a lot of lives, and for this reason alone it is worthy of appreciation, but it was not going to lead to the end of archism and not even, as we see, to the end of capital punishment in the United States. What we really need is abolition, something that is akin, once again, to Benjamin's discussion of the general strike in his "Critique of Violence." As Nica Seigel pointed out to me, the times that Benjamin was living in when he wrote that essay are somewhat analogous to our own in terms of rising authoritarianism and the breakdown of the normative liberal order. As previously noted, in the "Critique," Benjamin tells us that most strikes are in fact merely an accommodation with capitalism. Strikes, he tells us, are one of the few forms of violence (recall Benjamin is using the German term *Gewalt*, which means force and power as much as it means physical violence) permitted to non-state actors. As such, the strike is usually a way to use state violence against itself to get some material gains for the workers. The general strike, on the other hand, is a way of saying no to capitalism. It is nonviolent in the sense that it doesn't partake in the lies and exaggerations of mythic violence as such. In this way, the general strike is in fact a form of abolition.

Do we need the abolition of archism itself in order to have the abolition of state violence? I think that is a complicated question. While the Thirteenth Amendment formally abolished slavery, it also preserved it in its own language about being justified as a "punishment for a crime," leading to the vast prison carceral of today. I don't think we can ever have full abolition so long as archism reigns, but we can perhaps have something close to it in specific areas, and the death penalty could be one of those areas. I for one do not want to see the death penalty live on in its current zombie form. The emotional and physical costs to the subjects of that regime, as well as their families, are far too high. Even if executions effectively stop, as long as the regime of death continues with its death rows, lengthy appeals and the threat of execution hanging over the heads of condemned prisoners, we can't really speak of abolition. Of course, the fewer people that are executed the better, and if no one is executed, that is better still. If we think of abolition as a spectrum rather than an either/or (and I'm not sure it's a good idea to think of it that way, but the situation seems to demand that we do), we can try to be as close to true abolition as possible even while the siren song of archist power continues to demand lives to be sacrificed so that it can continue to assert its existence and, through that existence, rule over us.

In presenting this chapter to my coauthors, Austin Sarat asked me if abolition could ever be a legal act—that is to say, could the law as such ever give up this basic power? By way of answer, I would say that it depends on how we define the law. If we think of the law in a strictly conventional sense, as the current system, then I think the answer is no, the law is not able to give up its ultimate power and even its ultimate raison d'être. But if we think of the law in a broader sense (including, for example, Cover's thinking about those local and collective elements of law that our current court system competes with and seeks to destroy), then I would say that the answer is yes. Abolition is an act by the living to retrieve themselves from their status as mere life. This too is a form of law, but its power comes from rather than over the community of human beings. Really, what is being abolished in abolition is "mere life" itself. Abolishing that condition, one where our lives are held captive by a state and a law that is always ready to kill us, we are restored to a full humanity, our own collective and vital life. Anything less than that will be, like *Furman* itself, short-lived in the exact same way that the death penalty itself shortens (some) lives. Subject to a law that only ever seeks to kill, there are serious and built-in limits to how positive or benevolent any act from within that system can be.

NOTES

1. Jean-Baptiste Noé, "Le Tribunal révolutionnaire," June 22, 2019, https://www.jbnoe.fr/Le-Tribunal-revolutionnaire-3217.

2. I am indebted to Linda Ross Meyer for pointing this out.

3. Walter Benjamin, "Critique of Violence," in *Reflections: Essays, Aphorisms, Autobiographical Writings* (New York: Schocken Books, 1978), 242.

4. Niccolò Machiavelli, *The Discourses on the First Ten Books of Livy* (together with *The Prince*) (New York: Modern Library, 1950), 147.

5. *Id.* at 147.

6. Benjamin, "Critique," 297.

7. *Id.* at 250.

8. Maia Ramnath, *Decolonizing Anarchism* (Oakland, CA: AK Press, 2011), 7. I am grateful to Simmy Makhijani for referring me to Ramnath's work.

9. I don't want to romanticize this by any means. The very same cops who come to neighborhood barbecues are perfectly capable of then shooting and killing Black and Brown people in another context. In one context they are evincing their own humanity. In the other they are submerging that humanity into the requirements of the archist system that they serve.

10. Benjamin, "Critique," 243.

11. Robert M. Cover, "Violence and the Word," *Yale Law Journal* 95 (1986): 1607–8.

12. Benjamin, "Critique," 250. I would add that Robert Cover is also clearly not opposed to law per se (probably more clearly than Benjamin himself). He notes that "judges of the state are jurispathic [in] that they kill the diverse legal traditions that compete with the State." Cover, "Violence and the Word," 1610. It is these other laws that Cover, not unlike Benjamin, is trying to recover in the face of an overwhelmingly dominant and violent archist (my word, not theirs) form of law.

13. Benjamin, "Critique," 292.

14. Karl Marx, "On the Jewish Question," in *The Marx-Engels Reader*, ed. Robert Tucker (New York: Norton, 1978), 31.

15. *Id.*

16. *Id.* at 32.

17. *Id.*

18. *Id.* at 33.

19. Robert Cover's take on this is instructive: "The decade-long moratorium on death sentences may quite intelligibly be understood as failure of will on the part of a majority of the Court which had, at some point in that period, decided both that there was to be no general constitutional impediment to the imposition of the death sentence, and that they were not yet prepared to see the states begin a series of executions. Of course, throughout the period, new procedural issues were arising. But it does not seem far-fetched to suppose that there was also a certain squeamishness about facing the implications of the majority position on the constitutional issue." Cover, "Violence and the Word," 1622–23, n. 51.

20. See Jacques Derrida, "Force of Law: 'The Mystical Foundation of Legal Authority,'" in *Deconstruction and the Possibility of Justice*, ed. Drucilla Cornell, Michel Rosenfeld, and David Gray Carlson (New York: Routledge, 1992), 62.

21. "Incarceration Rates by Country 2023," World Population Review, October, 2021. https://worldpopulationreview.com/country-rankings/incarceration-rates-by-country.

22. Alexi Jones and Wendy Sawyer, "Not Just 'a Few Bad Apples': U.S. Police Kill Civilians at Much Higher Rates Than Other Countries," Prison Policy Initiative, June 5, 2020, https://www.prisonpolicy.org/blog/2020/06/05/policekillings/.

23. See Carol Steiker, "Capital Punishment and U.S. Exceptionalism," *Oregon Law Review* 81 (2002): 97. This populism can cut in various ways. In our increasingly mediatized age, the specter of lynching and other forms of extrajudicial killings do not bring the same responses that they might once have. The ubiquity of cell phones now means that these acts of killing are widely seen and noted by audiences that are not necessarily committed to archism and its violence.

24. Jacques Derrida, *Archive Fever: A Freudian Impression* (Chicago: University of Chicago Press, 1996), 2.

25. Furman v. Georgia, 408 U.S. 238, 271–81 (1972), http://law2.umkc.edu/faculty/pro jects/ftrials/conlaw/furman.html.

26. *Id.* at 305.

27. *Id.* at 289.

28. *Id.* See also Hannah Arendt, *Origins of Totalitarianism* (New York: Harcourt, Brace, Jovanovich, 1994), 298.

29. In our collective conversations about this volume, it occurred to me repeatedly that although death is indeed "different," it is not *that* different (I think this is a point that Linda Ross Meyer makes very clearly as well as John Bessler). The mere fact of being on death row itself, the psychological torture, and even nonlethal outcomes like life without parole are all forms of intense state violence that I think are on a spectrum where death is one extreme but not completely in a class by itself.

30. Carl Schmitt, *The Concept of the Political* (New Brunswick, NJ: Rutgers University Press, 1976), 19.

31. *Furman*, 408 U.S. at 293.

32. Corinna B. Lain, "The Highs and Lows of Wild Justice," *Tulsa Law Review* 50 (2015): 514–15. I am grateful to Corinna Lain for this reference.

33. *Id.* at 515. Lain's essay is a review of two books, including Evan Mandery's *Wild Justice: The Death and Resurrection of Capital Punishment in America*. This anecdote is drawn from his book.

34. Gregg v. Georgia, 428 U.S. 153, 183 (1976). Quoted in Lain, "Highs and Lows," 515.

35. John Bessler, *The Death Penalty's Denial of Fundamental Human Rights: International Law, State Practice, and the Emerging Abolitionist Norm* (Cambridge: Cambridge University Press, 2022), 274.

36. *Furman*, 408 U.S. at 300.

37. *Id*. at 303–4.

38. Michel Foucault, *Society Must Be Defended: Lectures at the Collège de France, 1975–1976* (New York: Picador, 2003), 241.

39. I am indebted to my former student Nick Thacker for these and other considerations of Pasolini's work and writings.

40. Pier Paolo Pasolini, *Salò: Or the 120 Days of Sodom* (1975 film).

41. *Furman*, 408 U.S. at 304.

42. I am indebted to Nica Siegel for this insight.

43. *Furman*, 408 U.S. at 344.

44. *Id*. at 343.

45. *Id*. at 356.

46. *Id*. at 238.

47. L. S. Tao, "Beyond Furman v. Georgia: The Need for a Morally Based Decision on Capital Punishment," *Notre Dame Law Review* 51 (1976): 722.

48. *Id*. See also Malcolm E. Wheeler, "Toward a Theory of Limited Punishment II: The Eighth Amendment after Furman v. Georgia," *Stanford Law Review* 25 (1972–73): 62; G. D. Crook, "You May Kill, But You Must Promise Not to Use Discretion: Furman v. Georgia," *Loyola of Los Angeles Law Review* 6 (1973): 526.

49. "United Kingdom Marks 50th Anniversary of Death Penalty Abolition," November 9, 2015. https://deathpenaltyinfo.org/news/united-kingdom-marks-50th-anniversary-of-death-penalty-abolition.

50. "The ECHR and the Death Penalty: A Timeline," Council of Europe, accessed 10 July, 2023, https://www.coe.int/en/web/portal/death-penalty.

51. *Id*.

52. "Death Penalty: Key Facts about the Situation in Europe and the Rest of the World," European Parliament, last updated July 28, 2020, https://www.europarl.europa.eu/news/en/headlines/world/20190212STO25910/death-penalty-in-europe-and-the-rest-of-the-world-key-facts.

53. "Abolitionist and Retentionist Countries," Death Penalty Information Center, accessed 15 May, 2023, https://deathpenaltyinfo.org/policy-issues/international/abolitionist-and-retentionist-countries.

54. See Tobias Smith, Matthew Robertson, and Sue Trevaskes, "(Not) Talking about Capital Punishment in the Xi Jinping Era," *International Journal for Crime, Justice and Social Democracy* 11, no. 3 (2022): 70–91. https://papers.ssrn.com/sol3/papers.cfm?abstract_id=4149068.

55. Jodi Dean, *Crowds and Party* (New York: Verso, 2016), 117.

Contributors

John D. Bessler has taught at the University of Baltimore School of Law since 2009. He has also taught at the University of Minnesota Law School, the George Washington University Law School, the Georgetown University Law Center, Rutgers School of Law, and the University of Aberdeen in Scotland. He clerked for U.S. magistrate judge John M. "Jack" Mason of the U.S. District Court for the District of Minnesota. He has written or edited ten books, six on the subject of capital punishment, including *Against the Death Penalty* and *The Death Penalty as Torture: From the Dark Ages to Abolition.*

Corinna Barrett Lain is a constitutional law scholar who writes about the influence of extralegal norms on Supreme Court decision making, with a particular focus on the field of capital punishment. Her scholarship, which often uses the lens of legal history, has appeared in the *Stanford Law Review, University of Pennsylvania Law Review, Duke Law Journal, UCLA Law Review,* and *Georgetown Law Journal,* among other venues. Professor Lain is an elected member of the American Law Institute and received the University of Richmond's Distinguished Educator Award in 2006.

James R. Martel is a professor in the Department of Political Science at San Francisco State. He teaches courses in political theory, continental philosophy, anarchism, postcolonial theory, and theories of gender and sexuality. He is author of eight books. His latest book is *Anarchist Prophets: Disappointing Vision and the Power of Collective Sight* (Duke University Press, 2022). He previously published *Unburied Bodies: Subversive Corpses and the Authority of the Dead, The Misinterpellated Subject, The One and Only Law: Walter Benjamin and the Second Commandment, Divine Violence: Walter Benjamin and the Eschatology of Sovereignty, Textual Conspiracies: Walter Benjamin, Idolatry and Political Theory, Subverting the Leviathan: Reading Thomas Hobbes as a Radical Democrat,* and *Love Is a Sweet Chain: Desire, Autonomy and Friendship in Liberal Political Theory.*

226 / Contributors

Sara Mayeux is Associate Professor of Law and Associate Professor of History at Vanderbilt University. She is author of *Free Justice: A History of the Public Defender in Twentieth-Century America* (UNC Press, 2020).

Linda Ross Meyer began teaching at Quinnipiac Law School in 1994 and taught criminal law, constitutional law, and legal theory, among other subjects. Before joining the faculty at Quinnipiac, Meyer served as a law clerk for Judge Charles A. Legge (N.D. Cal.), Judge William A. Norris (9th Cir.), and Justice Sandra Day O'Connor, and she spent her first two years of teaching at Vanderbilt University Law School. She is author of *The Justice of Mercy* and *Sentencing in Time* and many articles and book chapters on criminal responsibility, sentencing, and legal theory. Meyer is past president of the Association for the Study of Law, Culture, and the Humanities and recipient of the James Boyd White Award. She cofounded the Quinnipiac Prison Project.

Austin Sarat is William Nelson Cromwell Professor of Jurisprudence Political Science at Amherst College. He is former president of the Law and Society Association; former president of the Association for the Study of Law, Culture and the Humanities; and former president of the Consortium of Undergraduate Law and Justice Programs. He is author or editor of more than one hundred books, including most recently *Lethal Injection and the False Promise of Humane Execution*.

Carol S. Steiker received the J.D. in 1986 from Harvard Law School, where she was president of the *Harvard Law Review*, and an A.B. in history and literature from Harvard College in 1982. Steiker was a law clerk for U.S. Supreme Court Justice Thurgood Marshall from 1987 to 1988 and for Judge J. Skelly Wright of the U.S. Court of Appeals for the District of Columbia Circuit from 1986 to 1987. She served as staff attorney for the Public Defender Service for the District of Columbia from 1988 to 1992, where she represented indigent defendants at all stages of the criminal process—from arrest through trial, appeal, and application for postconviction relief. Her articles include "Punishment and Procedure: Punishment Theory and the Criminal-Civil Procedural Divide," *Georgetown Law Journal* (1997); "Counter-revolution in Constitutional Criminal Procedure? Two Audiences, Two Answers," *Michigan Law Review* (1996); and "Sober Second Thoughts: Reflections on Two Decades of Constitutional Regulation of Capital Punishment," *Harvard Law Review* (1995) (with Jordan M. Steiker). She is coauthor of *Courting Death*.

Jordan M. Steiker teaches constitutional law, criminal law, and death penalty law at the University of Texas and is Codirector of the Capital Punishment Center. He was a visiting professor at the Harvard Law School and has written extensively on constitutional law, federal habeas corpus, and the death penalty. His recent publications include "A Tale of Two Nations: Implementation of the Death Penalty in 'Executing' Versus 'Symbolic' States in the United States," *Texas Law Review* (2006) (with Carol Steiker); "The Seduction of Innocence: The Attraction and Limitations of the Focus on Innocence in Capital Punishment Law and Advocacy," *Journal of Criminal Law and Criminology* (2005) (with Carol Steiker); "Habeas Exceptionalism," *Texas Law Review* (2000); "Restructuring Postconviction Review of Federal Claims Raised by State Prisoners: Confronting the New Face of Excessive Proceduralism," *Chicago Legal Forum* (1998); and "Sober Second Thoughts: Reflections on Two Decades of Constitutional Regulation of Capital Punishment," *Harvard Law Review* (1995) (with Carol Steiker). He is coauthor of *Courting Death*.

Index

"Abolition in Our Time" (Steiker and Steiker), 183–184

abolition of death penalty: Amsterdam on, 26, 90n26, 92, 182, 183; Biden on, 10; Camus on, 51, 96; for certain categories of offenders, United States, 46; Enlightenment thought about, 22, 27, 30, 46; and future *Furman*-type decision possibility, 93, 123–125, 174; Garrett on, 37; by international community, 22, 39–40, 60n183, 100, 109, 111, 219; Marshall on "no rational basis" for capital punishment, 88n22; political context change since *Furman,* 114–120; Prejean on, 45, 147, 149; Senate Judiciary Committee testimony on (1968), 33; as unlikely, 91n39. *See also* Catholicism and death penalty; death penalty as state-sanctioned violence; public opinion on death penalty; state-level campaigns and abolition

abortion: and Catholic Church on death penalty, as inconsistent, 137–139, 144–147, 157–161; *Dobbs v. Jackson Women's Health Organization,* 137, 148, 158–159; "family values" issues of, 151–155; lay Catholic opinion on, 135, 142, 147–157; *Roe v. Wade,* 137, 138, 141, 144, 148–150, 153, 156–159

ACLU (American Civil Liberties Union), 116, 139, 151

Aikens, Earnest, 26

Aikens v. California (1972), 26, 96–97

Alabama: on abortion, 157; on psychological torture, 51

Alaska, on death penalty, 170

Alexander, Michelle, 75

Alito, Samuel, 36, 137–138, 156, 180

American Bar Association (ABA), 17, 103–104, 109, 175

Amnesty International, 3, 23

Amsterdam, Anthony, 26, 90n26, 92, 182, 183

antiabortion movement. *See* abortion

Anti-Terrorism and Effective Death Penalty Act (1996), 39

arbitrary application of death penalty: and death penalty as state-sanctioned violence, 209–212, 217–218; *Furman* vs. contemporary views of capital punishment, 94, 96–97, 100, 118–119, 121, 122; rarity of executions, 21–22, 36–47; "unusual" punishment as context for death penalty, 72, 74–78, 80. *See also* race and class bias

228 / Index

archism, 196–224; abolition of, 221; vs. anarchism, 199–201; defined, 199, 200; *Furman* as archist logic, 197, 208–216; and law as mythic violence, 15, 196–204, 218; and United States as global power, 218–222

Arendt, Hannah, 210

Arkansas, on abortion, 157

Army Field Manual, U.S. (1992), 44, 46, 49

Atkins v. Virginia (2002), 7–8, 112

Austria, on death penalty, 22

Badinter, Robert, 96

bail, excessive, 21, 28, 29

Baldus study, 38, 113

Barrett, Amy Coney, 123, 156

Bator, Paul M., 90n26

Bazelon, David, 141

Baze v. Rees (2008), 9, 70–72, 107

Beasley, Dorothy, 92

Beaumont, Gustave de, 205

Beccaria, Cesare, 22, 27, 30

Belarus, on death penalty, 219

Benedict XVI (pope), 146

Benjamin, Walter, 15, 196–209, 216, 218–221. *See also* death penalty as state-sanctioned violence

Bernardin, Joseph (cardinal), 149, 153–155, 160

Berrigan, Daniel, 153

Berry, William, 45

Bessler, John, 11, 168, 212, 218

Biden, Joe, on death penalty abolition, 10

Bill of Rights, British (1689), 21, 27, 70–72, 75, 79, 87n15

Bill of Rights, U.S., 27–29

Bill of Rights, Virginia, 28

Bird, Rose, 74

Black Lives Matter, 173

Blackmun, Harry: *Callins v. Collins*, 6–7, 65, 78, 82, 85; *Furman*, 11, 22, 32–33, 118–119, 217; *Jackson v. Bishop*, 31, 48

Blackstone, William, 30

Blake, Aaron, 151–152

Bloodsworth, Kirk, 38

Bork, Robert, 34

Branch, Elmer, 21

Brennan, Marjorie, 141

Brennan, William, and *Furman* opinion: Catholicism and death penalty, 13, 140–142, 156, 158, 160; contemporary views of capital punishment in context of, 95, 96, 97, 100, 111, 118; on cruelty of death penalty, 26, 28–29, 30–32, 35, 39, 48, 51; on death penalty as always unconstitutional, 5–6; human-rights-and-dignity framing by, 11, 31; state-sanctioned violence context of death penalty, 197, 204, 209–217; on "unusual" as normative, 12, 64–65, 71, 73, 77, 78–86

Breyer, Stephen, 9–10, 36, 96–99, 106, 119, 120, 124

Brown, Kate, 2

Brugger, Christian, 146

Bucklew v. Precythe (2019), 35–36, 87n12, 117, 120

Burger, Warren, 22, 32, 69–70, 74, 119, 142

Burton v. Livingston (1986), 40

Bush, George W., 156

cadena temporal (Filipino corporal punishment), 29

California: *Aikens v. California* (1972), 26, 96–97; on death penalty, 26, 94–95, 97, 115, 116, 173, 181; Proposition 17, 74

Callins v. Collins (1994), 6–7, 65, 78, 82, 85

Camus, Albert, 51, 96

capital punishment. *See* death penalty

Capital Punishment Project (ACLU), 151

Cardozo Law School, 110

Carolene Products case (1938), 82

Caste: The Origin of Our Discontents (Wilkerson), 75

Catholicism and death penalty, 135–166; abortion and death penalty views as inconsistent, 137–139, 144–147, 157–161; *Catechism of the Catholic Church*, 136, 137, 145, 146–147; Catholic Campaign to End the Use of the Death Penalty, 145–146; Catholic grassroots activism and public opinion, 147–157; Catholicization of Supreme Court, 137–138, 156, 183; Catholic Mobilizing Network to End the Use of the Death Penalty, 147–148; Church's and Supreme Court's convergence/divergence on death penalty, 13–14, 135–137; post-*Furman* and post-*Gregg*, 142–147; and Protestants on abortion and death penalty, 14, 140–141, 150–153, 155, 157; "seamless garment" speech (Bernardin), 153–155, 160; at time of *Furman*, 139–142

Center for Wrongful Convictions (Northwestern Law School), 110
Chatigny, Robert, 83–84
China: on death penalty, 219; United States' criticism of, 42
Christianity Today (magazine), on death penalty, 152
Civil Rights Act (1866), 46–47
Clark, Ramsey, 33, 95
class bias. *See* race and class bias
Cogley, John, 135–136
Coker v. Georgia (1977), 111
Colorado, on death penalty, 173, 181
Committee for Public Safety (France), 196, 206–207
Community of Sant'Egidio (Rome), 147
compounding pharmacies, 99, 180, 192–193n117
Connecticut, on death penalty, 173, 181
Constitution, U.S.: Bill of Rights, 27–29, 68, 79, 89n22; social contract theory, 71–72 (*See also* originalism); Thirteenth Amendment, 221. *See also* Eighth Amendment; Fourteenth Amendment; originalism; "unusual" punishments
Cooley, Thomas, 65, 86–87n5
Cover, Robert, 202, 218, 222, 223n19
"Critique of Violence" (Benjamin), 196–209, 216, 218–221. *See also* death penalty as state-sanctioned violence
Crowds and Party (Dean), 220
cruelty of death penalty: abolition movement and Enlightenment thought, 22, 27, 30, 46; arbitrary and discriminatory application of death penalty, 21–22, 36–47; and *Furman* as missed opportunity, 11, 21–25; international human rights campaigns on death penalty, 22–23, 39, 43–44, 46–50; NAACP strategy in *Furman,* 26–36; psychological torture of death penalty, 23–25, 30–34, 37–47, 50–51, 106; torture concept addressed by *Furman,* 22–25, 50–51. *See also* Eighth Amendment; torture
Cruz, Nikolas, 157
A Culture of Life and the Penalty of Death (USCCB), 145
Cupich, Blase (cardinal), 160

Danton, Georges, 196, 206–207
Dead Man Walking (film), 147

Dead Man Walking (Prejean), 45
Dean, Jodi, 220
The Death of Innocents (Prejean), 45
death penalty, 1–18; *Furman* legacy and scholarly debate about, 10; *Furman* ruling and subsequent upholding of, 4–6; Innocence Project on, 10; Supreme Court doubts about death penalty, in subsequent cases, 6–10. *See also* death row, exoneration from; death row inmates; public opinion on death penalty
death penalty, contemporary views vs. *Furman,* 92–131; death penalty for nonhomicidal offenses, 94, 100, 122; and future *Furman*-type decision possibility, 93, 123–125, 174; and political context change since *Furman,* 12–13, 14–15, 92–93, 97–99, 110, 114–120, 169–174; racial discrimination in death penalty, 93, 112–113, 122–123; and Supreme Court's changing constitutional methodology, 12–13, 92–97; and Supreme Court's conservative makeup, 93, 117–120, 122–123; and Supreme Court's Eighth Amendment capital jurisprudence, 110–114; and Supreme Court's role in death penalty transformation, 99–110. *See also* state-level campaigns and abolition
death penalty as state-sanctioned violence, 196–224; arbitrary nature of, 209–212, 217–218; archism and law as mythic violence, 15, 196–204; archist logic of, 197, 208–216; and "divine violence," 197–200; and eugenics, 217; murder as political category, 204–208; and retribution, 216–217; and rights in "On the Jewish Question" (Marx), 197, 205–206, 219; United States as global power and abolition, 218–222
Death Penalty in Decline? The Fight against Capital Punishment in the Decades since Furman v. Georgia (Sarat), book organization, 10–16
Death Penalty Information Center (DPIC), 1–3, 38, 41
Death Penalty (Megivern), 162n24
death penalty methods. *See* lethal injection
"death qualified" juries, 129n123

230 / Index

death row, exoneration from: contemporary rise after *Furman*, 3, 97–98; Earl Washington case, 191n88; Innocence Project, 10; National Registry of Exonerations, 38, 59n161, 110; in post-*Furman* era, 3, 97–98

death row inmates: death row phenomenon and death row syndrome, 41, 105–106; end-stage litigation for, 42–43, 59n162, 93, 107–108, 115–118; family members of, 41–43, 83–84; natural deaths of, 39; psychological torture of, 23–25, 30–34, 37–47, 50–51, 106; time spent on, 39, 57n137

Declaration of Independence, 36

"Declaration on the Protection of All Persons from Being Subjected to Torture and Other Cruel, Inhuman or Degrading Treatment or Punishment" (UN, 1975), 43

"Declaring the Death Penalty Unconstitutional" (Goldberg and Dershowitz), 23

Decolonizing Anarchism (Ramnath), 200

"Deconstructing *Dobbs*" (Tribe), 162n19

Delaware, on death penalty, 129n128, 173

Democracy in America (Tocqueville), 27–28

denationalization as punishment, 23, 31, 66, 68

Derrida, Jacques, 207, 208

Dershowitz, Alan, 23

deterrence and retribution: *Atkins v. Virginia*, 8; death penalty as state-sanctioned violence, 216–217; *Furman* and cruelty of death penalty, 27, 29, 32; *Furman* and "unusual" punishment, 73–74, 81, 88; *Furman* vs. contemporary views of capital punishment, 94–99, 102, 106, 112–115; proportionality of death penalty, 213–214

discriminatory application of death penalty. *See* arbitrary application of death penalty; race and class bias

"divine violence," 197–200

Dobbs v. Jackson Women's Health Organization (2022), 137, 148, 158–159, 162n19

Douglas, William O., 4, 26, 29, 35, 74–78, 112–113, 171, 216

Douglass, John, 177

Dow, David, 39

Dowd, Maureen, 162n19

DPIC (Death Penalty Information Center), 1–3, 38, 41

Dream Pharma, 179

Dred Scott v. Sandford (1857), 38

Drinan, Robert F., 143

due process. *See* Fourteenth Amendment

Durick, Joseph (bishop), 136

"The Dying Death Penalty" *(Time)*, 169, 172

Eichmann, Adolf, trial of (1963), 80

Eighth Amendment: *Atkins v. Virginia* on, 8; Brennan on *Furman* and, 140–141, 209–216; on cruel and unusual punishment/torture, 21, 25, 26–36, 37–38, 40, 43, 49, 51; and death penalty as always unconstitutional, 5; *Furman,* per curiam decision on, 4; *Furman* vs. contemporary views of capital punishment, 93, 95–97, 108, 110–112, 117–120, 123–125; Idaho on, 62–63n223; "incorporation" in Fourteenth Amendment, 65–66, 87n8; *Kansas v. Marsh* on, 9; Marshall on death penalty as per se violation, 48; state-level campaigns and abolition, 183. *See also* evolving standards of decency test; originalism; "unusual" punishments

emancipation, political vs. human, 206

Emmett Till Antilynching Act (2022), 47

End of Its Rope (Garrett), 37

end-stage litigation, for death row inmates, 42–43, 59n162, 93, 107–108, 115–118

Enlightenment philosophy, 22, 27, 30, 46

Enmund v. Florida (1982), 111–112

Erhlich, Isaac, 113–114

An Essay on Crimes and Punishments (Beccaria), 22

eugenics, death penalty as, 217

European Convention on Human Rights, 126n37, 219

European Union, and lethal drug production, 179

Evans, Timothy, 109

evolving standards of decency test: *Bucklew v. Precythe* on, 87n12; Catholic Church on, 136; cruelty and torture in context of, 8–9, 31, 34–36; *Furman* on, 68, 74, 79; *Furman* vs. contemporary views of capital punishment, 101, 102, 115, 119–120, 124; *Gregg* on, 73; *McCleskey v. Kemp* on, 77; "nose-counting" of state statutes for,

69; *Trop v. Dulles* on, 68, 70, 79; two-part inquiry of, 67–68
Ewing v. California (2003), 72, 74, 88n17

"family values" issues and abortion, 151–155
Faulder v. Johnson (1999), 42
Filártiga v. Peña-Irala (1980), 43
financial costs of death penalty: vs. life imprisonment, 98–99, 176–178; and regulatory oversight, 103–105; to states, 175–178, 181–184. *See also* state-level campaigns and abolition
First Things (journal), 160
Florida: on death penalty, 6, 181, 183; Parkland school shooting, 186–187, 195n161
Florida v. Cruz (2022), 157–158
Floyd, George, 37, 173
Food and Drug Administration, U.S., 179–180, 192n104, 192n117
Foreign Sovereign Immunities Act (1976), 25
Foucault, Michel, 214
Fourteenth Amendment: and cruelty of death penalty, 3, 22, 32, 36, 46; death penalty as violation of, 40, 49; equal protection by, 21–22; *Furman,* per curiam decision on, 4, 26, 32, 48; *Furman* vs. contemporary views of capital punishment, 93, 123; and *Gregg* as procedural due process, 86n3; "incorporation" of Eighth Amendment in, 65–66, 87n8; and "rational basis" test for death penalty, 73–74, 88–89n22; and *Robinson v. California,* 27
Francis (pope), 136, 146–147
Frankfurter, Felix, 23, 66
Franklin, Benjamin, 27
Fratelli tutti (2020 encyclical, Pope Francis), 147
Freedman, Eric, 39
French Revolution, 196–197, 206–207
Furman, William, 21, 32
Furman v. Georgia (1972): *Gregg* and resumption of executions, 6, 39, 48; individual death penalty cases addressed by NAACP in, 21, 26, 32; ruling, 1, 4–7, 10, 11–16; Supreme Court doubts about death penalty, in subsequent cases, 6–10. *See also* abolition of death penalty; cruelty of death penalty; death penalty, contemporary views vs. *Furman; Gregg v.*

Georgia (1976); public opinion on death penalty; "unusual" punishments

Gallup polls, 171
Garland, David, 10
Garland, Merrick, 2, 123
Garrett, Brandon, 37
Geneva Convention Relative to the Treatment of Prisoners of War (1949), 23, 43–44, 47
George, Ronald, 92
Georgia. *See Furman v. Georgia* (1972); *Gregg v. Georgia* (1976)
Germany, on death penalty, 39–40, 100
Gilmore, Gary, 38, 116, 144–145
Ginsburg, Ruth Bader, 7, 9, 96, 119, 123
Glossip, Richard, 42–43, 59n162
Glossip v. Gross (2015), 9–10, 98, 99, 106, 120, 124
God's Law and Order (Blake), 151
Goldberg, Arthur, 23, 122
Gorsuch, Neil, 117, 120, 123
Graham v. Florida (2010), 35, 69, 72, 74, 81–82
Granucci, Anthony, 70–72, 73, 75, 77
Great Britain: Bill of Rights, 21, 27, 70–72, 75, 79, 87n15; on death penalty, 216, 218–219
"Great Law" of 1682 (Pennsylvania), 22
Greenberg, Jack, 38
Greenhouse, Linda, 137
Greenpark Compounding Pharmacy and Gifts (Houston), 180
Gregg v. Georgia (1976): Catholicism and death penalty, 136, 144–145, 148, 151, 158; on constitutionality of death sentence, 47, 48; and contemporary views of capital punishment, 101–102, 105, 108, 109, 114, 119; due process in, 86n3; and guided-discretion statutes, 33–34, 168, 175–178, 185–187; on mass commutation of death sentences, 38; and originalist argument, 73; "regulatory project" of, 14; and resumption of executions, 6, 39, 48; and state-sanctioned violence context, 208, 211–212, 215–218. *See also* cruelty of death penalty
Grodin, Joseph, 74

Hamilton, Dawn, 38
Hancock, John, 30

232 / Index

Harmelin v. Michigan (1991), 71, 72
Harris, Robert Alton, 116
Harris poll (1965), 171
Harvard Law Review, "Declaring the Death
  Penalty Unconstitutional," 23
Hawaii, on death penalty, 170
Helling v. McKinney (1993), 34
Henry, Patrick, 27, 28
Hesburgh, Ted, 141
Higgs, Dustin, 118
Hindu law (ancient), on capital punish-
  ment, 76
Holland, Jennifer, 151
Holmes, Abraham, 28
Holocaust, 80, 100
Hope v. Pelzer (2002), 49
Hospira, 178–181, 192n104
Howard, John, 30
Hudson v. McMillian (1992), 34
human dignity. *See* Brennan, William, and
  Furman opinion; Catholicism and death
  penalty; cruelty of death penalty; interna-
  tional community on death penalty; tor-
  ture; "unusual" punishments

Idaho, on death penalty, 62–63n223
Illinois, on death penalty, 10, 97, 109, 173,
  181
India, on death penalty, 219
Innocence Project, 10, 110
In re Kemmler (1890), 29–30, 65–66
intellectually disabled defendants, death
  penalty as discrimination against, 3, 34,
  46, 101, 112, 115, 116, 191n88
international community on death penalty:
  abolition of death penalty by, 22, 39–40,
  60n183, 100, 109, 111, 219; Amnesty
  International on death penalty, 3, 23;
  cadena temporal (Filipino corporal punishment), 29; and Catholic European
  countries, 139, 142; European
  Convention on Human Rights, 126n37,
  219; European Union and lethal drug
  production, 179; Geneva Convention
  Relative to the Treatment of Prisoners of
  War (1949), 23, 43–44, 47; International
  Covenant on Civil and Political Rights,
  39, 47; UN Convention against Torture
  and Other Cruel, Inhuman and
  Degrading Treatment or Punishment
  (1984), 24–25, 43, 46–48, 50; United

States' criticism of other countries on
  human rights, 42. *See also individual
  names of countries*
Iowa, on death penalty, 170
Iran, United States' criticism of, 42
"Irish Eyes Aren't Smiling" (Dowd),
  162n19
Italy: death penalty prohibition in, 100; and
  lethal injection drug production, 179

Jackson, Lucious, 21
Jackson v. Bishop (1968), 31, 48
Japan, on death penalty, 219
Jefferson, Thomas, 27, 36
John Paul II (pope), 136, 146
Johnson, Lyndon B., 185
Jouet, Mugambi, 96
Jurek v. Texas (1976), 33–34
juries: "death qualified" juries, 129n123;
  guided-discretion, pre-*Furman* vs. contemporary, 174–175, 190n70; guided-discretion statutes, *Gregg,* 33–34, 175–178,
  185–187
Justice, Department of, death penalty moratorium, 2
juvenile offenders: death penalty prohibition, 8, 34, 46, 67, 101, 112; life-without-
  parole (LWOP cases), 69, 91n39

Kagan, Elena, 36
Kansas, death penalty repeal effort, 115
Kansas v. Marsh (2005), 9
Kavanaugh, Brett, 123
In re Kemmler (1890), 29–30, 65–66
Kennedy, Anthony, 8–9, 67, 74, 78, 79, 81,
  123, 160
Kennedy v. Louisiana (2008), 8–9
Kentucky, on death penalty, 35

Lain, Corinna Barrett, 14–15, 91n39, 211,
  213
Lawrence v. Texas (2003), 77
legal counsel: end-stage litigation for death
  row inmates, 42–43, 59n162, 93, 107–108,
  115–118; and guided-discretion statutes,
  33–34, 175–178. *See also* state-level campaigns and abolition
legislative role in death penalty: Anti-
  Terrorism and Effective Death Penalty
  Act (1996), 39; Blackmun on, 22, 217; and
  courts' on constitutional jurisdiction, 85,

89; on federal habeas review, 104; Senate Judiciary Committee testimony (1968), 33; Torture Victim Protection Act (1991), 25

lethal injection: botched executions, 3, 44–45, 99, 180; constitutionality of, 9, 35; and drug unavailability, 178–181, 192n104; Eighth Amendment challenge to, 117; three-drug protocol requirements, 107–108, 178

Liebman, James, 39

life sentences/life without parole: vs. financial cost of death penalty, 176–178; juveniles and life-without-parole (LWOP cases), 69, 91n39; public opinion on, 2

"lightning" analogy, 5, 22, 36, 94

Livermore, Samuel, 28, 29, 79

Lockett, Clayton, 10, 44–45

Louisiana: and *Furman,* 6; and *Gregg,* 33–34

Louisiana ex rel Francis v. Resweber (1947), 66

Lundbeck (Danish pharmaceutical company), 179–180

Luther, Martin, 140, 152

Machiavelli, Niccolo, 198–199

Marbury v. Madison (1803), 85

March for Life (1992), 156

Marjory Stoneham Douglas High School (Parkland, Florida), 186–187, 195n161

Marshall, Thurgood, and *Furman* opinion: on arbitrary and discriminatory practices of death penalty, 36; contemporary views of capital punishment vs. *Furman,* 95, 96–98, 101, 111, 113, 118, 129n108; on death penalty as always unconstitutional, 5–6, 26; on death penalty as a per se Eighth Amendment violation, 48; and death penalty in state-sanctioned violence context, 197, 212, 213, 216–218; dissents to capital punishment in subsequent cases, 140; on evolving standards of decency test, 35; on "gross injustices" of death penalty, 38; state-level campaigns and abolition since *Furman,* 171, 182; on torture, 41; and "unusual" context, 68–69, 73–74, 78, 88–89n22, 89n26

Martel, James, 15, 91n39

Marx, Karl, 197, 205–206, 219

Maryland, on death penalty, 173, 181

Massachusetts, corporal punishment (eighteenth-century), 30

Mayeux, Sara, 13–14, 183, 209

Maynard v. Cartwright (1988), 33, 34–35

McCleskey v. Kemp (1987), 6–10, 11, 38, 76, 113, 122

McCord, David, 181

McGautha v. California (1971), 36, 93

McKnight, Shawn (bishop), 148

Megivern, James J., 143, 144, 146, 149, 150, 162n24

Meltsner, Michael, 92

Meyer, Linda Ross, 11–12, 206, 213

Michigan, on death penalty, 130n128

Micke, William Joseph, Jr., 32

Miller v. Alabama (2012), 69

Mississippi. *See Dobbs v. Jackson Women's Health Organization* (2022)

Missouri, on death penalty, 35, 41

Montana, death penalty repeal effort, 115

moratorium on death penalty, federal (2022), 2

mythic violence, law as, 15, 196–204. *See also* death penalty as state-sanctioned violence

NAACP Legal Defense Fund: Catholicism and death penalty, 139; cruel and unusual punishment addressed by litigation of, 23, 26–36; *Furman* litigation and motivation of, 4–6; *Furman* litigation vs. contemporary views of death penalty, 92, 94, 101–102, 109, 114, 121, 122

The Nation, on *Furman,* 185

National Association of Evangelicals (NAE), 151

National Catholic Conference of Interracial Justice, 162n24

National Coalition against the Death Penalty, 151

National Coalition of American Nuns, 139

National Crime Commission, 170, 171

National Registry of Exonerations, 38, 59n161, 110

Nebraska, on death penalty, 173

Neufeld, Peter, 110

New Hampshire, on death penalty, 173

New Jersey, on death penalty, 114–115, 173

The New Jim Crow: Mass Incarceration in the Age of Colorblindness (Alexander), 75

234 / Index

New Mexico, on death penalty, 129n128, 170, 173, 181
Newsom, Gavin, 97
New York, on death penalty, 129n128, 170, 173, 181
New York Times: on abortion, 137, 157; on death penalty, 157, 185
Nixon, Richard, 171
nonhomicidal crimes: death penalty for, pre-*Furman,* 94, 122; death penalty prohibition, 8, 34–35, 100, 101, 111
Northam, Ralph, 97
North Carolina, on death penalty, 6, 33–34
Northington v. Jackson (1992), 40
Northwestern Law School, 110
Numa (Roman king), 198–199
Nuremberg trials (1945–46), 80

Obama, Barack, 156
O'Connor, Sandra Day, 7, 36, 77
Oklahoma, on death penalty, 35, 44–45, 182
"On the Jewish Question" (Marx), 197, 205–206, 219
Oregon, on death penalty, 115, 129n128, 170, 173
originalism: and abortion, 156–157; application-originalist version of "unusual," defined, 70–73, 88n20; Blackmun on *Furman* (1972), 217; Jefferson on Declaration of Independence for the living, 36; "unusual" punishments and death penalty interpretation, 64, 68–73, 79–82, 87n7, 87n12, 88n20, 89n22
Oxford English Dictionary, on torture, 25

Parkland (Florida) school shooting, 186–187, 195n161
Pasolini, Pier Paolo, 214
Penn, William, 22
Pennsylvania: on death penalty, 115, 173; "Great Law" of 1682, 22
People v. Anderson (1972), 26, 32, 47, 74
Pfizer, 180
Pizzuto, Gerald, 62n223
Planned Parenthood v. Casey (1992), 156
Plessy v. Ferguson (1896), 38
police violence, as "extrajudicial" state killing, 15, 201–203, 206–208, 213, 216, 218–220
Pontifical Commission for Justice and Peace, 144

poor defendants. *See* race and class bias
Porter, Anthony, 109
Powell, Lewis, and *Furman* opinion: contemporary views of capital punishment vs. *Furman,* 113; and death penalty in state-sanctioned violence context, 211–212, 216–217; dissenting/separate opinions of justices, 32; on justices' personal views, 22; state-level campaigns and abolition since *Furman,* 182; and "unusual" context, 70, 73, 76–77
Prejean, Helen, 45, 147, 149
Proffitt v. Florida (1976), 33–34
prolife movement. *See* abortion
Proposition 17 (California), 74
Protestants, evangelical vs. mainline, on abortion and death penalty, 14, 140–141, 150–153, 155, 157
public opinion on death penalty: abolition movement and change in, since *Furman,* 1–4, 171, 173, 184–185; of Catholics, 143, 147–157; and death penalty as cruel and unusual punishment, 212–213; and financial costs of death penalty, 98; *Furman* and backlash effect, 101; political context change since *Furman,* 114–120

Quakers, on death penalty, 22

race and class bias: and Catholic public opinion, 148; death penalty as arbitrary, 209–212, 217–218; death penalty as civil rights issue, 4; death penalty as racial discrimination, 3; *Furman* vs. contemporary views of capital punishment, 93, 112–113, 122–123; and police violence as "extrajudicial" state killing, 15, 201–203, 206–208, 213, 216, 218–220; state-level campaigns and abolition, 171–172; and "unusual" punishment, 74–78, 89n26
Ramnath, Maia, 200
"rational basis" test for death penalty, 73–74, 88–89n22
Reagan, Ronald, 155, 156
"Reflections on the Guillotine" (Camus), 96
Rehnquist, William, 22, 32, 81
religion: Hindu law (ancient), on capital punishment, 76; Protestants, evangelical vs. mainline, on abortion and death penalty, 14, 140–141, 150–153, 155, 157; Quakers on death penalty, 22; of Supreme

Court justices, 137–138, 156. *See also* Catholicism and death penalty
Reprieve (U.K.), 179–180
Reynoso, Cruz, 74
Roberts, John, 85, 137, 159
Robinson v. California (1962), 27, 87n8
Roe v. Wade (1973), 13, 137, 138, 141, 144, 148–150, 153, 156–159
Romero, Oscar (archbishop), 155
Roper v. Simmons (2005), 8, 69, 112
Ross, Michael, 83–84
Rucho v. Common Cause (2019), 85
Rudolph v. Alabama (1963), 122
rule of law, *Dead Man Walking* (Prejean) on, 45
Rush, Benjamin, 27
Russia, on death penalty, 219
Ryan, George, 10

Salinas (professor), 9
Salò, 120 Days of Sodom (film, Pasolini), 214
Sarat, Austin, 44, 45, 91n38, 221
Scalia, Antonin, and *Furman* opinion: Catholicism and death penalty, 138, 156; contemporary views of capital punishment vs. *Furman*, 112, 119–120, 123; and "unusual" context, 68, 70–72, 74, 79, 80
Scheck, Barry, 110
Schlafly, Phyllis, 153–155
Schmitt, Carl, 210
"seamless garment" speech (Bernardin), 153–155, 160
Seigel, Nica, 221
Sellin, Thorsten, 113
Senate Judiciary Committee testimony (1968), 33
shadow docket of Supreme Court, 117–118
Smith, William Loughton, 29
sodium thiopental, 108, 178–179, 192n104
Solem case, 72
Solesbee v. Balkcom (1950), 23
Sotomayor, Sonia, 35–36, 117, 156
Souter, David, 9
South Africa, on death penalty, 24, 40
South Carolina, on death penalty, 181
state-level campaigns and abolition, 167–195; and death sentencing decline since *Furman*, 170, 174–178, 190n70; and evolving standards of decency test, 69; and execution decline since *Furman*,

170, 178–181; vs. federal-level abolition, 167–168; financial cost to states, 175–178, 181–184; *Gregg* and guided-discretion statutes, 168, 175–178, 185–187; and public opinion change since *Furman*, 1–4, 171, 173, 184–185; sociopolitical context, 1972 vs. contemporary, 14–15, 169–174
Steiker, Carol, 12–13, 14, 175, 183–184, 186, 208, 218
Steiker, Jordan, 12–13, 14, 175, 183–184, 186
Stevens, John Paul, 8, 9, 81, 88n17, 106, 118–119
Stewart, Potter, and *Furman* opinion: contemporary views of capital punishment vs. *Furman*, 93–95; on cruel and unusual punishment, 34; and death penalty in state-sanctioned violence context, 216; "lightning" analogy, 5, 22, 36, 94; and separate concurrences of justices, 26; state-level campaigns and abolition since *Furman*, 169, 171; and "unusual" context, 74
Stop Lethal Injection Project (SLIP, Reprieve), 179–180
Supreme Court, U.S.: contemporary conservative makeup, 93, 117–120, 122–123; shadow docket of, 117–118; state-level campaigns vs. federal abolition, 167–168
Supreme Court Review, on *Furman* (1972), 172
Surovell, Scott, 97
Sword of the Lord (magazine), on death penalty, 152

Tao, S., 217–218
Taylor v. Riojas (2020), 40
Texas, on death penalty, 6, 94, 116, 124, 182, 183
Third Geneva Convention (1949), 23, 43–44, 47
Thirteenth Amendment, 221
Thomas, Clarence: contemporary views of capital punishment vs. *Furman*, 120; Eighth Amendment and "unusual" context, 64, 68–72, 79–82, 84–85, 89n22
Thomas Aquinas (saint), 142, 154
Time magazine: "The Dying Death Penalty," 169, 172; "Why the Era of Capital Punishment Is Ending," 172
Tocqueville, Alexis de, 27–28

236 / Index

torture: definitions, 24–25, 43; *Furman* concurring/dissenting opinions on, 22–25; mock execution as, 11, 25, 40, 43–44, 48; psychological torture, defined, 41; psychological torture of death penalty, 23–25, 30–34, 37–47, 50–51, 106; UN Convention against Torture definition, 50. *See also* international community on death penalty

Torture Victim Protection Act (1991), 25

Tribe, Laurence H., 162n19

Trop v. Dulles (1958), 23–24, 31–32, 35, 66–71, 79, 80, 119–120

Trump, Donald, 35, 117–120, 122–123, 156

Tuscany, on death penalty (1786), 22

UN Convention against Torture and Other Cruel, Inhuman and Degrading Treatment or Punishment (1984), 24–25, 43, 46, 47–48, 50

Uniform Code of Military Justice (Army Field Manual, 1992), 44, 46, 49

United States v. Briggs (2020), 36

United States v. Carolene Products Co. (1938), 82

United States v. Morrison (2000), 85

"unusual" punishments, 64–91; "cruel and unusual" addressed by NAACP strategy in *Furman*, 26–36; "cruel" and "unusual" as different standards, 64–65; "cruel and unusual" as evolving standard, 65–68; and frequency of death penalty, 68–70; *Furman* justices' varied interpretation of, 11–12; originalist interpretation of death penalty, 64, 68, 70–73, 87n7, 87n12, 88n20, 89n22; and "rational basis" for death penalty, 73–74, 88–89n22; "unusual" as normative term, 12, 64–65, 71, 73, 77, 78–86; "unusual" as "unprincipled," 74–78

U.S. Code: 10 U.S.C. § 855 ("Cruel and Unusual Punishments Prohibited"), 49–50; on torture, 25

U.S. Conference of Catholic Bishops (USCCB), 136, 143–147

Utah: death penalty repeal effort, 115; Gilmore's execution, 38, 116, 144–145; *Weems* (1910) on death penalty in, 65

Vatican II, 136, 138, 143–144. *See also* Catholicism and death penalty

Vermont, on death penalty, 129n128, 170

Virginia: Bill of Rights, 28; on death penalty, 115, 173, 176–178, 181, 183; State Crime Commission, 176

Vladeck, Steven, 118

Voltaire, 30

Warden, Rob, 110

Warren, Earl, 31, 64, 68, 122, 142

Washington, Earl, 191n88

Washington, George, 27

Washington Post, Schlafly on Bernardin's speech, 153, 155

Washington (state), on death penalty, 173

Watts v. State of Indiana (1949), 23

Weems v. United States (1910), 29–31, 65–69, 79

We Gather Together (Young), 151

Weigel, George, 160

Weisberg, Robert, 114

West Virginia, on death penalty, 170

White, Byron, 5, 26, 73, 74, 93–95, 169, 216

"Why the Era of Capital Punishment Is Ending" *(Time)*, 172

Wilkerson, Isabel, 75

Wilkerson v. Utah (1879), 29–30, 65, 66

Williams, Daniel K., 153

Williams v. Taylor (2000), 175, 176

Yale Law Journal, Greenberg on *McCleskey*, 38

Yick Wo v. Hopkins (1886), 75

Young, Neil, 151